PRACTICAL
SOLITARY
MAGIC

PRACTICAL SOLITARY MAGIC

Nancy B. Watson

☥ WEISERBOOKS

York Beach, Maine, USA

First published in 1996 by
Weiser Books
P. O. Box 612
York Beach, ME 03910-0612
www.weiserbooks.com

Library of Congress Cataloging-in-Publication Data

Watson, Nancy B.
    Practical solitary magic / Nancy B. Watson.
      p. cm.
    Includes bibliographical references (p. 237) and index.
    (pbk. : alk. paper)
    1. Magic. 2. occultism. I. Title.
BF1611.W38 1996
133.4'3--dc20
96—24394   CIP

ISBN 0-87728-874-7
BJ

Printed in the United States of America

08 07 06 05 04 03 02 01
11 10 9 8 7 6

Cover art is "Vergessenes Ritual." Copyright © 1996 Ananda Kurt Pilz. Walter Holl Agency, Germany.

Quoted material from Murry Hope's *Ancient Egypt: The Sirius Connection* copyright © 1996 Murry Hope and used by permission of Element Books. Shaftesbury, Dorset, England.

The paper used in this publication meets or exceeds the minimum requirements of the American National Standard for Information Sciences—Permanence of Paper for Printed Library Materials Z39.48-1992 (R 1997).

For my dear Teacher,

MURRY HOPE

TABLE OF CONTENTS

FOREWORD xi

ACKNOWLEDGMENTS. xiii

INTRODUCTION xv

PART ONE: THE PSYCHOLOGY AND ETHICS OF MAGIC

CHAPTER 1. MAGIC AND THE MIND 3
   Magic and Psychology, 4
   How Magic Works, 5
   The Importance of Temperament, 6
CHAPTER 2. MAGIC AND ETHICS 9
   Magic and Personal Relationships, 12
   Ethical Magic, 13

PART TWO: THE ARCHITECTURE OF MAGIC

CHAPTER 3. THE FOUR PLANES. 17
   The Physical Plane, 17
   The Emotional Plane, 18
   The Mental Plane, 19
   The Spiritual Plane, 19
   The Cellar, 19
CHAPTER 4. THE MENTAL PLANE 23
   Setting Your Goal, 23
      Defining Your Goal, 24
      Anticipating Consequences, 26
      Expressing Your Goal Safely, 29
      Writing Down Your Goal, 30
   Divination, Affirmations, and Incantations, 32
   Oracles, 33
   Astrology, Numerology, and Magic, 36
   Creating and Using Affirmations, 37

Three Steps to Effective Affirmations, 39
    Exercise 1: Positive Energy Affirmation, 42
    Exercise 2: Receptivity Affirmation, 44
    Tips on Using Affirmations, 45
    Prosperity Affirmations, 46
Magical Incantations, 47
Summary, 50

CHAPTER 5. THE SPIRITUAL PLANE 53
Choosing Archetypes, 55
    Exercise 3: Using the Pendulum, 61
    Exercise 4: Seeking Pendulum Advice, 61
    Establishing a Bond with Your Chosen Archetype, 63
    Working with Celtic Deities, 65
Effective Prayer, 66
    How to Pray, 67
    The Pin and Candle Rite, 68
Contacting the Archetype Within, 71
    Assuming the God-Form, 71
    Ego and Archetype, 76
    Protecting Yourself, 79
    Exercise 5: How to Seal Your Aura, 80
Building the Magical Personality, 81
    Exercise 6: Assuming the Magical Personality, 83
    Life of the Magical Personality, 83
Summary, 84

CHAPTER 6. THE EMOTIONAL PLANE 87
Visualization Techniques, 88
    Exercise 7: Visualization, 92
Magical Feeling, 94
    The Rite of Aphrodite's Girdle, 95
Clearing, 100
    Visual Clearing Method, 101
    Exercise 8: Clearing Technique, 102
    Clearing Fear, 103
    Exercise 9: Etheric Clearing, 104
    Letter Clearing, 106
    Murry Hope's Rite of Tears, 107
Summary, 109

CHAPTER 7. THE PHYSICAL PLANE 111
The Four Elements in Nature, 112
The Four Elements in Ritual Magic, 113
The Four Elements in Psychology, 114
Elementals, 117
    Dealing with Elementals, 119
The Fire Element, 121
    Candle Magic, 123
Salamanders, 127
    Gifts for Salamanders, 130
The Air Element, 131
    Incense Magic, 133
    Wildcrafting Herbs for Incense, 134
    Substitutions for Incense, 135
    When to Use Incense, 138
Sylphs, 139
    Gifts for Sylphs, 143
The Water Element, 144
    Water Magic, 145
    Using Water to Wash Away Emotional Negativity, 145
    Exercise 10: How to Charge (Magnetize) Water, 147
    Cleansing the Atmosphere, 148
    Exercise 11: Murry Hope's Cleansing Visualization, 149
    Using Water to Create a Positive Emotional Attitude, 150
Ondines, 152
    Gifts for Ondines, 156
Meeting Your Personal Ondine, 156
    Astral Travel, 157
    Exercise 12: The Journey, 159
    Meeting Salamanders, Sylphs, and Gnomes, 164
The Earth Element, 165
    Earth Magic, 167
Gnomes, 172
    Gifts for Gnomes, 174
Overview, 174

PART THREE: THE PRACTICE OF MAGIC

CHAPTER 8. TIMING AND TIDES 179
    Using the Solar and Lunar Cycles, 179
    Using Power Days, 181
    Using Days of the Week, 183
    Using Planetary Hours, 184
    Exceptions to the Rules, 184
    When to Expect Magical Results, 186
    Why Some Magic Fails, 187
CHAPTER 9. RITUAL 191
    The Four Phases of Ritual, 192
    Casting a Magic Circle, 194
    Consecrating Magical Tools and Implements, 199
    Using Magical Instruments, 201
CHAPTER 10. A PROSPERITY RITE 203
CHAPTER 11. CONTINUING YOUR STUDIES 213
    High Magic, 214
    Finding a Teacher, 214
    Finding a Group, 221
    Growing into Magic, 223

APPENDICES

APPENDIX A: TEMPERAMENT QUESTIONNAIRE 227

APPENDIX B: PERSONAL SYMBOL EXERCISES 233
             GOD/GODDESS SYMBOL EXERCISES 235

BIBLIOGRAPHY 237

INDEX 241

ABOUT THE AUTHOR 249

FOREWORD

In spite of the abundance of metaphysical literature that has flooded the market of late, the dearth of good solitary magic primers emphasizes the need for an expert to make a contribution in this particular field. And here she is, in the person of Nancy B. Watson, magician of over thirty-five years practical experience. Watson presents her subject matter in an easily readable style, her eminently sane and well-grounded approach incorporating her extensive study of Jungian psychology with her proven expertise in the field of practical magic.

Practical Solitary Magic is not just for the specialist few, but rather for anyone who, through diligence and self-discipline, is brave enough to confront the unseen worlds via the power of his or her own mind. Learning to identify, understand, and negotiate these subtle energies can be the deciding factor as to whether we elect to become the masters of our own destiny, or remain among the flotsam that is forever tossed aimlessly back and forth on the waters of life.

Watson is careful to define the ethics involved in all magical practices. Rather than effect moral judgments, she places her emphases on safety precautions and individual karmic responsibility. Her simple rites and exercises, which echo the mystical practices of more profound early disciplines and magical systems, such as those of ancient Egypt, Greece, Celtica, Northern Europe, and Polynesia, are both psychologically sound and spiritually safe.

Nancy Watson does me the honor of referring to me here as her "Teacher." After reading *Practical Solitary Magic,* I rather feel she has a lot to teach me!

—Murry Hope

ACKNOWLEDGMENTS

My sincere thanks go to:

Dion Fortune, wherever she may be, for pointing the way.

Murry Hope, who has so generously allowed me to share with readers much of what she has taught me at the personal level, and for permission to publish some of her private rituals.

Louis M. Vuksinick, my psychiatrist, who appears to know nearly everything there is to know about human nature, for sharing some of this knowledge with me.

My fiancé, James J. Nordhoff, for his suggestions, patience, and most of all, for his unstinting support.

Grateful thanks are also due to The C. W. Daniel Co., Ltd., Inner Traditions International, Samuel Weiser, Inc., and especially to Element Books, Ltd., for allowing me to quote liberally from their publications.

INTRODUCTION

This book is written for the individual who wishes to learn how to practice magic safely and effectively on a solitary basis.

It has never been easy for solitaries to learn the principles of magic. In the late 50's and early 60's, when I began my magical studies, the majority of books on magic were written by authors who were affiliated with occult groups, and since such organizations usually extracted from members an oath of secrecy regarding their teachings, scarcely any practical instruction found its way into print. What did appear amounted to a secret code which the student had to decipher before he could begin experimentation on his own.

Fortunately, a lot of people were willing to do the work and as a result, many carefully guarded teachings have been exposed to public view in recent years. In fact, today's would-be magician is overwhelmed by the amount of study material accessible. Separate books on the subjects of affirmations, visualization, folk-magic, ritual, and a dozen other magical topics are available today. Since even advanced magicians sometimes express confusion when confronted with the multiplicity of magical techniques, it's easy to sympathize with novices who, without the guidance of a teacher, have no idea where or how to make a start.

Beginners face other problems as well. Most modern works do not explain the principles behind magical practice, so unless students are willing to study dozens of procedures in an attempt to discover the rules which underlie them, they are restricted to using the ready-made techniques contained in the text they are currently studying. And since no single book—or even a single collection of books—contains magical formulas designed to cover every conceivable goal, novices are liable to find themselves without the knowledge or means to achieve their personal desires.

To further complicate matters, the terminology used by modern writers bears little resemblance to that used by the classical authors, so even if ambitious students manage to digest all the current material, they still find themselves perplexed when they approach the classics.

There remains for the beginner the most critical problem of all: the issue of safety in magic. The greatest disadvantage to practicing magic on a solitary basis is that the student does not have a teacher to help him or her over rough spots. And rough spots abound. It is true that magic can be dangerous.

This book is designed to help the student overcome these difficulties. First, practical magic is here given a structure into which all magical techniques fit neatly. Second, all procedures are described in both modern and classical terms. Third, the principles underlying all procedures are clearly explained, so that students will be able to create effective magical operations for themselves. And fourth, safety measures are stressed. Having made all the mistakes myself over the years, I know where the danger areas lie and can help the student to avoid them.

The reader may wish to know something of my own magical background. My studies began in San Francisco when I was 15. A neighbor interpreted my horoscope, introduced me to the tarot, gave me a little book called *It Works*, and took me to lectures given by a man named Neville, who taught visualization techniques.[1] I immediately began astrological studies, and tried to get my hands on a deck of tarot cards.

In the late 50's there was only one metaphysical bookstore in the city, and its atmosphere was calculated to give visitors a distinct case of the creeps. I nervously ascended two floors in an antiquated cage-like elevator to emerge in a dusty room dimly lit by a few crusty Victorian lamps. Books were stacked higgledy-piggledy on tables, chairs, sofas, and the floor. Overseeing the disarray was a strange little man who sometimes proved uncooperative. When I tried to purchase a tarot deck—the Waite pack was the only one available then—he wouldn't sell it to me. He insisted that I study Papus' *Tarot of the Bohemians* before beginning work with the cards.

---

[1]R. H. Jarret, *It Works* (Marina del Rey: DeVorss, 1976).

I couldn't afford the book, so I joined a metaphysical library—located down the street and featuring another rickety elevator—borrowed the book, took it home, and knowing nothing about copy machines (which were, in any case, scarce in those days), laboriously typed out the entire text.

I visited the library often, but its shelves were filled with classical texts on metaphysical subjects which were, for the most part, totally beyond me. In time, I began experimentation with *It Works* and visualization techniques. Eventually I was allowed to purchase a tarot deck.

Books by Wiccan authors (Doreen Valiente, Patricia Crowther, etc.) began to appear in the United States in the early 60's. Wicca, being magically based and pro-feminine, greatly appealed to me, and for two years I wrote impassioned letters to anyone I thought could help me find a group that I could join. It was to no avail: either the groups didn't exist in my area (the movement was still young), or my letters put people off. Finally, a kindly Wiccan from the Midwest supplied me with an extensive reading list and told me that I could consider myself an honorary Wiccan if and when I managed to absorb all the material on the list. Since many of the books were out of print or otherwise unavailable—it took years to find them—the challenge wasn't easy.

At the top of the list, however, were the books of Dion Fortune, mostly available, and these I read and reread until I knew them almost by heart. Studying these, and those of her associates and former Golden Dawn colleagues, I managed over time to decipher the code in which they were written. Then my real magical experimentation began. I was on the lookout for a teacher all the while, but Fortune sets a high standard of excellence, and it was to be many years before I found one. It was a lonely time.

I took up Hatha and Raja Yoga in my early 30s. Several years later, I placed myself under the guidance of an exceptionally brilliant Jungian psychiatrist and, with his help, have worked for individuation ever since. Psychiatry proved to be an important development in my magical career, because the knowledge gained from it enabled me to correlate classical magical teachings with the various functions of the human psyche, which is, after all, the source of all magical results. I also learned why some magical practices are dangerous and others not.

The greatest disappointment of my magical career was that I was never able to study with Dion Fortune, who died when I was 2 years old. I vowed early on that if I ever ran across some-one of her caliber, I would move heaven and earth to study with that person, but by the time I had been practicing magic for twenty-six years, I had pretty much given up on finding a teacher. Then I read Murry Hope's books, and knew the long search had ended. It was with Murry's help that I was able to complete my magical education.

To read about magic in the abstract is one thing; to hear stories recounted by flesh-and-blood magicians is quite another. In my early years as a solitary magician, I yearned to hear about the personal experiences of those who were knowledgeable on the subject. I learned more from the personal anecdotes contained in Dion Fortune's *Psychic Self-Defense* than I did from all the rest of her books combined.[2] I have worked ever since on the theory that there is nothing so instructive as a real-life tale—a theory borne out by several years of teaching students who appeared to crave the same thing I had when starting out. It's for this reason that there are many personal anecdotes scattered throughout this text. I hope the reader understands that these are included for educational, not egoistic, reasons.

An old metaphysical maxim states that "When the student is ready, the teacher appears." An astounding number of people today are interested in magic. It is my most deeply held wish that solitary magicians will find what follows to be of value.

---

[2] Dion Fortune, *Psychic Self-Defense* (York Beach, ME: Samuel Weiser, 1992).

PART ONE

The Psychology and Ethics of Magic

CHAPTER 1

MAGIC AND THE MIND

We do not affect fate by our magical operations, we affect ourselves; we reinforce those aspects of our nature which are in sympathy with the powers we invoke.[1]

— *Dion Fortune*

There have been many excellent definitions of magic given over the years by metaphysicians and those who study esoteric tradition, but the best (and certainly the most complete) that I have read is Murry Hope's:

> Magic is concerned with the conversion of universal energies into practical frequencies that can be utilized according to the needs of the occasion. These energies in themselves are totally neutral, having no affiliation with any belief, system or personality either here on Earth or anywhere in the cosmos, their manifestation at the magical level being coloured entirely by the nature and intention of the user.[2]

Hope's definition makes it clear that the practice of magic is essentially nonreligious. You need not hold any formal (or even informal) religious beliefs in order to practice it. This doesn't mean, however, that spirituality plays no part in magic. On the contrary, there are important magical techniques which depend upon spirituality for their effectiveness. But the means of expressing this spirituality—whether you choose to work with deities or not, for instance—may always be freely chosen.

---

[1]Dion Fortune, *Sane Occultism* (London: Aquarian Press, 1967), p. 56.
[2]Murry Hope, *Practical Greek Magic* (London: Aquarian Press, 1985), introduction.

MAGIC AND PSYCHOLOGY

To practice magic is to set a goal and to perform actions symbolic of its achievement. Symbols have a profound effect upon the human psyche, a fact well known to psychologists and politicians. Since magicians have always made lavish use of symbols in their work, it might be assumed that they, too, are consciously aware of their impact upon mind and heart. But this isn't always the case. Many magicians do not understand the mechanism whereby psychological change produced by the use of symbols translates into desired external results. For them, magic is purely a matter of formula, strictly adhered to. As an inexperienced magician who wishes to attract a lover, for instance, you might read in some magical text that to burn a pink candle for ten minutes every day for a week will produce the desired effect. So you purchase a candle and dutifully burn it according to instructions. Your operation will almost certainly fail, however, because you haven't yet learned that *it is the psychological work that accompanies magical (symbolic) action, not the action itself, which produces results.*

The great magicians have always recognized the link between psychology and magic. In modern times, the practice of one discipline has frequently led to a profound interest in the other. Dion Fortune, for instance, was a psychoanalyst before she was a magician:

> As soon as I touched the deeper aspects of practical psychology and watched the dissection of the mind under psycho-analysis, I realised that there was very much more in the mind than was accounted for by the accepted psychological theories. I saw we stood in the centre of a small circle of light thrown by accurate scientific knowledge, but around us was a vast, circumambient sphere of darkness, and in that darkness dim shapes were moving. It was in order to understand the hidden aspects of the mind that I originally took up the study of occultism.[3]

---

[3]Dion Fortune, *Psychic Self-Defense* (York Beach, ME: Samuel Weiser, 1992), pp. 18–19.

Israel Regardie, another great name in modern magic, was first a magician, then a practicing psychologist. He was quite specific about the links between the two disciplines when he wrote in 1938:

> Analytical Psychology and Magic comprise in my estimation two halves or aspects of a single technical system. Just as the body and mind are not two separate units, but are simply the dual manifestations of an interior dynamic "something" so psychology and Magic comprise similarly a single system whose goal is the integration of the human personality. Its aim is to unify the different departments and functions of man's being, to bring into operation those which previously for various reasons were latent.[4]

This may sound somewhat abstract to the reader interested in practical magic, but in fact the fusion between magic and psychology of which Regardie speaks and its result are of great importance to magicians on a practical level.

HOW MAGIC WORKS

To understand how magic works, you must first understand the difference between the conscious and the unconscious minds.

We are all very familiar with the conscious mind, which is your ordinary everyday walking-around consciousness. When your body goes to sleep at night, your conscious mind goes to sleep as well, and your unconscious mind wakes up, becomes active, and begins to communicate through dreams which your conscious mind may remember upon waking. The same process occurs during meditation when both your conscious mind and your body are stilled: your unconscious mind becomes active and begins to communicate through waking visions, hunches, or significant insights. Given the opportunity, your unconscious mind is a good communicator. It constantly sends helpful suggestions to your conscious mind in the hope that they will be heeded and acted upon.

---

[4]Israel Regardie, *The Middle Pillar* (St. Paul, MN: Llewellyn, 1985), p. 16.

To practice magic is to reverse the process. As a magician, you set a goal with your conscious mind, and attempt to communicate your desire to your unconscious mind in the hope that it will heed and act upon it. Provided your communication is clear, your unconscious mind will take the instructions it is given and go quietly to work to produce the desired result in material reality. We don't know how the unconscious accomplishes its task, only that it does. What you need to know as a magician is how to clearly and directly communicate desire to your unconscious mind. The unconscious does the rest. This is the essence of magic.

There are as many methods for communicating desire to the unconscious as there are people who wish to use them. Provided only that the communication is clear and direct, there is no right way or wrong way to give instruction to the unconscious. There are, however, some archetypal communication techniques which have proven effective for magicians for literally thousands of years. It is primarily these techniques—or variations thereof—on which we will concentrate in this book.

THE IMPORTANCE OF TEMPERAMENT

You will find that some methods presented here work for you and that others don't. This is to be expected, given that each individual is unique in temperament, interests, and skills. Finding what works for you comes only with experience—and experience can't be gained unless all techniques are tried.

At first, you may experience some failures. But you will also have some successes. Naturally intuitive types may have trouble with some of the physical techniques, but will probably excel in spiritual practices.[5] Practical, down-to-earth people (sensate types) may find spiritual procedures difficult, but sail through the physical ones. Intellectual (thinking) types will probably find methods appropriate to the emotional plane hard going, but will find mental plane work easy. Individuals who tend to "think with the heart" (feeling types) may find purely mental work such as goal analysis

---

[5]To establish your type, see the Temperament Questionnaire in Appendix A.

difficult, but exercises involving the emotions exceedingly simple. None of this is predictable. I know highly spiritual types who revel in physical magic, as well as intellectuals who excel in emotional techniques.

Don't be discouraged when you fail. Keep trying, because you will eventually find the methods which will always work for you. You should perfect these to the best of your ability. Your education shouldn't stop, however, with those techniques which you find easily effective. In fact, the methods which initially seem difficult or out-of-character are those that will eventually bring you notable—perhaps even your greatest—successes.

Dion Fortune thought that candidates for initiation into magical societies should be sorted out by temperament. Those who were naturally psychic should receive instruction in magic, while natural magicians should receive instruction in psychism. Ideally she felt, this "cross-grain" training would develop those facets of the candidate's character which were undeveloped and therefore unreliable. Fortune's principle is sound because to develop skills which are not natural to the temperament is to develop a system of checks and balances which can help offset the dangers inherent in the path one naturally follows.

Natural psychics don't need instruction on how to be psychic; the gift and skills are already there. Psychics tend to be too receptive. They need to learn how to generate positive energy so that they don't become unwitting victims of any negative influences which happen to be floating around in their vicinity. On the other hand, natural magicians easily generate energy and tend to be willful. They need to learn how to be receptive to incoming impressions, so that they don't attempt to achieve goals in the face of subtle but insuperable obstacles.

Solitary practitioners of magic may never be forced by a magical society to learn skills foreign to their natural temperaments, but this doesn't mean they can afford to ignore this very important principle. On a practical level, learning difficult skills means greater safety in magical practice, because the use of these skills allows you to achieve a goal without being forced to deal with unexpected or unwanted phenomena at the same time. This alone makes learning seemingly difficult techniques worthwhile. But there are other benefits as well.

When you deliberately go against temperament in order to master difficult skills, you automatically develop new facets of your character, and this allows you to achieve goals in every area of life. By contrast, if you have an imbalance in your character—you may be too intellectual, for instance—you may only achieve success in certain areas of life. For practical purposes, then, it's important that you stretch yourself in every way you can. For those who aspire to the highest levels of magic, there is an additional but less practical, benefit to be gained. Magicians with well-rounded temperaments become candidates for what is termed high magic, a form of magic which has little to do with the achievement of mundane goals.[6]

Novices should work through all the techniques contained in this and other books and, should concentrate initially on those which prove successful. This will bolster your self-confidence. When you have a number of successes under your belt and know that you are working with power, you can tackle those techniques which originally proved difficult.

Along the way, you should do everything possible to develop the intuitive, intellectual, emotional, and earthy aspects of your character so that you become a well-rounded, healthy human being, capable of achieving goals in every area of life.

---

[6]Readers drawn to this path are referred to a short discussion of the subject contained in chapter 11.

CHAPTER 2

MAGIC AND ETHICS

Any attempt to dominate others, or in any way to manipulate their minds without their consent, is an unwarrantable intrusion upon their freewill and a crime against the integrity of the soul.[1]

— *Dion Fortune*

Most readers probably realize that it is morally wrong to harm another being through the use of magic, and that there are severe penalties to be paid for such behavior. You may not realize, however, that it is equally wrong to help others without their conscious knowledge and without first obtaining their explicit permission. This may make some readers indignant, especially those who are amateur healers, or who take part regularly in healing circles.

If you have difficulty believing it's wrong to help someone who is in obvious need, but who has not requested assistance, try putting the shoe on the other foot. Imagine that you have a friend who, being very conservative and perhaps religious in the traditional sense, disapproves of metaphysical pursuits in general, and of magic in particular. This person discovers with great alarm that you are reading this book and privately decides to save your soul from damnation. To this end and on a regular basis, your friend mentally beams to you the thought that magic is dangerous and should be given up. If you discovered these efforts to "save" you, how would you feel? Those who have no knowledge of, or belief or interest in, the powers of the human mind might be faintly amused or mildly contemptuous, but others—you, presumably, since you are reading this book—might feel quite differently. For who has the right to intrude upon your thoughts, even if the motive for doing so is "good"?

[1]Dion Fortune, *Psychic Self-Defense* (York Beach, ME: Samuel Weiser, 1992), pp. 141–142.

The same principle applies to "absent" healing. As Dion Fortune unequivocally stated:

> It may be laid down as a maxim in spiritual healing that no one has the right to apply any alterative mental treatment to another without that person's consent .... It has been argued that surely anybody would welcome relief from pain. But this is far from being the case. Many people have profound religious convictions, and would consider such interference blasphemous. Even if we do not agree with them, we ought to respect their opinions.[2]

Religious convictions aside, people don't like to be manipulated. Furthermore, people know on some level (perhaps not conscious) when an attempt is being made to manipulate them, and they pull away from the manipulator. The fastest way to lose your friends is to practice magic on them.

I once knew a man who, despite considerable knowledge of healing and magical tehniques, was unable to find a way to practice his skills professionally. Frustrated, he attempted to fix his friends' problems on a psychic level. Sometimes he did this in the presence of the person, more often not. He never asked permission to help, and apparently didn't consider his actions intrusive. I was one of his targets and, when I realized what was going on, my reaction was to carefully conceal any troubles I might have had, and to avoid him. Desperate to uncover information about my personal life, he tricked a mutual friend into giving him my horoscope, presumably with the hope that it could tell him what I would not. That put an end to our friendship. Since then, he has lost other friends for similar reasons, and no longer has any standing in the metaphysical community.

As this story suggests, the desire to help others often stems from something other than purely altruistic motives. Compulsive do-gooding usually masks a deep need for power, which may

---

[2]Dion Fortune, *Sane Occultism* (London: Aquarian Press, 1967), p. 144. Another factor to consider is that illness often serves a positive purpose. This will be discussed in chapter 4.

manifest as a desire to control others, or as a desire to attract admiration.[3] Either version of the power motive creates problems for victim and perpetrator alike.

As anyone who has studied history or mythology knows, saviors usually end up as martyrs to the causes they have espoused. Power-types who manage, by whatever means, to control the thoughts and actions of those around them eventually find themselves so burdened with responsibilities that they have little time to meet their own needs. When the man mentioned earlier found his source of "patients" drying up, he single-handedly attempted to heal the entire planet and to prevent, through magic, its destruction by "threatening" groups. It's no coincidence that he was constantly ill and that his marriage was in trouble. The demands made by an inflated ego can be prodigious and exhausting.

Unwilling victims of power-types suffer from intrusion into their personal lives, but it's much worse for willing victims. Those who are very happy to hand their responsibilities over to someone whom they see (or claim to see) as superior pay a great psychological price, because the level of their self-esteem drops each time they ask to be rescued.

The metaphysical law which underlies the problems attendant upon magical meddling is known as The Law of Rebound, which states that if you direct a force—any force, even a benign one, such as love—toward another human being and it is not accepted or absorbed by that individual, the force boomerangs back to you with three times its original power.[4] The results are invariably unpleasant.

---

[3] Individuals whose horoscope features a prominent Saturn, Neptune, or Pluto (or signs and houses relating to these planets) often seek to control others. Magicians with such placements should do everything they can to overcome their manipulative tendencies. This may require therapy. Also helpful are three books, written by knowledgeable therapists: Liz Greene, *Saturn: A New Look at an Old Devil* (York Beach, ME: Samuel Weiser, 1976); Marilyn Waram, *The Book of Neptune* (San Diego, CA: ACS Publications, 1992); and Donna Cunningham, *Healing Pluto Problems* (York Beach, ME: Samuel Weiser, 1991).

[4] Also called the Law of Three by Wiccans.

To illustrate this law with an image, imagine that you, the magician, are standing at one end of a long, dark, and narrow corridor. At the other end of the corridor is a door opening onto a room belonging to one of your acquaintances. Because of the darkness and length of the corridor, you can't see whether the door opposite you is open or closed. You project a magical force toward the person at the other end of the corridor. It travels down its length. If the door is open (as it might be if your friend has asked for help), the force enters freely and is absorbed by the person. If the door is closed, however, the force slams against the door and makes its way back, hitting you with three times its original power. And you are ensnared in your own net.

An ambitious actress I once knew decided she needed a powerful theatrical mentor who could give her career a needed boost. She fixed on a man, the managing director of a theatre, whom she found mildly attractive. She knew something of magic and decided to bewitch him so that he would find her requests for assistance irresistible. She went to work magically, and in the process fell madly in love with him. He failed to fall in love with her, however, so she had a very uncomfortable case of unrequited love on her hands. She was, as the saying goes, hoist on her own petard.

The actress' case is classic, because the force she projected rebounded on her in its purest form. She wished him to fall in love with her; she fell in love with him. It's not always so neat. Sometimes a rebounding force changes its nature midstream, so to speak, and manifests in a startling manner. The male healer mentioned earlier, for instance, was not, as far as I know, suddenly subject to psychic intrusion by others; he simply lost all his friends.

MAGIC AND PERSONAL RELATIONSHIPS

It is never wise to help others without their permission; but what if a friend asks for magical assistance? My opinion, based upon personal experience, is that the request should be denied. This is, of course, very difficult to do, for you don't want to turn your back upon a friend who is genuinely in need. Nor do you want to see the end of the relationship, something which could occur if it appears that you've abandoned a friend in the midst of a crisis. Acceding to your friend's request, however, may pose an even greater threat to your relationship.

When one individual acts as savior and the other as helpless victim, the relationship between the two lacks balance, and resentment may develop on both sides. The needy person wants help and, getting it, naturally wants more. Though grateful for assistance in the beginning, your friend may eventually come to resent someone who is able to accomplish things that he or she cannot. This is unavoidable, for no one likes to be compared unfavorably with another. In the meantime, you (the "savior"), faced with an escalating number of demands for help, may become resentful of the time and effort required and increasingly contemptuous of an individual who cannot seem to cope with problems. Unless both you and your friend can break your patterns of behavior, your relationship is doomed, for resentment is corrosive.

Turning down a request for help may lead to trouble; granting it may be even more dangerous. It's a no-win situation. There is, however, a way out.

If you are asked for magical assistance by a friend who is normally self-sufficient, you might offer to teach that person how to perform his or her own magic. You needn't give a comprehensive course in the subject; a few pointers will usually do. Or, you might wish to recommend a book which can teach some magical techniques. (The book approach is probably best taken with individuals who are constantly needy and demanding.) If your offer is accepted, well and good. If it is rejected, then you must assume that your friend, for whatever reason, is unwilling to participate in the process. Either way, the responsibility no longer rests with you.

ETHICAL MAGIC

Never attempt to harm or dominate another individual by magical means. The penalties for such behavior are severe. It is never necessary to manipulate another human being magically in order to achieve a goal. *When you desire something, work on yourself rather than on other people.* Remember: if you can communicate your desire clearly and directly to your unconscious mind, you can attain anything you want in life. The following chapters contain all the communication techniques you will need.

PART TWO

THE ARCHITECTURE
OF MAGIC

CHAPTER 3

THE FOUR PLANES

Events shape and take form on the Inner Planes long before they appear as actual happenings on the plane of manifestation in matter.[1]

— *Dion Fortune*

To get successful results from magic, work must be done upon all four of the planes. In ascending order, these are the physical plane, the emotional plane, the mental plane, and the spiritual plane. Each of these planes, and the magical techniques appropriate to it, will be discussed in detail in coming chapters. For now, it's important to get an overview of them.

THE PHYSICAL PLANE

When you practice magic, you work with a structure which is similar to a four-story house. First there is a ground floor which represents the physical plane. You might imagine that this floor contains a number of rooms, each representing a particular magical technique appropriate to this plane. There is a room where oils are blended and poured, a room where candles are molded and consecrated, a room where waters are created, a room where powders and incense are compounded, and a room where crystals are cleansed and charged with energy. Each of these rooms is dedicated to a particular element, so that as you work with these physical tools you learn about the four elements and their correspondence to the various facets within your character.

---

[1]Dion Fortune, *Sane Occultism* (London: Aquarian Press, 1967), p. 82.

There is a kitchen with a large hearth; this is your laboratory. And there is an herb garden just outside the kitchen. There is also a storage room which contains supplies of magical tools. As a novice, you will, of necessity, spend more time obtaining supplies for magical practice than in creating the supplies themselves. Later, when you are more experienced, you may decide to specialize in the creation of one or more magical tools. Finally, there is a small room which serves as a temple where, after all your preparations, you may practice your magic.

Those who know little of magic often think that physical plane magic—the lighting of candles, the sprinkling of powders, etc.—is what magic is all about. This is because they aren't privy to what goes on behind the scenes, so to speak, on the other planes.

There are two important reasons to practice magic on the physical level. First, physical materials such as herbs and incense stimulate your senses, which in turn activate certain areas of your psyche and create an emotional state in you conducive to the practice of magic. Second, the use of physical materials grounds energies generated on the higher planes so that you obtain tangible results from your magical operations.

THE EMOTIONAL PLANE

The second floor of this imaginary house represents the emotional plane and, like the first, contains a number of rooms. There is a quiet room in which you can daydream and visualize what it is you want to achieve. There are studios where you can experiment with music, dance, or the visual arts to see what effect these have upon your emotional state. And there are a variety of therapy rooms available so that you may release the emotional stresses which are the primary cause of physical illness and pain.

Since it is emotion (desire) which motivates anyone to practice magic in the first place, the emotional plane plays a pivotal role in magic. Desire to achieve a goal urges you to move up one level to the mental plane where you can plan your magical operations for optimal results.

THE MENTAL PLANE

The third floor is a symbol of the mental plane. This story is a vast library, with books of knowledge on all subjects, not just metaphysics and magic. There are chairs and couches so that you can mull over your goals and plans in comfort. And there are plenty of writing desks, where you can create affirmations and incantations. The only sound tolerated here is the muffled shuffle of cards and the click of runes or coins as oracles are consulted. The analysis and planning you do on this level are critical to the safe achievement of your goals through your practice of magic.

THE SPIRITUAL PLANE

The fourth and top floor—the penthouse, so to speak—represents the spiritual plane. This is a large and very lovely room, filled with paintings, friezes, and sculptures of all that has ever been held sacred on Earth. There is a beautiful brazier, containing the fire of purification and creativity. The roof opens, like the dome of an observatory, on clear starry nights. A spiral ladder climbs to the open sky so that you may without hindrance observe the stars, offer prayers, and receive the influx of divine inspiration. It is generally a quiet place, except for those times when chants and music may be heard. Work you do on the spiritual level affects all lower levels, and gives depth and permanence to your magical operations.

These four planes or stories comprise the formal architecture of magic. There is, however, one other place that we should visit.

THE CELLAR

This is a dark and labyrinthine place. It contains all your instincts and personal memories. It also contains those feelings, thoughts, and urges you choose to deny or ignore. Its ways are difficult to negotiate without a guide. But negotiate them you must. Your sanity and the quality (even the quantity) of your energy depend on this, for what goes on in the cellar will eventually affect, for good or ill, the emotional plane. The cellar is otherwise known as your personal unconscious.[2]

It is imperative that you have a thorough grounding in psychological principles and, more importantly, a deep knowledge of what is going on in your own psyche if you wish to practice magic. The work of those best known in magic—Dion Fortune, Israel Regardie, and Murry Hope, to name three—is psychologically based. Fortune was one of the first practicing psychoanalysts in England; she wrote two textbooks on psychology, both of which are still in print today.[3] Murry Hope, England's foremost contemporary occultist, has written two magic-related psychology books, both of which are used as textbooks in the British school system.[4] Israel Regardie expressed his vehemence on this subject when he wrote in 1937:

> I have seen absolutely nothing in the past thirty years to deflect me from my primary conviction that psychotherapy, regardless of type of school, needs to be made a part of the curriculum of every Mystery School. Arguments that meditative techniques, astrological

---

[2]Modern psychology no longer refers to the subconscious or the superconscious, but combines the two concepts in the term unconscious. The cellar described here is similar (but not identical) to the Freudian subconscious, while the open sky viewed from the penthouse is similar to the Freudian superconscious. In keeping with modern usage, I have used the term unconscious when referring to that part of the psyche which seems to produce mysterious urges and intuitions. As discussed in chapter 1, it is the unconscious to which we appeal when we practice magic.

[3]Dion Fortune, *The Machinery of the Mind* (York Beach, ME: Samuel Weiser, 1980) is an excellent primer of psychology. *The Problem of Purity* (York Beach, ME: Samuel Weiser, 1980), also by Fortune, is marred by a distinctly Victorian view of sexuality, but is worth reading, particularly for those who choose to lead a celibate life. Both books were originally published under Fortune's real name, Violet M. Firth. Fortune's extensive psychological knowledge didn't preclude her needing personal help on occasion. William Gray, who knew Fortune personally, wrote me that she had made an appointment to see a Freudian psychiatrist just prior to her death. The cause of her distress (if it existed) is not known.

[4]See Murry Hope, *The Psychology of Ritual* (Shaftesbury, England: Element Books, 1988) and *The Psychology of Healing* (Shaftesbury, England: Element Books, 1989).

insights, and visionary experience lead in the direction of self-knowledge are true enough. I have no argument with these facts. But the subtle effects of ego inferiority, concealed as it is within the unconscious depths of the psyche, are so extensive and insidious that unless the student has a guru of first class quality, his meditations and insights and visions will become totally distorted without his even being aware that such is the case.[5]

In 1970, Regardie wrote that his opinion hadn't changed over the years, and that he had undergone psychotherapy himself and acquired some of the qualifications necessary to practice it. He further stated that he wouldn't even consider discussion of magic with a student until that student had experienced some form of psychotherapy.[6]

The point here is that if you wish to practice magic safely, you must have a deep knowledge of what is going on in your personal unconscious. I know of no better way to gain this knowledge than to consult a psychotherapist.

With this architecture of magic in mind, we are now ready to look at the magical techniques appropriate to each of the four floors or planes. We'll begin on the third floor, with the mental plane, since that is the starting point for any well-planned (and therefore ultimately effective) magical operation.

---

[5]Israel Regardie, *My Rosicrucian Adventure* (St. Paul, MN: Llewellyn Publications, 1971), p. 5.

[6]See Israel Regardie, *The Middle Pillar* (St. Paul, MN: Llewellyn, 1985), p. viii. This book is subtitled "A Co-relation of the Principles of Analytical Psychology and the Elementary Techniques of Magic."

Chapter 4

THE MENTAL PLANE

The most important rule is to formulate, *clearly and precisely,* the goal to be reached, *and then to* retain it unswervingly in mind *throughout all the stages of the execution, which are often long and complex.*[1]

—*Roberto Assagioli*

Mental plane work consists of meditation, self-analysis, goal analysis, written expression of the goal, creation of affirmations and magical incantations—in fact, of anything which involves thought and words, either written or spoken. Divination is also included in mental plane work, since consulting an oracle is an important part of planning prior to the actual performance of a magical operation.[2]

SETTING YOUR GOAL

The work you do upon the mental plane is critical to the safe achievement of your goal. It's possible to get by with errors made upon the spiritual, emotional, and physical planes. If you pray to the "wrong" deity for assistance, for instance, or design a weak or faulty visualization, or use the wrong incense, there's still a possibility that you can achieve your goal—or at least partially achieve it. But errors made upon the mental plane can mean that you will

---

[1]Roberto Assagioli, *The Act of Will* (Baltimore: Penguin, 1974), pp. 178–179.

[2]Not all authorities on magic associate divination with the mental plane. It's sometimes assigned to the spiritual plane, since the seeker is presumably contacting a higher power when consulting an oracle. Sometimes it's assigned to the physical plane because oracle consultation usually involves manipulation of physical objects such as cards or runes.

have to cope with unwanted and unintended consequences after your goal has been achieved. With thought and planning—that is, with careful mental plane work—such consequences can easily be avoided.

DEFINING YOUR GOAL

You must know what you want before you can attain it. This may sound simplistic, but there are an amazing number of people who have, at best, only a vague idea of what they want. Vague ideas produce vague results.

Suppose your goal is to enjoy greater financial prosperity. Fine, but how do you define prosperity? It might mean having a million dollars in the bank. Or it might mean earning a good living doing what you most love to do.

Let me illustrate the goal-definition process with a personal example. Many years ago, I decided I wanted to be financially independent. I had worked for twenty-five years in jobs which meant nothing to me personally, and while they paid the rent, I was sick to death of it. I wanted the freedom to call my time my own.

Not too long after I had settled on this goal, I realized its impossibility. My mother had died when I was young and my father, whose finances I managed, had very little money; so inheritance was out of the question. My marriage of many years had broken up and I had no desire to remarry. The job I held as an office manager certainly wasn't going to make me rich, and I've never been lucky with the lottery. My goal was clearly impossible. I went to work on the project anyway, using techniques which this book describes.

Then it occurred to me that what I needed was not financial independence, but a schedule which would allow me to do what I wanted, when I wanted. Basically, this meant working for myself.

So now I had a new goal. But what kind of business should I go into? There was really only one answer—something I loved! There was only one thing I really wanted to do, and that was to become part of the metaphysical world. I had been making herbal concoctions for years, for myself and for others, and they had proven both effective and useful. The owner of the local metaphysical store expressed an interest in seeing my potions. She liked what she saw and said she could sell them. The small batch I gave her were sold within an hour, and thus I began my business, Nancy B. Watson's Potions. I quit my job one month later.

The point here is that my original goal—financial independence—was gradually changed and redefined until it became something quite different and more realistic. Is your goal realistic? You have set your sights too high if you can't imagine achieving your goal without the aid of a miracle. Scale down your goal if you have to, as I did. There is nothing wrong with achieving a goal in stages.

Suppose, for instance, that your goal is to have a million dollars in the bank. Can you really imagine having a million dollars in the bank? One part of you obviously can—the part that has set the goal. But another part of you may balk at the idea. "Impossible," this part says, "you can never have a million dollars in the bank. You're not worthy of it. You don't deserve it. You could never earn that much. It'll never happen." *When one part of you says it can't happen, it isn't going to happen.* So scale down the goal—to half a million dollars, perhaps. Can you and your pessimistic part imagine this? "No, it's still too much." All right, then, how about one hundred thousand dollars? "A hundred thousand's okay." Aha! You and your pessimistic part are comfortable with this amount, so your new goal is to have one hundred thousand dollars in the bank. When you have this amount, you'll probably find that your pessimistic part has no trouble imagining half a million dollars in the bank, so you can go to work on that. And this can continue until you reach your ultimate goal.

After you've decided on a goal, always set aside some quiet time and casually mull the goal over in your mind. Listen to any objections issuing from the pessimistic part of you. Take whatever it says seriously. If you attempt to override its voice, it will attempt to sabotage your work, so listen carefully. If you need to rethink and redefine your goal in order to accommodate your pessimistic part, do so.

Take a lot of time formulating your goal. Rethink it three, fifteen, fifty times if necessary; but get it right. If you follow the advice in this book, you have an excellent chance of attaining your desires. So make sure you really want what you say you want before you start lighting candles or muttering incantations.

If you find this business of setting goals very difficult, you are probably a feeling type. In that case, I recommend that you read Roberto Assagioli's *The Act of Will*.[3]

ANTICIPATING CONSEQUENCES

Try to anticipate negative repercussions which might occur as a result of achieving your goal. A force, like a coin, always has two sides: one positive, one negative. You cannot invoke a positive force without invoking its negative side as well. This is metaphysical law.

Suppose that your goal is to attract a new romance into your life. A new romance is a positive force, but please be aware that achievement of your goal will require some sacrifice on your part. If you are an independent or private person, for instance, a new romance will require that you forego some of your independence and privacy. This is the price you will pay to attain your desire. It is the negative side of the force (of love) which you have invoked. How much privacy are you willing to give up when you attain your goal?

Perhaps you want to be more prosperous. Prosperity is the positive force that you want. Be aware that increased prosperity usually carries with it additional work or responsibility, which represent the negative side of the force you have invoked.

A former boss of mine became a self-made millionaire over the many years I worked for him. I watched him go from a fairly easy-going and fun-loving person to a man obsessed with money. He worked an average of ten hours a day in the office. In the

---

[3]See note 1 on p. 23.

mornings, before he came to work, he studied the stock market. He did the same after work. He bought every fancy gadget invented, and he spent most of his spare time taking these things to and from repair shops. In short, he was run by his money. I don't really think this is what most of us envision when we think of prosperity. I think most of us imagine having enough leisure time to do exactly what we want to do. This man had no leisure time. Twice a year he'd go to the tropics for a vacation. He took computer manuals with him to read on the beach. Some vacation. How much work are you willing to take on in order to achieve the prosperity you want?

Perhaps you want to overcome a health problem. With this goal, you are attempting to banish a negative force—an illness. But remember that every force has two sides. We often give ourselves physical diseases in order to take care of ourselves psychologically. If you find yourself stuck in a rut, or in an unpleasant situation from which you wish to escape, or if you are very tired, or need more love and attention, you may contract a physical disease in order to take care of yourself emotionally.

Obviously, giving yourself a physical disease is not the best way to take care of your emotional needs. There are better ways, but these require, first, that you understand what your needs are and, second, that you make some changes in your life so these needs can be taken care of. If you are in a rut, it's time to make a change. This may mean quitting a job of many years, which is always a frightening proposition. If you are in an unpleasant situation, it may mean you have to directly confront people or circumstances which you would rather not confront. If you are very tired, you may have to look at your work habits and change them. If you need more love and affection, you must try to understand why you don't have as much as you want. Perhaps you are afraid of being vulnerable, in which case you are going to have to take some risks. Perhaps you don't like to ask for affection outright, in which case you are going to have to speak up. It takes honesty to understand what the real cause of a disease is, and it takes courage to make needed changes. Sometimes it's easier simply to suffer the disease.

Back in 1974, I moved into a new house. I hoisted furniture and fifty-pound sacks of earth, and my back began to ache. Then I developed numbness in my leg and foot and I was put into the hospital for nine days for treatment of a slipped disc. My favorite thing has always been to curl up in bed with a book and to read for hours. Imagine my surprise when I was told that the only known cure for a back problem is prolonged bed rest!

On doctor's orders, I stayed in bed and read for three months. It was bliss. It was also thought-provoking. It was clear that my tendencies to impatience and hyperindependence had gotten me into trouble. I had taken on too much of a burden, and the burden wasn't all physical. At the time, I was living with a very demanding man, working for a very demanding boss, and caring for a very demanding father. So it's not too surprising that I developed a disease which demanded that I do my favorite thing.

The downside was that a slipped disc is a chronic problem which could conceivably have threatened my financial survival. Bosses don't look with favor on employees who land in the hospital every few months. So the experience convinced me that I had to curb my impatience, ask for help when necessary, and lie down and read at every opportunity—all of which I have tried to do, with good results so far. Looking back, I realize that if I hadn't been forced by injury to take it easy, I would probably have had a nervous breakdown, something I consider much more serious than a slipped disc.

If overcoming physical illness is your goal, try to figure out what benefits you are getting from your illness before you try to banish the disease by magic, because if you banish the disease, you banish the benefits as well. Then try to figure out how you can achieve those same benefits without getting sick. When you've figured this out, you can cure the disease magically—if you're still suffering from it. You probably won't be.

No matter what your goal, try to anticipate how its achievement is going to affect not only you, but those around you. Try to anticipate negative reactions others might have to your achievement. If you attract a new romance, your friends may be hurt when you don't see them as often as you have in the past. If you become more prosperous, your friends and family may be envious, and envy is never easy to handle. It's almost impossible, of course, to anticipate every little thing that could happen, but do your best.

EXPRESSING YOUR GOAL SAFELY

Once you have anticipated all the possible negative repercussions which might occur when you achieve your goal, you can attempt to prevent their occurrence by the use of safety clauses. This is formally known in magic as "binding the baser aspect."[4] The principle here is to state your primary goal (love, prosperity, etc.), along with secondary goals (privacy, leisure time, etc.) which are also important to you.

Assume your goal is a new romance, and that you are a private and independent person. You want the new romance, but you don't want to give up all your privacy or independence. Your goal might be: "I want a new romance *and* to maintain some independence and privacy." Or, perhaps you want greater prosperity, but don't want to become a slave to your money. Your goal might be: "I want greater prosperity *and* enough leisure time to enjoy it." If your goal is better health and you have determined that it was your need for more affection which produced your ill-health in the first place, your goal might be: "I want perfect health *and* plenty of affection."

It's also important that you make use of "generic" safety clauses. These are clauses such as: "and may everyone benefit," or "and may it be for the good of all," or "and may it be for my highest good and greatest joy." If your goal is to have one million dollars in the bank and you don't use a generic safety clause, you might find yourself in the hospital after an auto accident, paralyzed for life, with a million dollars of insurance money in the bank. Generic safety clauses can be tacked onto the end of any goal. A completely expressed goal thus might be: "I want one million dol-

---

[4]Medieval magicians physically bound talismans representing their goals with leather thongs or cords in an attempt to prevent the negative side of the invoked force from manifesting.

lars in the bank and lots of leisure time to enjoy it—and may everyone benefit."

WRITING DOWN YOUR GOAL

There are entire systems of magic based solely upon formulating and writing down a goal. This suggests that the power of the written word should never be underestimated.

My very first experience with magic involved formulating and writing down a goal. I was 15, and had been introduced to that little book I mentioned earlier called *It Works*, which maintained that any goal could be achieved if you knew exactly what you wanted and wrote your desire down in detail. At the time, I was attempting to work my way up through the theatrical ranks as an actress and as yet hadn't gotten very far. It was November or December of 1961 and I was playing a walk-on in a production. I had a terrific crush on an older man in the cast named Ron. The show was about to close, and I was concerned because I didn't think I'd ever see him again. I decided to put *It Works* to the test. My goal was to see Ron again, so I wrote down, "I want to see Ron again." The book said to be specific, so I had to decide when I wanted to see him. I had developed an interest in astrology and had heard that on February 4, 1962, there was to be a major conjunction of planets which, according to some astrologers, could signal the end of the world. I decided that I might as well see Ron on the day the world came to an end, so I wrote: "I want to see Ron again on February 4th." Remembering the need for specificity, I had to fix a time and so arbitrarily picked one o'clock in the afternoon. My final written goal was: "I want to see Ron again on February 4th at 1:00 P.M." As I wrote this, I had no idea on what day of the week February 4th would fall, nor any idea what I would be doing on that day. Our show closed on schedule and some time later I was invited to attend a theatrical gathering on the afternoon of February 4th. (This was unusual, since most theatrical gatherings take place late at night.) On February 4th, I walked into the theatre and looked at the box office clock. It was 12:59 P.M. I walked down the stairs into the lobby and walked right into Ron, who opened his arms and shouted with joy at the sight of me: "JUDY!" Since my name is Nancy, this was something of a letdown. Clearly I should have included a safety clause in my written goal, "and he will know who I am when he sees me." However, *it worked*. In fact, it worked beyond all belief. I didn't see Ron for a year. On February 4, 1963, I ran into him at a restaurant. Another year intervened and on February 4, 1964, I saw him yet again. I haven't seen him since, but I think of him every February 4th. This experience hooked me on magic.

Students often ask how specific they should be when they set their goals. There are two schools of thought on this. One school—reminiscent of *It Works*—says that one should be as specific as possible. This means that a written goal (safety clauses included) will often run to many lines, sometimes even a page or so. The other school maintains that goals should be rather openended. Dion Fortune belonged to the open-ended school of thought. In her *Practical Occultism in Daily Life*, she spoke specifically about setting monetary goals, but her words might well apply to all goals:

> [I]t is never wise to work for a specific sum of money. By so doing we limit the whole range and scope of opportunities that might otherwise have been available for us. Supposing, for instance, we worked for a hundred pounds, which we conceived to be the sum necessary to solve our immediate problems, and . . . a hundred pounds came our way . . . [W]e have got our hundred pounds, it is true, but . . . if we have been able to set in motion cosmic power sufficient to produce a hundred pounds, we have started off a chain of causes that might have led anywhere if we had not checked them at the hundred pound limit."[5]

[5]Dion Fortune, *Practical Occultism in Daily Life* (London: Aquarian Press, 1969), pp. 47–48.

Fortune is essentially saying that there is such a thing as too much control. It is sometimes best to allow the unconscious, or any other energies working on the project, to decide the best way a goal should be fulfilled. You set goals with the conscious mind, but the unconscious mind is in many ways more wise than the conscious, and for this reason can be trusted to make important decisions.

I think each method has its place, and the one to use depends on the goal. If your goal is a romantic one, for instance, and if you know the qualities you want in a mate or lover, it is probably wise to list all of those qualities in the goal. I have known people who have specified that they wanted intelligence, a sense of humor, trustworthiness, etc. in a lover, but neglected to specify that the lover should be free of other romantic entanglements, and then have found themselves pursued by individuals intelligent, humorous, trustworthy, but very definitely married. With this type of goal, being specific pays off.

On the other hand, if your goal involves money, it is probably best not to specify how you will receive the money. Let your unconscious decide how it's going to provide for you. The unconscious usually takes the shortest possible (the most efficient) route to produce results in material reality.

> Writing down goals is powerful magic.
> Be careful what you write.

DIVINATION, AFFIRMATIONS, AND INCANTATIONS

> Divination is . . . a spiritual diagnosis whereby we try to discover what subtle influences are at work in our affairs. It can be exceedingly helpful if rightly done . . .[6]

---

[6]Dion Fortune, *Practical Occultism in Daily Life* (London: Aquarian Press, 1969), p. 38.

When you have formulated and written down your goal to your satisfaction, you must determine if it is appropriate for you to pursue the goal at this time. This is done by performing divination, which is also known as consulting an oracle.

ORACLES

The oracle you choose is entirely up to you. You might want to consult the tarot, the Cartouche, the Medicine or Olympus Cards, the runes, or the I Ching. Choose that with which you are most comfortable. If you don't have any divination skills as yet, but are anxious for information, or if you have no real talent for divination, I recommend the *I Ching Workbook* by R. L. Wing.[7] This contains clear and simple instructions and invaluable advice.

I do not recommend the use of a pendulum for this work. It's important to use some device over which you have little conscious control (such as cards, runes, or I Ching coins), because your great interest in achieving your goal may lead you to manipulate the pendulum in such a way that it tells you exactly what you want to hear. It's too easy to cheat with a pendulum.

For the same reason, I do not recommend purely psychic methods in this instance, because it's too easy for one part of your mind to tell another part of your mind exactly what it wants to hear. You want the truth, not the advice given by a conscious mind fired up with ambition and desire.

If you don't have any divination skills and can't (for whatever reason) use the *I Ching Workbook*, you have no choice but to consult with someone who has the necessary skills. This should be a professional, not someone you just happen to know. Well-intentioned family members or friends who have the requisite skills may have a stake in your goal, and their advice might be more biased than honest.

---

[7] R. L. Wing, *I Ching Workbook* (New York: Doubleday, 1979).

I once met a woman who insisted that she be the one to give oracle advice to her 16-year old son, who was working on a prosperity goal. She explained that she knew her son better than anyone else, and that she had his best interests at heart. I reminded her that very often we think we know what's best for someone else, when in fact we don't. She didn't want to hear this, became quite livid, and threatened in public to direct negative energy my way. I didn't cringe, but I did feel very sorry for her son, whose goal probably involved getting enough funds together to allow him to escape from his manipulative mother. Any similar situation is one you want to avoid.

Consulting another individual, even a professional, is an inferior way to get the information you need after you have set a goal. It is your own unconscious mind which speaks to you through the oracle, and your unconscious is an expert, like no other, on the subject of your well-being and happiness. Its advice will be truthful and can be trusted. Besides, the essence of magic is self-help. The true magician is as self-sufficient as he possibly can be.

The purpose of consulting an oracle after you have set a goal is to determine if pursuing the goal at a given time will benefit you in the way you wish. This is an important safety measure. We often enthusiastically choose a new goal and rush headlong to achieve it, never stopping to consider if our timing is right or if there are obstacles, subtle perhaps, standing in our way. And then, when we don't get what we want, we are disappointed. We can save ourselves a lot of grief by asking the oracle for its advice before we start magical procedures.

Your discussion with the oracle might sound like this: "Oracle, here is the project I have in mind," and you state your written goal. "If I pursue this goal, what can I expect?" Or, "What are your comments?" Then shuffle the cards or throw the runes or coins, and interpret the result.

Most of the time, the oracle will respond by saying something like: "This is a pretty good idea. But there are a couple of factors you haven't taken into consideration, and these are . . . ," and it will tell you what you have neglected to consider in formulating your goal. This kind of response is known as a qualified go-ahead. You should seriously consider any factors you may have overlooked and, if necessary, rethink and rewrite your goal. When you have done this, consult the oracle once again to be sure you haven't overlooked anything else, then proceed with your plans.

Sometimes, the oracle will respond: "This is the worst idea you've ever had. Don't even consider pursuing this goal." This is, of course, very disheartening. With this kind of response, the oracle is telling you one of two things: either your timing is bad, or your goal is ill-chosen.

Bad timing is a common problem. Your goal may be appropriate, but you may have chosen to pursue it at a time when it cannot be achieved. In this case, the oracle is trying to save you a lot of time, energy, and disappointment by telling you not to pursue it now. You might be entirely unaware of temporary circumstances that exist which make achieving your goal impossible. There might be some emotional blockage within you which will prevent you from attaining what you desire. Or the stars and numbers may be temporarily adverse (see page 36). In the face of the oracle's opposition, don't proceed with your plans, but don't be entirely discouraged either. Ask the oracle at regular intervals if you can pursue the goal. When the time is right, it will let you know.

If you ask the oracle many times if it's appropriate to pursue the goal and its advice is invariably and vehemently negative, this is a strong signal that you may have chosen a goal which is entirely unsuitable—one which could prove disastrous to you or to those for whom you care. Please remember that it is *your* unconscious which speaks to you through the oracle, and that your unconscious has *your* best interests at heart; it wants to see you well and happy. It knows more than you do on the conscious level, and is seeking to protect you from harm. Its advice, though disappointing, is ultimately to your benefit, if you will heed it. I've known people who have gone to work magically on a goal even after an oracle has cautioned them many times against it. The results were not good. We magicians tend to be willful, sometimes to our detriment.

Now for the good news. Sometimes the oracle will respond to your query with: "This is the best idea you've ever had! Go for it!" Congratulations—and carry on!

ASTROLOGY, NUMEROLOGY, AND MAGIC

We must now consider the subjects of astrology and numerology in relation to the practice of magic. Dealing with them is like dealing with the weather. You don't usually plan a picnic in the dead of Winter for obvious reasons. As a magician, you should always be aware of astrological and numerological "weather" conditions before you embark on a major magical project. If your goal is to find a new romance and transiting Saturn happens to be sitting on your natal Venus, or if you are pursuing prosperity and you happen to be in a Seven Personal Year, you haven't a hope of achieving your goal under current conditions. Knowing what is going on with the stars and numbers can save you a lot of energy.

Ideally, you should learn to be your own astrologer and numerologist so that advice is always available when you need it. (You'll also save yourself a lot of money; astrological and numerological advice isn't cheap.) But I recognize that both disciplines—astrology, particularly—require a good deal of study before they can be mastered. For younger students, these studies may of necessity lie in the future. The study of astrology today is a great deal easier, however, than it was when I began it. Astrologers who have access to a computer no longer have to do tedious calculations. This simplifies the subject considerably, particularly for those, like myself, who hate arithmetic.

If you do not yet have astrological skills, my advice is to consult a good astrologer once a year and ask to have your transits calculated for the coming twelve months. Tell the astrologer to advise you at which points during the year it would be best to work on prosperity goals, romantic goals, health goals, etc. And ask to be advised when it would be best *not* to work on these goals. This will give you a good time frame for your magical operations. Still, your ultimate goal should be to become your own astrologer. The salespeople in any good metaphysical bookstore can help you choose a textbook. Many of these stores offer astrology classes as well.

There don't seem to be many numerologers around, so you may be forced to become your own consultant, which isn't a bad thing at all. Numerology gives valuable advice on timing and superb information on character as well. It's also great fun and easy to learn. There are many fine numerology books on the market. For beginners, I particularly recommend Florence Campbell's classic *Your Days are Numbered*, and for those who already know the basics, *Numerology, the Complete Guide*, by Matthew Oliver Goodwin.[8] Goodwin's work is probably the most complete treatment of numbers I've ever seen and is superb—but it's not for beginners.

Having consulted your oracle and considered astrological and numerological conditions, it's time to start working with affirmations.

CREATING AND USING AFFIRMATIONS

When you have settled on and written out your goal, and have been given the go-ahead by an oracle, your next task is to choose or construct affirmations for daily use.

Affirmations are statements describing the positive state you want to attain by achieving your goal. They are important in magical work because they enable you to reverse much of your early negative conditioning. As Dion Fortune points out:

> The effect of . . . rhythmic repetitions of significant phrases is very great, as Coué showed in his system of auto-suggestion and as the Catholic Church has always known and taught in the repetition of prayers upon the beads of the rosary.[9]

As a child, you loved and trusted your parents, and took whatever they told you as absolute truth. You also imitated their behavior.

---

[8]Florence Campbell, *Your Days Are Numbered* (Marina del Rey, CA: De Vorss, 1958); Matthew Oliver Goodwin, *Numerology: The Complete Guide* (North Hollywood, CA: Newcastle, 1981),

[9]Dion Fortune, *Practical Occultism in Daily Life* (London: Aquarian Press, 1969), p. 14.

But parents aren't perfect, and with maturity, you may have discovered that what you were taught has not benefited you as an adult. You may have inherited a bad attitude about money, for instance, and find yourself perpetually on the brink of poverty. This is tiresome and stressful, so you eventually decide to increase your prosperity. You set a financial goal and go to work on it magically, but nothing happens. You've done your magical work, but you still wonder where next month's rent is coming from. What has gone wrong? Early conditioning is the culprit, and self-sabotage is the result. The part of your psyche that is bound up with your early childhood has refused to relinquish its control over your attitudes and behavior, and it has sabotaged your magical efforts.

There are only two ways I know of to get rid of self-sabotage: psychotherapy and a combination of affirmations and emotional clearing.[10] If you come from a severely dysfunctional family, I strongly recommend you see a therapist in addition to doing affirmations or emotional clearing work.

Before you can create and use effective affirmations, you must first be aware of your capacity for self-sabotage. This involves taking an honest look at your childhood and what you were taught by your parents. This isn't easy, but it's necessary if you want to achieve your goals.

Suppose your current goal is to find a happy romantic relationship. Take a look at your previous romances. If your former romantic partners were abusive, then you can be pretty sure that your parents abused you in some way, and that you are unconsciously repeating a childhood pattern. An affirmation to help break the pattern might be: "I am surrounded by gentle, loving people."

Perhaps you continually find yourself poverty-stricken and want greater prosperity. Why are you always poor? Look at your childhood, and at your parents' attitude toward money. Perhaps they subscribed to the widely held puritanical notion that unless you slog away for fifteen hours a day you don't deserve money. This is balderdash! If you work creatively and efficiently for a

---

[10]Emotional clearing will be covered in chapter 6.

shorter period of time, you can earn just as much and have more energy for other pursuits. Or perhaps your parents felt that people who had money were evil. This is ridiculous. There are at least as many evil poor people as there are evil rich people. Perhaps your parents felt guilty about having money, and passed this on to you.

Both of my parents were born to wealth and never had to worry about money in their early years. Unfortunately, all the money was gone by the time I was born. My mother, who knew nothing about money because she had never had to deal with it, did the only thing she could, which was to warn me that I would be on my own financially when I grew up. I can still hear her words: "There will never be any money for you, Nancy." She must have said this a thousand times. And she was right: there was never any money for me, not even when I worked long and hard. Her words had programmed me to poverty. It took me years to grasp this, but once I did, I immediately went to work to reverse the conditioning. The affirmation I used (and still use) is: "There is always plenty of money for you, Nancy."

When you have set a new goal, look back over your life to see how successfully you have achieved similar goals in the past. If you don't like the pattern you see, you can be fairly sure that self-sabotage is your problem, and that you need to work with affirmations.

THREE STEPS TO EFFECTIVE AFFIRMATIONS

Creating affirmations is a personal process, driven by each individual's own character and goals. Indeed, the more personal your affirmations, the more effective they will be. Most successful affirmations, however, have several things in common. The following simple steps will help you to maximize the effectiveness of your own personal affirmations.

1. **Always phrase an affirmation in the present tense:** An affirmation such as "I will be wealthy" won't work because your use

of the future tense conveys to your unconscious mind that it needn't produce wealth in the present, only at some unspecified time in the future. You want money now, so instead try: "I *am* wealthy." But this will be effective only if you truly believe that you are wealthy while you say the words.[11] If you cannot feel wealthy when you say this, forget it. Instead, work with: "I am wealthier every day," which puts no terrific strain on your credulity or emotional state.

2. **Never use a negative word in an affirmation:** I once had a friend who discovered the joys of doing affirmations. She called me, very excited, to tell me her first, which was: "I have a healthy, sexy body, free of disease." A disaster. To understand where she went wrong, close your eyes for a moment and mentally say the word "disease" to yourself. If you're normal, the word will bring up very unpleasant pictures or feelings.

Let me explain the mechanism at work here. The unconscious mind does not understand words. It belongs to an earlier phase of evolution than the conscious mind—a preverbal phase. The only things the unconscious mind understands are pictures and feelings. Words are important in magic because they conjure up pictures and feelings. If you use a word with happy connotations (such as "love" or "prosperity"), that word calls up happy pictures and feelings. Your unconscious takes these and goes to work to reproduce them for you in material reality. But the reverse is also true. If you use words which conjure up unpleasant pictures or feelings, your unconscious will go to work to reproduce these in material reality. Your unconscious produces in material reality whatever pictures or feelings you give it—good, bad, or indifferent. You must therefore choose your words carefully.

3. **Be sure you are entirely comfortable with the affirmations you choose or create:** A year before I quit my nine-to-five office job, I used Louise Hay's *Feeling Fine* affirmation tape

---

[11]Instructions on how to dredge up appropriate feeling will be given in chapter 6.

every morning.[12] I loved this tape, but there was one affirmation on it which I positively detested: "Every day is fun for me!" Every day was *not* fun for me—every day was hell, and there was no way I was going to convince myself otherwise. I remember repeating the affirmation with extreme sarcasm at first, then finally refusing to repeat it at all. I actively resented the affirmation because the anticipation of hearing it spoiled my enjoyment of the rest. This situation illustrates the disadvantages of using affirmations someone else has created.

Some affirmations just aren't going to sit well with you, and these should be dropped from your repertoire as soon as possible. When you choose or create a new affirmation, spend a little quiet time, repeat the affirmation to yourself, and listen to what various parts of you have to say about it. If your new affirmation is: "I am vibrantly healthy!" and you hear an inner voice muttering sarcastically, "Sure you are!" you had better figure out another affirmation to use. Using affirmations which produce aggravation or disbelief can be counterproductive.

~

People often ask me how many affirmations they should create to cover a single goal. My inclination is to answer "several," meaning anywhere from three to ten, or even more. The number depends on how complex your goal is and what kind of obstacles—particularly those relating to your early conditioning—you have to overcome. But if you create too many affirmations, you may not do them because of time limitations, so keep the number down to something manageable.

A list of sample affirmations relating to prosperity goals is given at the end of this chapter (see page 46). You may use them if you wish, but it would be much better if you created your own, because you know your goal and your background much better than I do. Furthermore, the more you put into your magic, the

---

[12]Louise Hay, *Feeling Fine* (Carson, CA: Hay House), audiotape.

more you will get out of it. There are, however, two affirmations which I recommend you use in addition to your own creations, and we will discuss these shortly.

Magic has two poles: active and passive. When you operate from the active pole, you generate positive energy in the form of goal writing, affirmations, and magical incantations. Eventually the energy you expend comes back to you, laden with all the good that you desire. When this happens, you must be receptive to the good. When you are receptive, you operate from the passive pole of magic. If you are not receptive, you block the good energies and do not experience them. This is self-sabotage.

Some people are very good "senders." They operate naturally from the active pole of magic. They enjoy the process of setting goals and creating affirmations and incantations, and they easily generate lots of positive energy. Others are very good "receivers." I had a friend who hadn't worked for years and who sat around at home watching soap operas and reading trash novels. I've got nothing against soap operas and trash novels, except that they are spectator sports which don't call forth a lot of energy from the spectator. My friend never did anything creative. He was slowly going broke, but he was absolutely convinced that a fortune would soon drop into his lap.

This man was a champion receiver. Indeed, he was eventually saved from bankruptcy by a former wife who took over the reins, financial and otherwise. This says something about the power of emotional conviction. The problem was that the man didn't much care for his ex-wife, so he really only exchanged one form of bondage (poverty) for another. With a little creative thought and effort, I think he could have done better for himself.

Most people seem to be better receivers than senders. Whatever your natural inclination, you should work on activating both poles of magic within yourself.

EXERCISE 1: POSITIVE ENERGY AFFIRMATION

An affirmation designed to activate the positive part of your personality might be: "I am a creative center which gives off benefits to everyone." You'll understand the power of this affirmation after doing the following exercise.

• Take the phone off the hook and go someplace where you can be quiet and relaxed. Sit or lie down and make yourself as comfortable as possible.

• Go within and make contact with the great energy source you find therein. You might see this as a great light deep in the center of your being. Or you might simply feel the energy deep within you. You may also, if you wish, imagine that there is a beautiful golden crystal emitting rays of intense energy from your solar plexus area. It doesn't matter how you make contact with the energy, as long as the contact is made.[13]

• Imagine that this internal energy is flowing outward from your center. It is flooding your entire body. It is flooding your heart. It is flooding your mind. It is flooding your consciousness. You are entirely filled with beautiful golden energy.

• Let the golden energy flow out from your body. It begins to fill your aura. Expand your aura. Let the golden energy fill your expanded aura.

• You are now surrounded by your own self-generated energy. A sphere of radiant energy envelops you.

• Realize how wonderful this feels. You feel terrific. You are generating positive energy and it is flooding the area around you. Anyone entering the room would feel this energy, and it would make him feel wonderful, because energy, like laughter, is contagious. You feel radiant and positive and optimistic and full of vigor and life, and so do those around you. When you generate positive energy, you benefit others. You really are a creative center which gives off benefits to everyone.

---

[13]Some people do not find the energy within, but rather outside themselves. This presents no problem. Draw the outside energy in through the crown of your head, down into your solar plexus area and make contact with it there.

• Slowly come back to normal consciousness. Wiggle your toes, flex your fingers, open your eyes, stretch and yawn. Repeat the affirmation aloud: "I am a creative center which gives off benefits to everyone."

You needn't do this exercise every time you repeat the affirmation, but do it often. You'll find it very beneficial. It will not only make you feel wonderful, it will also make you irresistible to the world-at-large, because people love to be around those who are generating lots of positive energy.[14] I recommend that you do this exercise prior to any practical magic work, before going to job interviews or auditions, and before asking for a raise or for a favor.

Always repeat this affirmation before you repeat those you have created for yourself.

EXERCISE 2: RECEPTIVITY AFFIRMATION

The affirmation designed to activate the receptive side of your nature is: "I am totally open and receptive to _____."
[Fill in the blank with whatever good you desire.]

It's best to stand or sit while you repeat this affirmation. Raise your arms and open your palms to the ceiling. Lift your chin a little and look up. Feel how open you are in the Heart Chakra area. With arms and chin still raised, repeat the affirmation. If you are working on a prosperity goal, you might say, "I am totally open and receptive to prosperity and abundance!" You might even imagine that dollar bills or gold are raining down upon you from above.

This affirmation should always be repeated at the end of the affirmation list you have created for yourself.

---

[14]An abundance of positive energy—charisma, in fact—has always been a mark of the adept, or high-ranking magician.

TIPS ON USING AFFIRMATIONS

Affirmations are long-term work. Louise Hay says that doing an affirmation is like planting a seed in the ground: if you plant a seed one day, you don't expect to see a full-grown plant the following day.[15] Affirmations must be done every day, as many times a day as possible, for at least three months before you can expect to see results. Three months may seem a long time, but think about the fact that you've lived your whole life up to now with attitudes that haven't produced the benefits you desire. To be able to turn those attitudes around in three months is just short of a miracle.

I recommend that you do your affirmations in the morning. Affirmations give you an emotional lift so that you start the day feeling upbeat. If you run or walk in the morning, try whispering them while you exercise. Passersby will think you're crazy, but that's their problem. If you don't exercise in the morning, I recommend you do your affirmations directly after getting out of the shower. Don't do them in the shower; water, as we shall see later, alters emotional energy, and you certainly don't want to wash away all the positive energy you have generated with your affirmations.

It's a good idea to record your affirmations on a tape. Leave adequate space between the recorded affirmations so that you can repeat them leisurely. I find the most convenient time to use a tape is after a shower, while I'm putting on makeup, doing my hair, and getting dressed.

It's best to repeat affirmations aloud. Let your unconscious hear those positive words! If you have privacy problems, whisper them. And do your affirmations with feeling. Repeating words by rote, without emotion, won't make much of an impression on your unconscious. Remember: the unconscious understands and acts upon feelings.

Writing affirmations is also good. Louise Hay writes out several affirmations before she goes to sleep at night.

---

[15]Louis Hay, *Feeling Fine* (Carson, CA: Hay House), audiocassette.

Do not neglect this daily work. Repetition gets through to the unconscious mind. Your affirmation work will eventually filter down through the emotional plane (altering your feelings) to the physical plane. It is the physical plane which produces material results.

PROSPERITY AFFIRMATIONS

Following are some examples of prosperity affirmations. By all means, feel free to experiment with them. But remember that personally composed affirmations are always the most effective, so don't hesitate to "customize" any of these to fit your own character and goals.

I am a creative center which gives off benefits to everyone.

I attract all the good things in life that I deserve.

I give thanks for all of the riches that come to me.

I am surrounded by money-making opportunities.

I believe in the power of my mind.

I am a channel for riches and abundance.

People pay me good money for my services and products.

Every dollar I spend returns to me three-fold.

I claim my share of universal abundance.

I am as I believe I am.

Riches of all sorts are drawn to me.

Whatever I do prospers.

I attract my share of wealth and possessions.

I am thankful for all the good that comes to me.

I welcome my prosperity with open arms.

I am totally open and receptive to abundance.

MAGICAL INCANTATIONS

Just as the repetition of affirmations has a profound effect upon your unconscious mind, so do rhythm and rhyme, which is why so many magicians make use of magical incantations.

The best-known magical incantation in the English language is from Shakespeare's *Macbeth*. Act Four, Scene One opens with three witches, bent on serious mischief, stirring up a poisonous brew containing (for starters) "Eye of newt and toe of frog, / Wool of bat and tongue of dog, / Adder's fork and blindworm's sting." They incant as they stir the pot:

> "Double, double, toil and trouble;
> Fire burn, and cauldron bubble."[16]

I certainly don't condone the intention of these malevolent beings, but the construction of their incantation is perfect. One expects perfection, of course, from Shakespeare, and while none of us can emulate his mastery of the language, we can still learn a lesson or two about the construction of incantations from him.

1. **State your magical intention as briefly as possible:** Please note that Shakespeare's witches don't go on and on about their intention. They don't say, for instance, "We want to create a lot of toil and trouble in the lives of those who come into contact with us and in order to do this we are putting some thoroughly nasty ingredients into our cauldron and . . . ." They keep it short and to the point.

During a series of classes I gave on practical magic some time ago, I taught the art of constructing magical incantations, but apparently didn't make myself clear about the importance of brevity. One of my students showed me an incantation that had taken a

---

[16]William Shakespeare, *The Tragedy of Macbeth*, IV, i (Boston: *The Riverside Shakespeare*, 1976), lines 10–11.

week to compose, and it was three pages long! The student was so proud of the composition and had obviously worked so hard on it that I didn't have the heart to say it was completely useless—as an incantation, anyway. The thought that had gone into it was probably very productive.

One of the reasons for keeping incantations short is so they can be memorized easily. During the performance of a magical operation, body and mind are both busy. The mind must be kept focused on the work at hand, and the body is usually busy lighting candles and incense, drawing talismans, etc. If an incantation is very long and imperfectly memorized, you will probably have to break away from what you are doing in order to refer back to it. A break in concentration during ritual work is never good. A magical ritual should flow from start to finish, and at some point it should build to an emotional climax. It is this emotional intensity which "speaks" to the unconscious mind. If you must break away from the ritual in order to refresh your memory on an incantation, the climax won't occur, and your chances of magical success decrease. Repeating an incantation should, in fact, keep your mind focused on the work at hand, not force a break in concentration. As a good rule of thumb, an incantation should be no longer than four short lines.

2. **Give your incantation plenty of rhythm and rhyme:** The following superb incantation is taken from William Gray's *Magical Ritual Methods*:

> Earth without and Earth within,
> Make the Mill of magic spin,
> Work the will for which we [I] pray,
> Io Dio, Ha He Yay[17]

---

[17]W. G. Gray, *Magical Ritual Methods* (York Beach, ME: Samuel Weiser, 1980), pp. 215–216. Used by permission. Mr. Gray wrote me that his incantation was based upon one originally written by Wiccan author, Doreen Valiente.

This invokes the magical earth element. There are other similar verses, each of which invokes one of the elements, and they are perfect for elemental work, which will be discussed in later chapters. But for now, it's important that you get a feel for good incantation. Read the above aloud several times until you feel the verse worming its way into your unconscious mind. A message expressed in rhythm and rhyme is easily accepted by the unconscious.

Here is the incantation I use when I am in the process of creating Love Water. It's not Shakespeare, but it will serve:

> Bring them love
> Bring them romance
> Make them lusty
> Make them dance!

This conjures up (for me at least) a picture of happy people frolicking about naked and having a wonderful time. I find the rhythm irresistible. Try repeating this incantation while you are standing, and watch what happens.

Don't let writing poetry intimidate you. The object here is not great literature. In fact, great literature is irrelevant. Bad poetry makes terrific incantations. Of course, if writing bad poetry really offends you, then by all means write good poetry. The more you put into your magic the more you get out of it.

~

Magical incantations are best repeated during the actual performance of a ritual. They are most helpful when you are doing something physical or repetitive. They may be chanted, for instance, while you are lighting candles or incense, sprinkling magical waters or powders about, consecrating a talisman (such as a crystal) with the four elements or creating some kind of magical potion and stirring the pot, like Shakespeare's witches.

Incantations may also be used outside of ritual work. After I slipped a disc, I designed a healing visualization and always accompanied the visual image with a chant:

> Discs aligned,
> My back is fine.

It's not elegant, but it's stuck with me (as a good incantation should), and to this day when I say the words I can see in my mind's eye a spinal column containing perfectly aligned discs. If my back bothers me, I go to bed and, before I go to sleep, I say the incantation and the visual image automatically appears. Remember: the unconscious mind reacts to visual images; and words are important because they call up visual images.

SUMMARY

In summary, let us compare the creation and functions of written goals, affirmations, and incantations:

A *written goal* can be as lengthy as you want it to be. If your goal is very complex, its expression may run to many lines, perhaps even to a page.

An *affirmation* is a statement describing a spiritual, mental, emotional, or physical state which you want to achieve. Affirmations are generally not too lengthy. They are repeated on a daily basis for at least three months.

A *magical incantation* is a short, pithy statement of magical intent, filled with rhythm and rhyme. Incantations are repeated during the actual performance of a magical ritual. Sometimes they may be used outside of ritual for healing or other purposes.

1. Define your goal.

2. Anticipate possible negative repercussions which may occur when you achieve your goal.

3. Redefine your goal if necessary.

4. Write down your goal. Use safety clauses.

5. Perform divination to establish if pursuit of your goal is appropriate.

   (a) With qualified go-ahead from oracle, go back to 3.

   (b) With negative advice from oracle:

      (1) Consult oracle again until positive advice received.

      (2) If oracle consistently gives negative advice, start over with a new goal.

   (c) With positive advice from oracle, go to 6.

6. Create or choose affirmations. Do affirmations daily for three months.

7. Create magical incantations for use when ritual is performed.

CHAPTER 5

THE SPIRITUAL PLANE

[E]very technique of Magic is intended in different ways to open the conscious ego's field of vision to the deeper, more spiritual aspects of the divine nature . . .[1]

—Israel Regardie

Having done all your mental plane work, it is wise to immediately place your project on the level of the spiritual plane. Spiritual plane work adds depth and permanence to your magical operations. Although it is possible to perform magic without any assistance from the spiritual plane, the results obtained from such operations are likely to be temporary. Initially successful results may mysteriously vanish, as if they had never existed at all.

There are three basic types of magical techniques appropriate to the spiritual plane:

1. Prayer, with which almost everyone is familiar;

2. "Assuming the god-form," an advanced spiritual plane technique not as well known as prayer; and

3. "Building the magical personality," which just barely qualifies as a spiritual plane procedure.

It may surprise you to see prayer listed as a magical technique, but in fact it is a very practical one. Murry Hope maintains that all prayers are heard, and I agree with her. The question is: who or what hears the prayers?

---

[1]Israel Regardie, *The Middle Pillar* (St. Paul, MN: Llewellyn, 1985), p. 71.

The answer to this question lies entirely with the individual. Spiritual plane matters are private and intensely personal. No person, system, or institution has the right to dictate how an individual should conduct his spiritual life, and I shall not intrude in this area.

What I propose to do in this chapter is to advise you on how to effectively approach the various archetypes which exist on the spiritual plane. I shall also indicate how to choose the Western archetype most appropriate to the goal you wish to achieve.[2] But the ultimate choice of archetype, and the method of approaching it, is entirely up to you.

∽

Before continuing, you should turn to Appendix B, which contains Murry Hope's personal and god/goddess symbol exercises. Read these and perform them. The exercises have appeared in several of Ms. Hope's books, but those reprinted here—the most sophisticated versions—are taken from her *Ancient Egypt: The Sirius Connection*.[3]

Performing these exercises serves two practical purposes. First, the symbols which surface from your unconscious may well tell you those archetypes with which you can most easily work. Since choosing archetypes can sometimes be confusing for the beginner, this is a real boon. Second, and more important, the symbols provide you with excellent personal protection. As Ms. Hope states: "Once established, personal and god/goddess symbols should be used when undertaking any form of psychic or occult

---

[2] I have worked extensively with the Greek, Roman, Egyptian, Norse, and Celtic pantheons for many years, and the advice I give relating to these deities is based upon my own personal experience. Though I have great respect for all other archetypes, I have no personal experience with them and therefore cannot presume to advise the student how best to choose or approach them.

[3] Murry Hope, *Ancient Egypt: The Sirius Connection* (Shaftesbury, England: Element Books, 1990).

work, time travel, or meditation. These are your security codes which will ensure you safe passage through the unfamiliar territories of altered states of consciousness."[4]

When you have performed the two exercises, you will be ready to explore the spiritual plane. There is no greater adventure.

CHOOSING ARCHETYPES

If you were reared in, and are comfortable with, the Judeo-Christian tradition, then you probably already know which archetypes to call upon for assistance in achieving your goals.[5] There are many people today, however, who are no longer comfortable with this tradition, and it is for them that this chapter is written. As Murry Hope writes:

> Because one man or woman capitalizes the first letter of the word "god," and another prefers to say Jesus instead of Llew, Apollo, Arthur or Horus, does not make him or her a better or more enlightened person, for in the final analysis it will not be the names, fashions, political expediencies or earthly dogmas of the human collective that will be the deciding factor, but the truth, light and love in the heart of the individual for his or her god or goddess.[6]

You may not wish to work with an identifiable deity at all. You may prefer not to anthropomorphize spiritual energy. This is fine. It is possible to appeal to spiritual energy for help (through the use of prayer) without personifying it in any way. I myself have done this many times when, for whatever reason, I have chosen

---

[4] *Ancient Egypt: The Sirius Connection*, pp. 132–135. Used by kind permission.
[5] These include God, Jesus, the Holy Spirit, the Virgin Mary, archangels, angels, and saints.
[6] Murry Hope, *Practical Celtic Magic* (London: Aquarian Press, 1987), p. 136.

not to work with any particular deity, and this has proven effective on a practical level.[7]

You may want to work with the higher self, or with a spiritual guide. This, too, is fine. Or you may want to work with the well-established and highly personified deity-figures found in Western mythologies. There are hundreds of these gods and goddesses, and each is very capable of aiding you with your goals, provided that:

1. You choose an archetype which, *given its nature*, is able to help you with your chosen goal, your general aim in life, or balancing your character.

2. You establish some kind of bond with the deity prior to asking it for favors.

The personal and god symbol exercises contained in Appendix B may help you identify the archetype(s) with which you can most productively work. Then again, they may not. If the exercises don't point in the direction of any particular deity, then you will have to approach the project intellectually.

Choosing an appropriate Western archetype demands some knowledge of mythology. If this isn't your area of expertise, I recommend that you purchase or borrow from the library the *New Larousse Encyclopedia of Mythology*.[8] This covers myths from all over the world (not just the West), and is lavishly illustrated.

Murry Hope's *The Way of Cartouche, Practical Egyptian Magic, Practical Celtic Magic, Practical Greek Magic, Practical Atlantean Magic,* and her *Olympus, Self-Discovery and the Greek Archetypes* are all invaluable sources because they clearly indicate the particular strength of each god or goddess, making it very easy to choose ar-

---

[7]Students who prefer not to work with any form of spiritual plane archetype may find the technique described later in this chapter of particular interest.

[8]*New Larousse Encyclopedia of Mythology* (London: Hamlyn, 1968).

chetypes appropriate to your goals.[9] I wish Ms. Hope would write a book on practical Norse magic to complete the set, so to speak, but it looks as if that isn't going to happen. There has been a recent renaissance of interest in Norse archetypes and there are now several books available on rune magic, some of which contain descriptions of the Norse deities and indicate their functions. If you are interested in Norse lore you should carefully sift through these. I highly recommend Kevin Crossley-Holland's *The Norse Myths* which, while it is not in any sense a book about magic, does give a very complete description of the various Norse archetypes in their mythological context.[10]

If you are interested in the Greeks, you should purchase or borrow Robert Graves' *The Greek Myths*, undoubtedly the most comprehensive book ever written on the subject.[11]

If you find the prospect of searching for an appropriate archetype overwhelming, it might help to know that each Western pantheon has a character all its own and that, with a little self-analysis, you can narrow your search considerably.

It may be helpful at this point to turn to Appendix A and take the "Temperament Questionnaire." The results will tell you whether you are, by nature, an intuitive, thinking, feeling, or sensate type. When you have determined this, use the following profiles to assist you in choosing a spiritual patron.

Intuitive types: Egyptian gods and goddesses appeal to highly spiritual people who probably need to develop the earthier side of

---

[9]Murry Hope, *The Way of Cartouche* (New York: St. Martin's, 1985); *Practical Egyptian Magic* (New York: St. Martin's, 1984); *Practical Celtic Magic* (London: Aquarian Press, 1987); *Practical Greek Magic* (London: Aquarian Press, 1985); *Olympus, Self-Discovery and the Greek Archetypes* (London: Aquarian Press, 1991). Ms. Hope's *Practical Atlantean Magic* (London: Aquarian Press, 1991) in which she has resurrected the original Atlantean deities pre-figuring the Egyptian, Greek, Roman, Celtic and Norse archetypes will be of interest to magicians fascinated with this important prehistoric era.

[10]Kevin Crossley-Holland, *The Norse Myths* (New York: Pantheon, 1980).

[11]Robert Graves, *The Greek Myths* (Baltimore: Penguin, 1968).

their natures. If you're new to magic and are an intuitive type, choosing an Egyptian archetype will benefit you greatly. But if you're an experienced magician, you should consider a Norse deity.

Thinking types: The Greek and Roman deities appeal to those who are by nature intellectual, and who probably need to acknowledge and express their emotions with greater ease. If you're new to magic, a deity from the Greek or Roman pantheons will benefit you. If you're experienced in magic, you should probably seriously consider choosing a Celtic deity—but first see the cautionary note concerning the Celtic archetypes on page 65.

Feeling types: The Celtic archetypes appeal to those who are by nature emotional, and who probably need to develop their capacity for rational thought. If you're new to magic and are a feeling type, a deity from the Celtic pantheon will be a good choice. (Again, be sure to read the note concerning the Celtic deities on page 65.) If you're an experienced magician, consider choosing an archetype from the Greek or Roman pantheons.

Sensate types: Norse deities appeal to naturally earthy, practical people who probably need to elevate their energies to a spiritual level. If you're new to magic and are a sensate type, a Norse archetype will be of benefit. But if you're an experienced magician, you should probably look to the Egyptians.

If you are new to the practice of magic, you will benefit most by choosing a pantheon which is closest to your natural temperament. If you are an experienced magician you will benefit most by choosing a pantheon opposite to your natural temperament. Once you have chosen the pantheon, the search for an appropriate archetype within that pantheon must begin.

Choosing an Archetype that Supports Your Goal: Imagine that your goal is to attract a new romance. Logic would dictate that you choose an archetype which embodies the spirit of love— the great Greek goddess Aphrodite, for instance, or her Roman counterpart Venus. In the Egyptian pantheon, you might want to choose Hathor. The Norse goddess Freya would also be appropriate, as would the Celtic Guinevere. Men might invoke the lusty Zeus (Roman counterpart, Jupiter), or Aphrodite's lover Ares (Roman counterpart, Mars). Adonis would also serve well, as would the Celtic figure of Lancelot.

If your goal is greater prosperity, you need to look for a deity which has a strong relationship with the earth element, which governs abundance: the Greek Earth Mother Gaia, for instance, or Demeter, a grain goddess whose Roman counterpart is Ceres. In the Egyptian pantheon, the luxury-loving cat-goddess Bast would be appropriate; in the Norse, Freya (who loves gold) or Frigga, an earthier figure. Male archetypes include the Roman Pluto, whose name means "wealth," and his Greek cognate Hades, Lord of the Underworld.[12]

If your goal is better health, there are innumerable healers among the gods and goddesses of antiquity. In the Greek and Roman pantheons these include Apollo, Pan (or Faunus), and Artemis (or Diana). The Egyptian healers include Horus, Bast, and Thoth.

Choosing a Patron Archetype: You may prefer to choose an archetype, not for a specific purpose, but rather for assistance with your general aim in life—a patron deity, so to speak.

A woman whose major goal in life is to be a good mother might look to the Greek Demeter or to the Egyptian Isis. A craftsperson might choose the Greek Hephaestus or the Roman Vulcan; a military sort the Greek Ares or Athena, the Roman Mars or Minerva, the Norse Thor, or the Egyptian Neith. Scholars and writers might gravitate to the Celtic Merlin, the Greek Hermes, the Roman Mercury, the Egyptian Thoth, or the Norse Odin.

---

[12]The ancients equated the depths of Mother Earth with wealth, probably because she is the source of precious minerals and gemstones, but also because the Earth provides us with everything we need in order to exist on the physical level—food and materials for shelter.

Athletes might find inspiration in the Egyptian Horus, the Greek Heracles, or the Norse Thor. There is, in fact, an archetype for every occupation.

If you decide to choose an overall patron deity, be aware that your chosen archetype will probably not be able to provide you with assistance in every area of your life. A businessman who chooses the administrative Zeus as his patron, for instance, won't be able to get healing help from his deity, because Zeus cares little for health matters. Similarly, a businesswoman who chooses Athena as her patroness will not be able to appeal to the deity for romantic help because Athena's relationships are of a platonic sort. It is important that you understand your patron deity's limitations before you place yourself under its sponsorship, and that you make allowances for these.

It is possible to adopt a patron for general purposes and to choose, when needed, another archetype for a specific goal. But your patron deity and the secondary archetype should be compatible. If they aren't, you risk offending your patron. Be aware that some deities are "disliked" by other deities. Ares, the Greek god of war, is detested by all his fellow gods—except Aphrodite, who likes macho lovers. Hades isn't popular either.

It's probably best for beginners not to mix pantheons. If you are an animal lover, for instance, and have chosen the Greek Artemis as your patroness but need some help on a writing project, it would be best to choose the Greek Hermes as your secondary helper, rather than the Egyptian Thoth.

Later on, when you are more experienced, you can try combining deities from different pantheons. But you should know that some pantheon combinations are better than others. The Egyptian and Norse pantheons tend to work well together, as do the Greek and Celtic. As an experienced magician, you could successfully choose the Norse Freya as your patroness, for example, and ask for additional help from the Egyptian Bast on occasion. The Norse/Egyptian combination works well, and both archetypes are cat-goddesses, so they have much in common.

One good way to choose a secondary archetype is to ask your patron to make the choice for you. This involves using a pendulum.

EXERCISE 3: USING THE PENDULUM

The following instructions assume the reader to be right-handed. Left-handed individuals should hold the pendulum in their left hands.

• Take the pendulum in your right hand. Rest your right elbow on some stable surface, such as a table. Holding the end of the pendulum's chain, let it dangle an inch or so above the table. Try to keep it absolutely still.

• When the pendulum is motionless, ask it to show you a "yes" response. The pendulum may swing forward and backward, in relation to the perpendicular line of your body. It may swing in a clockwise circle. Or, it may move in some other manner unique to you and your pendulum.

• Now ask your pendulum to show you a "no" response. It may swing from side to side, parallel to your body. It may swing in a counterclockwise circle. Or, again, it may move in some other manner unique to you.

Once you have determined your pendulum's positive and negative responses, you have all the skills you need. But it is imperative that you understand that the "magic" is not in the pendulum; it is within you. The unconscious mind, which always rejoices when it has a chance to give good advice, is what activates your pendulum.

EXERCISE 4: SEEKING PENDULUM ADVICE

When you are comfortable working with your pendulum, you may ask your patron deity's advice on an archetype that can help you achieve the specific goal you have in mind.

Perhaps you are a woman, a writer, and you are unhappily married to a man who tends to be violent when crossed. Your goal is to get out of the marriage with your skin intact. Your patron deity, the Egyptian Thoth, generously gives you guidance and support for your writing, but he is unable to help you with your marital problems. You need assistance from an archetype who can help you leave your husband safely—a female deity, perhaps, who understands your problems, and who can assist you as well as protect you. Reading through some myths, you come up with the following possibilities: Greek Artemis, whom the Black Sea Amazons revered; Egyptian Neith or Greek Athena, both leaders of the Libyan Amazons; The Morrigan, a Celtic battle-goddess; and Norse Freya, in her role as leader of the Valkyries.

Write down these names on a piece of paper, and place it by your left hand. Mentally go within and ask your patron deity, Thoth, for guidance. Ask him to indicate, through the pendulum, which archetype he thinks is most appropriate to you and your goal, one with whom he can easily work.

Take up your pendulum in your right hand. Point with your left hand to each of the names on the list, and ask the pendulum to signal "yes" or "no" to each name. If your patron, through the pendulum, signals "yes" to one name, you have found your secondary archetype. If your patron signals "yes" to two or more names, the choice is up to you. If you get only "no" responses from your pendulum, you will have to search out further possible archetypes and go through the procedure again.

Choosing an Achetype that Balances Character: As a magician, you should do everything you can to balance your character. Doing so produces a well-rounded personality, one which is capable of achieving goals in every area of your life.

Suppose, for instance, that you are a fiercely independent and very private woman, who would like, perhaps for the first time in your life, to marry and settle down. Your natural temperament is akin to that of Artemis, who prefers solitude to human company. You would benefit by inviting Hera, the Greek goddess of marriage, into your life.

Perhaps you are an over-civilized male who wishes he could let go and have some fun for a change. Your natural counterpart in the spiritual realm is Apollo. You'd benefit from calling in Dionysus, who likes an occasional orgy. Or you're a bookworm and your lifestyle could use some fresh air. You're too much like Hermes. Try invoking wild, natural Pan.

The trick is to "know thyself"—a motto emblazoned upon all of Apollo's temples—and to know what you need in order to balance your temperament. By invoking the aid of an archetype opposite to your natural temperament, you can activate undeveloped energies within you.

I recommend Jean Bolen's *Goddesses in Everywoman* and *Gods in Everyman* for readers who would like to choose archetypes in order to balance their temperament.[13] Bolen is a Jungian therapist, and her psychological studies of the major Greek gods and goddesses are both fascinating and fun to read. The Greek deities have their counterparts in every major Western pantheon, so even if you're not specifically interested in the Greeks, you'll still find Bolen's information useful. Female magicians will also be interested in Murry Hope's analysis of the Greek goddesses in the "Dragons and Serpents" chapter in her *Essential Woman*.[14]

ESTABLISHING A BOND WITH YOUR CHOSEN ARCHETYPE

No matter which archetype you choose, you must establish a bond with the deity before you ask it for assistance. You wouldn't walk down the street and ask a complete stranger for help with your love life, for obvious reasons. And if you would hesitate to make such a request of a fellow human, you should hesitate to ask the same of a spiritual archetype. Why should a deity grant your request for assistance when you have never before given the deity any thought or regard?

The laws of courtesy which exist in human society also exist in the relationship between archetype and human, and these must be scrupulously observed if you hope to attract assistance from

---

[13]Jean Bolen, *Goddesses in Everywoman* (San Francisco: HarperCollins, 1984); *Gods in Everyman* (San Francisco: HarperCollins, 1989).
[14]Murry Hope, *Essential Woman: Her Mystery, Her Power* (London: Collins/Crucible, 1991).

the spiritual realm. The relationship between deity and human must be mutually beneficial. We humans must give in order to receive.

Fortunately, most deities are easy to please. All archetypes love attention. They love to be thought about, meditated upon, admired, and respected. You may wish to give them small gifts, such as flowers or fruit, or you may want to consecrate the flame of a candle to them. Actually, it's not the gift that's important, but the intention behind it. In magic, intention is everything.

Please note, however, that archetypes do *not* like blood sacrifice. They put up with this savagery in the old days because the human race was young and didn't know any better. But we're beyond this sort of thing now, and archetypes expect us to act with love and respect toward all life forms, including ourselves.

Having earned its regard, always treat a deity with courtesy. To command an archetype to do a favor for you is unthinkable. Pray or plead, but don't demand. Moreover, deities don't like to be badgered. Tell them clearly three times what you want and ask for their assistance, then leave them alone.[15] They need time, space, and privacy in which to go to work on your behalf. If you plead with them too often, you will alienate them.

Please understand that your chosen archetype will not personally help you with your goal. Archetypes are busy and don't have time to help everyone who appeals to them. They will assign their own assistants to perform whatever labor is necessary to see that your project is successfully completed.[16] It is a great honor to be granted such an assistant, and your helper should be accorded all the courtesy and regard, even the love, that you would give to the archetype itself.

Spiritually inclined magicians who have developed clairvoyant, clairaudient, or clairsentient abilities will be aware of their

---

[15]See page 68 for a discussion of the Law of Three Requests.
[16]Sometimes elementals are assigned to the work at hand. These will be discussed at length in chapter 7.

helpers, and will establish a close relationship with them.[17] But if you're new to magic and mythology, you probably will not be conscious of the fact that you are being assisted from the spiritual plane. No matter. If you have a genuine regard for your deity and have appealed to it in the proper manner, and if your goal is successfully achieved, you may assume that you have received assistance. You may be justly proud of this, because it means that you have merited the attention of your chosen archtype.

Be sure to offer thanks to your helper and to your archetype. Genuine gratitude attracts great blessings.

WORKING WITH CELTIC DEITIES

Celtic archetypes will not respond to a human's need for assistance in the same way that a Greek, Roman, Norse, or Egyptian deity will. Celtic archtypes prefer to choose their own votaries, and no amount of human pleading or persuasion will change this.

The best you, as a magician, can do is to study the entire Celtic pantheon and the stories relating to it, and then hope that you will be adopted by the deity of your choice. But don't be surprised if a deity other than the one you have chosen puts in an appearance and offers to help. Being ignored by your preferred deity can be disappointing, but it's wise to assume that the deity who does offer assistance can do the job required. Be sure to accept all offers of help with grace and gratitude.

Students sometimes ask how they will know when they have been adopted by a Celtic archetype. There's no pat answer to this. The archetype may appear in a dream. There may be several synchronous happenings which lead in the direction of a particular deity. There may be a waking vision of the archetype acting in a helpful mode.

---

[17]A close relationship between magician and helper can simplify the practice of magic to the degree that very little physical plane magic need be used in order to achieve goals. Nonphysical magic—mind magic, as it's called—is usually practiced only by advanced magicians; beginners ordinarily need physical props to focus their mental energies.

I worked with the Arthurian archetypes for years, always with the hope that one or another would put in an appearance, but it didn't happen. Natural progress eventually led me from the Celts to the Egyptian and Norse pantheons. Then one day, years after my work with the Celts, I felt the need of a helper who could assist me with psychic self-defense. In asking for this helper, I didn't specify that it should come from any particular pantheon, as I had by this time worked with all of them and would have been comfortable with whatever appeared. A ferocious warrior-woman arrived on the scene and, because I had most recently worked with the Norse deities, I assumed her to be of that pantheon. But then I discovered her name was Celtic and realized she was a representative of The Morrigan, the Celtic battle-goddess.

The Morrigan is a very ancient archetype—much older than the Arthurian figures with whom I had worked years before. In my Arthurian days, I had paid little attention to the older deities, so when The Morrigan's representative appeared, I had to do a lot of reading in order to understand that with which I was dealing. While doing the study, I found myself enmeshed in a whole series of synchronous events. I had been experiencing a health problem and had just discovered an herbal remedy which might possibly solve it. I was at the same time reading a novel about a fictional family of occultists, whose last name was the same as the herb in question. One of the most compelling characters in the book was a worshipper of The Morrigan. I was (am) really thrilled to be assisted by a Celt, because I tend to be too intellectual and need the balance provided by the emotional Celtic archetypes.

EFFECTIVE PRAYER

When you have chosen, and established a bond with, a suitable archetype, you must know how best to approach that deity so that its energies can be called upon to assist you. Some deities are best approached by prayer. Others are not. Those to whom prayers can effectively be directed are the Judeo-Christian archetypes, the deities of the Greek pantheon, the Roman archetypes, the Celtic deities, and the lesser, or more personal, archetypes such as the higher self, an inner guide, or a great teacher. Egyptian and Norse archetypes prefer a different approach (see page 78), but this doesn't mean they can't be appealed to through prayer; it simply means that prayer isn't necessarily the best way to call upon their energies.

HOW TO PRAY

I once had a client who confessed to me that she did not know how to pray. Since there may be others like her, I shall define prayer here as a personal plea for assistance from a revered spiritual plane archetype such as a god or goddess. To create an effective prayer, you must:

1. Tell your chosen archetype what your problem is.

2. Tell the deity how you are working to overcome the trouble. It's important that the archetype know you are taking responsibility for your problem, and not leaving all the work up to the spiritual plane.

3. Ask for the archetype's assistance.

4. Make your plea emotional.

Imagine that you frequently suffer from gastritis, which can be very painful. Your goal is to overcome the problem. You have written down your goal, complete with safety clauses. You have done the intelligent thing and seen a doctor, who has prescribed medication (which you are taking), and who has advised you to watch your diet (which you are doing). The doctor has warned you that the condition could lead to an ulcer, and has also told you that the problem could be psychosomatic—that your mind and emotions may have created the condition.

On reflection, you realize that your relationship with a spouse who is subject to violent mood swings is probably the culprit. You realize that you must learn to relax in the midst of difficulties, and perhaps you decide to take instruction in meditation in order to do so. But you feel that you need help from an archetype to overcome the problem. You are a thinking type much drawn to the Greek pantheon, and in reading about the various Greek archetypes, you set your sights on Artemis, who can bestow emotional distance. You establish a relationship with her.

You are now ready to make your appeal. Your prayer to Artemis might sound like this: "Dear Artemis, I have gastritis, which is very painful. I'm taking medication and eating bland foods. But I realize that the problem exists because of my relationship with my spouse, whose mood swings are extremely upsetting to me. I know I must gain some emotional perspective, and I'm meditating daily. But I'm new to this and need your assistance. Please help me!" If your plea is emotionally felt, it will surely be heard and acted upon.

But you mustn't leave it there. According to the Law of Three Requests, all pleas for help should be repeated three times. The theory behind this law is that the first request alerts the conscious mind, the second request alerts the unconscious mind, and the third request alerts the cosmic mind—that is, the part of the psyche that links in with the collective unconscious, where the archetypes can be contacted.[18]

The three requests for help are most effectively made in one session, because each request helps to further focus your mind. With the third request, your mind is fully concentrated on the appeal. *In magic, there is no substitute for mental focus.*

THE PIN AND CANDLE RITE

Prayer is a rather plain procedure. If you wish to dress it up a bit, you might enjoy using the following folk-magic technique:

Materials needed: One candle

One straight or map pin

---

[18]Murry Hope, who taught me this law, describes it a little differently in her *Practical Celtic Magic*: "At first utterance the conscious mind is alerted, the repeat engages the reasoning faculties, while the third statement makes direct contact with the psyche or soul force" (pp. 218–219).

Optional: Scented oil or magically prepared water

Preliminaries: The candle you use should not be encased in glass. It can be thick or thin (thin is probably best). Its color is important (see the color chart on page 122 for the relationship between colors and various goals). Try to pick a color which correlates to your goal. If you are appealing to an archetype for help with your love life, for instance, you might want to choose pink, red, or orange. Or, you may choose a color which resonates with your chosen deity.

An ordinary straight pin is fine for this rite, but I prefer to use a map pin (a straight pin with a small bead on top) because it's more aesthetically pleasing. Map pins can be purchased in any stationery store.

Magicians experienced in physical plane magic will want to anoint their candles with a scented oil or water (for complete instructions on consecrating candles see chapter 7). You may skip ahead to learn the procedure before performing this rite, or if you prefer, simply perform the rite as described here.

The Rite:
• Invoke your personal and god symbols (see Appendix B).
• Do Exercise 1 (page 42) to activate positive energy.
• With your prayer well in mind, light your candle. Be aware as you do so that the kindled flame alerts spiritual plane entities to your presence.
• Place the pin in the palm of your dominant hand and fold your fingers over it.
• Gaze at the flame for some time and meditate upon the archetype you wish to contact.
• Focus your mind and say your prayer. Be emotional.
• Pause.
• Repeat your prayer a second time. Be more emotional.
• Pause.
• Repeat your prayer a third time. Be as emotional as possible.
• Take your pin and stick it into the side of the candle, as close to the top as possible without burning yourself.

- Remain before the candle for a few minutes.
- Return to normal activities.
- When the pin drops from the candle, you will know that your prayers have reached the spiritual plane and have been heard by your chosen deity.
- Extinguish the candle before leaving your home or retiring for sleep. The candle should not be used again.

Variations on this simple rite have appeared in many spellcasting books, but in none that I have seen has there been an explanation as to why the procedure is effective.

The fire element has always been used in conjunction with the spiritual plane, and it's not difficult to understand why. A flame leaps upward, as if striving to reach a higher plane, and it carries with it heat and light.

Metal retains magnetism. Go to a psychometrist for a reading, and you will probably be asked for a piece of jewelry (such as a wedding ring) belonging to the person for whom the reading is being given. Sensitives can pick up and interpret the energy contained in the metal and give advice based upon their findings.

The mechanism behind the ritual, therefore, is this. The metal pin becomes charged with your emotional appeal. When you stick the pin into the candle, the emotion is transferred to the wax. When the wax is burned by the flame, your message dissipates into the atmosphere, and is received and heard by your chosen spiritual plane archetype, which then goes to work on your behalf. Whether or not the technique is actually effective through this mechanism is debatable. What matters is that the psychology involved is sound.

When you have appealed three times to your archetype, your work on the spiritual plane is over. Do not make another appeal. Assume that your prayer has been heard, and that it is being acted upon by the appropriate powers. Leave them in peace to do whatever is required. Worrying, doubting, or fretting about the outcome seriously interferes with the work in progress. Get on with your magic. After all, there's still a great deal to be done before you can achieve your written goal.

CONTACTING THE ARCHETYPE WITHIN

If you have chosen to work with a Norse or Egyptian archetype, you need to learn about a technique not as widely practiced as prayer. In certain eras of the Egyptian magical past, priests and priestesses who served in the ancient temples went about their daily business wearing the masks of the deities whom they served. A priest of Anubis wore the mask of a jackal; a priestess of Hathor wore the mask of a cow. To a visitor, it must have seemed that the gods themselves walked the temple halls. And, in a sense, they did. When the priestess donned her mask, she laid aside her ordinary, everyday personality and became a representative of the goddess whom she served. Every sacred act that she performed inside the temple was dedicated to, and infused with the power of, the deity whom she represented. To those who came for healing or worship, she *was* the goddess. She had assumed the god- form.

> The god-nature exists within each of us; we are gods in the making and identification with the principles they represent can only help us toward the knowledge and understanding they embrace at their higher octaves.[19]

Modern-day magicians who wish to achieve a goal with the help of the Egyptian or Norse deities must, like the ancient priests, put aside their everday personalities and step into the shoes, so to speak, of the archetype whose assistance they desire. Then, acting with the power of the deity, they perform their magic.

ASSUMING THE GOD–FORM

Assuming the god-form is entirely different from prayer. With prayer, you ask an archetype to intercede for you, to help you to achieve what you desire. In assuming the god-form, you tem-

---

[19]Murry Hope, *Practical Egyptian Magic* (New York: St. Martin's, 1984), p. 127.

porarily act as deity, and in this role you perform symbolic actions designed to bring about desired results.

Assuming the god-form is not easy—and it's not for beginners. Nor, as we shall see later, is it for those who suffer from low self-esteem. It requires a great deal of preliminary work. To begin with, you must know as much as possible about your chosen archetype, for you must know how it would act under most circumstances. Nothing but extended study and meditation can provide this knowledge.

More importantly, you must find the archetype *within yourself*, for if it does not exist within you, how can you effectively act the role? A gentle, peace-loving man who cannot find within any brawling instinct will not be able to assume Thor, the Norse god of thunder. Similarly, a highly spiritual woman who cannot find within herself any materialistic urges had better not attempt to assume Freya, an archetype known for her love of gold.[20]

Feeling and intuitive types will probably find assuming the god-form relatively easy. Thinking and sensate types may have greater difficulty with the technique.

Each individual assumes the god-form differently. We can learn something about the technique by looking to the acting profession, for actors are called upon to assume a character in much the same way that the magician is called upon to assume the god-form.

Some performers are known as "technical" actors. This type of actor first decides how a character will appear physically and then endeavors, in rehearsal, to establish the "look" of the character before starting to work on the emotional content of the role. Delivery of lines in the early rehearsal period is usually pretty dreadful because there is, as yet, no emotional tone to the character. When the "look" is right, the rest of the character begins to

---

[20]Individuals who are not in touch with their basic instincts (such as survival, sex, aggression) are suffering from psychological problems which must be sorted out in therapy before they can safely attempt to assume the god-form. In the interim, prayer may be used as a substitute.

emerge. These actors work, in other words, with externals first, then move inward.

Similarly, magicians who are by nature technicians will initially spend a good deal of time getting together their props and working on the physical aspects of their archetype. When they are satisfied with these, they wait patiently for the emotional content of the archetype's energies to surface from within—or, to use magical terminology, for "the power to come down."

Readers would do well to study carefully a scene from Dion Fortune's novel, *Moon Magic*, in which a great female magician (or "adept") makes lavish use of magical paraphernalia during the performance of a solitary rite designed to call upon the energies of Egypt's great lion-goddess, Sekhmet.[21] The purpose of the ceremony is to liberate from emotional bondage a man (not physically present) who is destined to act as her magical partner, or priest.

On the physical level, the adept is robed in black, crowned with a silver diadem, and equipped with both an ankh and a wand; she stands before a lamp and a figure of the goddess, beneath a hanging "perpetual" light. Incense is burning somewhere. On the astral (imaginative) level, her accoutrements are more elaborate, and consist of a robe which befits her exalted magical grade, a Uraeus serpent on her brow and a silver kestos on her hips.

As the ceremony begins, the adept draws pentacles upon the air, uses her ankh to similarly inscribe moon signs, and intones various Names of Power. The power comes down and manifests as an aura of light about the ritual furniture and ornamental symbols. As the room brightens, she traces a fire symbol upon the air with her wand. Knowing that she is working with power, she calls upon Sekhmet, and over her head she feels "the head of a lioness formulate." This places her in a position to draw upon the archetype's energy. She inscribes a magic circle and triangle of art with her ankh, calls upon the spirit of her priest until he appears before her, and, using her wand, draws a circle of fire about them both.

---

[21]Dion Fortune, *Moon Magic* (York Beach, ME: Samuel Weiser, 1978), pp. 86–87.

The ring of fire rises and emits great heat. She fixes her eyes upon her priest and, speaking with the authority of Sekhmet, she declares: "You and I are alone in the circle of fire where none can intervene. You will do your own will and no one else's." The flames die down; the priest's figure fades; she performs a proper banishing; the rite is over. The work is ultimately effective.

Throughout *Moon Magic* and its companion volume, *The Sea Priestess*, Fortune lays great emphasis on the physical trappings related to assuming the god-form. Not coincidentally, I think, the heroine of these two books is a former actress who clearly understands the value of a good stage setting and effective props. This doesn't mean, of course, that her approach to the archetypes is superficial; far from it. The physical paraphernalia of magic serve to fire her imagination. This in turn puts out a call to her chosen archetype, which responds by lending its authority to her as she performs her magic.

Don't be intimidated by the scene's formal ritualism. Fortune, in her early occult career, was a member of the Society of the Golden Dawn, and her practice of magic was much influenced by that Society's highly stylized and lavishly mounted group rituals. When her heroine traces pentacles and moon-signs and invokes Names of Power and so on, Fortune is referring to practices that she herself learned during her tenure with the Golden Dawn.[22] If you have never worked with a Golden Dawn-type magical society, you need not feel inadequate because you don't know about pentacles and moon-signs and such. But you *should* pay careful attention to the props you use in your own magic, for it is the skillful use of these which allows you to temporarily identify with the archetype you are invoking.

The male magician who wishes to assume the god-form of Odin may want to purchase, and use during magical operations, a blue cape and a floppy hat, two of Odin's physical attributes. The

---

[22]Readers interested in this form of magic are referred to Israel Regardie, *The Golden Dawn* (St. Paul, MN: Llewellyn, 1984).

female magician who wishes to assume Nephthys may want to purchase and consecrate for magical use a beautiful goblet, Nephthys' primary magical tool. She will also wish to carefully study the sitting and standing postures of the Egyptian archetypes, and to imitate these when performing magic.

But technical magicians must not place so much emphasis on external trappings such as props and costumes that they neglect the interior work. If they cannot "feel with" or "think with" their chosen archetype, they will not be able to assume its form, and their magic will be ineffective.

Let us now consider the technique of "method" actors. If technical actors work from the outside in, so to speak, method actors do just the reverse. From the very first, they live the character they mean to portray. This can lead to serious problems in their personal lives, for they do not leave their character in the rehearsal hall, but take it home with them and subject their families to whatever temperamental characteristics belong to the role they are playing. It is only later in the rehearsal period—if at all—that they begin to develop the physical or technical aspects of their role. Critics often heap abuse on method actors whose speech is so unintelligible that it cannot be understood by the audience, but they usually can't complain about the emotional content of a method actor's performance, which can be quite brilliant.

Method–type magicians feel so closely aligned with their archetypes that they may forego the use of props and costumes altogether, and work only with mind and heart. This is fine, provided they don't identify so closely with the archetype that they forget their purpose, which is to achieve a goal on the practical level. Dion Fortune's heroine did not become so caught up in mystical union with her archetype that she forgot the reason for invoking it in the first place.

Props and costumes can be useful for method–type magicians because they belong to the physical plane and keep them grounded in reality. They will also remind them that, though they may be privileged enough to temporarily channel their archetype's energy, they are still only playing a role.

EGO AND ARCHETYPE

Just as method actors who play murderers must not identify so closely with their role that they actually kill someone, so you, as a magician, must retain some sense of personal identity when you assume the god-form. Otherwise you run the risk of confusing your own ego with the energy of the archetype you are invoking, which can lead to some serious psychological problems—to delusions of grandeur or megalomania, for instance.[23]

Archetypes are not known for their patience when dealing with mortals who think themselves permanently on a par with the gods. Greek mythology is littered with tales of what happens to mortals who exhibit *hubris*, a Greek word meaning excessive pride or arrogance.[24] The old expression, "Those whom the gods wish to destroy they first make mad," is worth remembering here. Megalomania is a form of madness which can be regularly encountered on big-city streets in the form of "divinely inspired" (usually drunk) prophets who shout to all and sundry that the world is fast shuddering to a halt. In the metaphysical world, there are dozens of self-proclaimed prophets of one sort or another, and we are inundated with advice from apparently privileged individuals who channel the supposed wisdom of superior intelligences from other galaxies.[25]

Magicians who have weak egos risk becoming too identified with the role they are playing when they assume the god-form. Their deep sense of insecurity makes them crave the feeling of power they experience when they contact the archetypal energies, and they have a hard time giving up their role, so that (like method actors) they end up playing it twenty-four hours a day for days, weeks, or months on end. This essentially puts them on a par

---

[23]The American Heritage Dictionary defines *megalomania* as "a psychopathological condition in which fantasies of wealth, power, or omnipotence predominate."

[24]*Hubris* originally meant "violence." For some examples, see the stories of Arachne, Ixion, and Icarus.

[25]I am not condemning all channelers here. Some I believe to be genuinely inspired. But others, I fear, are deluded, power-mad, or simply in it for the money.

with the street-crazies. Obviously, you must make every effort to avoid this pitfall.

As a magician, you act as a filter, so to speak, for the energies of your chosen archetype when you assume the god-form. What comes through is affected by the quality of the filter. If the filter is flimsy—if your ego is weak—then it may be swamped by the energies coming through, which can result in a massive inflation of the ego (as we have already discussed) or, even worse, in its annihilation. And if the filter is dirty—that is, if your character is base—then what comes through in the form of power will be contaminated.

History provides an excellent example of a weak and dirty filter in the form of Adolf Hitler.[26] It is widely known, of course, that Hitler despised Jews. It is not so well known that he had contempt for Christianity, which he considered to be a religion for weaklings. Hitler was determined to create a Master Race which would be utterly ruthless and brutal. This Master Race could not be nourished on Christianity or Judaism, so Hitler and his cronies (Himmler, in particular) turned to the old Norse deities for spiritual support.[27]

Anyone who reads a comprehensive biography of Hitler cannot fail to be struck by the fact that those who knew him well and those who never met him had almost identical impressions of the man. They all say, again and again, that when Hitler spoke, it was as if he were a man possessed—as if some power greater than himself took over and spoke through him. Since Hitler's oratory was the basis of his popularity, and since it was his popularity, to a great degree, which brought him to power, the matter of his speech is of some interest. Assuming that Hitler was, as so many people suggested at the time, taken over by some force stronger than himself,

---

[26]Many psychological studies have been made of Hitler. All of them stress his deep insecurities due to his early upbringing and later humiliation in Vienna. There can be no doubt that he was a megalomaniac.

[27]See Joachim Fest, *Hitler* (New York: Harcourt Brace, 1992); Nicholas Goodrick-Clarke, *The Occult Roots of Nazism* (London: Aquarian Press, 1985); or any book covering the history of the S.S.

what was this force? Surely not the Hebrew Yahweh or the Christian God. One of the Norse deities? I think so. It's my opinion that Hitler assumed the god-form when he spoke publicly. Whether he did this on a conscious level or not, I do not know.

Some occultists maintain that Hitler was a black magician who knew exactly what he was doing, and there is some evidence to support this theory; but it's also possible that an eager Norse archetype recognized Hitler as an open, unconscious channel and took advantage of the situation. In either case, that which dominated when Hitler assumed the god-form was the basest aspect of the archetype, because Hitler himself was base.

It's easy to say, "Oh, well, Hitler, yes. He was evil, and he had the power to do some real damage. But I'm just an ordinary person, and I'm not evil. Even if I were and could assume the god-form the way he did, nothing much would come of it. All this stuff about Hitler doesn't apply to me." But it *does* apply. We all have aggressive and vengeful urges on occasion—they are part of our survival equipment—and they can get you into serious difficulties if you don't curb them. If you assume the god-form while feeling vengeful or malicious, you will eventually have to contend with the Law of Rebound.

It might appear from the foregoing that the Norse archetypes are dangerous to assume; and in a sense, this is true. But this doesn't mean that they are evil. The Norse archetypes are no more (or less) evil than the deities of any other Western pantheon. *Every* archetype—Greek, Roman, Egyptian, Celtic, or Norse—has its dark side. The quality of the energy brought through when you assume the god-form depends entirely upon your character, which acts as a filter for the archetypal energy. If Gandhi (or someone of equal spiritual caliber) had assumed a Norse archetype, the results would have borne no comparison to those that Hitler produced.

The Norse archetypes have tremendous vitality. They are vigorous and bursting with energy. They love earthly life; it's almost as if they can't wait for you to open yourself to them so that they can take over and take action. The Egyptian archetypes, by comparison, are very courteous and gentle. They wouldn't dream of intruding on your psyche beyond your desire for them to do so.

They don't have the Norse passion for earthly life. Their eyes, so to speak, are turned toward the stars and to the cosmos.

PROTECTING YOURSELF

If the prospect of assuming the god-form makes you uneasy, fearful, or anxious, don't do it. As the magical maxim has it: "When in doubt, do nought." Use prayer instead. If you do choose to assume the god-form, remember the following protective measures:

1. Never assume the god-form when you are feeling angry, spiteful, malicious, jealous, or envious.

2. Before you assume the god-form, ask your archetype to limit its manifestation to a specific time and place. If, for instance, you anticipate that your magical operation will take half an hour, tell your archetype that it must not manifest beyond this time. Specify also that it must not manifest in any place other than the one you have set aside for the ritual. This is particularly important when you are working with the Norse archetypes.

3. If you are working with costumes or props—and it's wise to do so—use them as an actor would. Put on your costume and go to work. If you wish to assume Bast, for example, put on your cat mask and begin your magical operation. When you remove the mask, the performance is over and it's back to reality.

4. You may, if you wish, signal to your unconscious that you wish to return to normal consciousness by the use of a key word. Any word will do, as long as you have established it ahead of time. I have used the word "claptrap" for years. When I complete my ritual, I clap my hands and say "claptrap!" It immediately brings me back to reality.

5. Clapping your hands together, stamping your feet on the ground, and eating or drinking something immediately after magical work are all good ways to close down the psychic centers through which the archetypes manifest.

6. You can seal your aura after assuming the god-form.

EXERCISE 5: HOW TO SEAL YOUR AURA

Grounding:

- Stand comfortably, with your feet slightly apart. Take a couple of deep breaths and relax.
- Focus your attention on your feet.
- Focus on the floor beneath your feet.
- Focus on the Earth beneath the floor.
- Imagine that there is a flap in the middle of each foot.
- Open the flaps.
- Imagine that roots are growing from your feet.
- The roots grow down into the Earth. They grow long and thick. They reach down into the center of the Earth.
- Pause.
- Feel how stable you are.

Sealing:

- Using both hands and physical gesture, draw an imaginary circle of little leaping flames on the ground around you.
- You are enclosed in a small circle of leaping flames.
- Pause.
- Using your hands, draw the flames up and over your head. (Hands remain above your head.)
- You are enveloped by protective flames.
- Tie a knot in the flames above your head. (Hands remain above your head.)
- Mentally formulate a sacred symbol or a sphere of radiant energy above your head.
- Using your hands, draw energy from the symbol or sphere down through your crown, into the solar plexus area. If you wish, draw the energy down all the way to Earth (floor) level.
- Pause.
- Know that you are safe from all intrusion.

This technique seals your aura for about four hours, and it may be used on a daily basis. Use it whenever you feel you need protection. The exercise may seem lengthy or cumbersome at first, but with practice you will be able to perform it in the space of a minute. Repeat every four hours, or as needed.

BUILDING THE MAGICAL PERSONALITY

Building the magical personality qualifies as a spiritual plane technique because it requires you to work with a self-created ideal.[28] The procedure closely resembles assuming the god-form, but is useful for those who do not wish to work with an archetype. Others will also find it effective. Building the magical personality is a role-playing procedure. The difference between it and assuming the god-form is that when you build the magical personality, you act out an idealized version of yourself rather than that of an archetype.

To successfully build your magical personality, you must decide what qualities you would like to personify as a magician. These might include an ethical approach to magic, good powers of concentration, or proficiency in various magical techniques. You must also decide what you would like to achieve as a magician. I'm not referring here to personal goals, but to a choice of specialty in the magical field. You might envision yourself, for instance, as a healer, or as an expert in the magical use of herbs, or as a clairvoyant.

If you are a beginner, of course, you probably don't have any idea what your specialty is or will be, but you probably do feel a pull from some specific magical direction. Go with it. As Roberto Assagioli tells us, "*We are*, essentially and genuinely, *what we will to be*, even if we often fail to manifest it."[29] If herbs excite you, build herbal knowledge into your magical personality. Envision yourself as a great expert on the subject—and start studying at the material level.

---

[28]All ideals belong to the spiritual plane.
[29]Roberto Assagioli, *The Act of Will* (Baltimore: Penguin, 1974), p. 144.

When you have decided what general characteristics you want to include in your personality, and what your specialty will be, it is time to think about appearance. Props and costumes are important because they help you to *feel* like a magician. Decide what kind of robe you would like to wear. Purchase or make one if you are able. You may want to wear some magical insignia, such as a pendant or diadem or bracelet. You may also want to invest in some magical tools, such as a wand, dagger (or sword), goblet, or pentacle for use in your rituals.[30] Most metaphysical stores carry tools and jewelry appropriate for magical work, but if you can't find the equipment you want, or can't afford it, use your imagination. In fact, imagination is often more effective than the real thing.

You will also want to choose a magical name for yourself.[31] This can be taken from mythology, folklore, nature, or history. It should be a name you really love and which has some symbolic meaning for you.

Take time to make these decisions. You may wish to write down a complete description of your personality—a sort of imaginary biography.[32] Remember the power of the written word as you do so.

Once you have settled on qualities, speciality, appearance, equipment, and name, work with these for some time. Your magical personality needs time to gel in your imagination. The more it has gelled, the more effective it will be.[33]

---

[30] These tools symbolize the four elements and will be discussed in chapter 9.

[31] Golden Dawn members were required to choose a motto rather than a name. Dion Fortune chose "Deo Non Fortuna" (which I take to mean "God, not chance") and later shortened it for use as her pen name.

[32] Many actors write biographies of the characters they are to portray before they begin the rehearsal process.

[33] Readers are advised to read Dion Fortune's *The Sea Priestess* and its sequel, *Moon Magic* (York Beach, ME: Samuel Weiser, 1978), to further understand the process of building the magical personality. In these two books, an adept—undoubtedly one of the greatest female characters ever written—builds her personality so that she can perform a magical act designed to benefit humanity. No insignificant magical projects for her!

EXERCISE 6: ASSUMING THE MAGICAL PERSONALITY

- Invoke your personal and god symbols (see Appendix B).
- Do Exercise 1 (page 42) to activate positive energy.
- Standing, bring to mind your magical personality.
- Picture your idealized personality standing in front of you. Make the image as vivid as possible.
- Now imagine that your body is hollow.
- Imagine that the air about you is filled with your magical name.
- Inhale deeply. Breathe in your magical name. Fill your hollow body with your magical name.
- Keep breathing in your magical name until your body feels full-to-bursting with it.
- With one long, drawn-out exhalation, sound your magical name aloud. Sound the name slowly and with force, from deep within your diaphragm area. Finish sounding the name as you finish your exhalation. When done properly, the sound will physically vibrate through the length of your torso. Feel the vibration of the sound.[34]
- Step forward and mentally merge yourself with the idealized personality before you.
- Acting now as your magical personality, perform your magic.

LIFE OF THE MAGICAL PERSONALITY

Dion Fortune maintained that building the magical personality was a safe procedure, at least for those with a "well-integrated personality."[35] But since not everyone is so favored, it's best to assume that the same dangers which attend assuming the god-form also attend this technique. Magicians who suffer from low self-

---

[34]Some practitioners maintain the vibration should be felt in the hands and feet, but I don't think this is necessary. This technique is known as "vibrating" a name or word, for obvious reasons. Singers and actors familiar with breath and voice control will find the procedure easy, but others may have to practice before it feels effective.

[35]See "A Magical Body," in Dion Fortune, *Applied Magic* (London: Aquarian Press, 1979).

esteem can become so enamored of the power-rush they feel when they identify with their personality that they have trouble giving up the role and strut around as Great Magicians day in and day out.[36] The cautions are the same here as they were for assuming the god-form. It would be wise for anyone (well-integrated or not) to follow the safety procedures mentioned on page 79 in order to ensure a safe return to normal consciousness and reality after performing this exercise. You may, if you wish, use your magical personality in conjunction with prayer or with assuming the god-form. To do this, first assume your magical personality. Then pray to your chosen archetype, or assume the god-form. Finally, perform your magic.

You may find that you eventually outgrow your magical personality. This is to be expected. In fact, it is to be desired. An urge to create a new personality indicates that you are growing, and that you are beginning to recognize your true magical talents and interests. A new personality should be created, and a new name taken, when the old ones feel outworn.

SUMMARY

Work upon the spiritual plane lends permanence to the results you achieve through magical operations. Remember that as you leave behind your ideal self and beloved archetype and turn to that which is decidedly human: the emotional plane.

1. Perform personal and god symbol exercises (Appendix B).

2. Choose an archetype (from any pantheon or tradition) which can help you to:
   a. Achieve a specific goal, or
   b. Act as your patron (for general purposes), or

---

[36]To be fair, I have seen some individuals of confessed low self-esteem positively bloom after having worked with their magical personalities for a while. The magical personality appears to give them the confidence they have long needed.

c. Balance your character.

3. Establish a relationship with your archetype.

4. If your chosen archetype is Greek, Roman, Celtic, Judeo-Christian or personal (higher self, spiritual guide, etc.), use prayer.

5. If your chosen archetype is Egyptian, Norse, or from a shamanic tradition (African, Native American, etc.), assume the god-form.

6. If you wish, build your magical personality and use it in combination with either step 4 or 5.

CHAPTER 6

THE EMOTIONAL PLANE

*[F]eelings are the causes of the actions and circumstances of
. . . life.*[1]

—Neville

*The emotions have their sources in the instincts; indeed, an
emotion may be said to be the subjective aspect of an instinct.*[2]

—Dion Fortune

Practicing magic is rather like planning, and then embarking
upon, a journey. When you set your goal, you decide on your destination. But just knowing where you are headed will not get you
there. You need an itinerary, and just as a traveler needs to use
some form of transportation, so you need power in order to arrive
at your magical goal. Emotion is the moving force of magic. It is
emotion—desire—which motivates you to practice magic in the
first place.

The stronger your desire to achieve a goal, the better your results. Magic cannot be successfully practiced without passion. It's
important that you care deeply about your goal. Several years ago,
a student told me that she was having trouble setting her goal. "I
know I really should work for prosperity for the family," she said.
The word *should* is always a red flag to me. It implies duty, which
usually doesn't evoke much enthusiasm. I asked if there wasn't
some other goal that she could happily pursue, and of course there

---

[1]Neville, *Feeling Is the Secret* (Los Angeles: G & J Publishing, 1966), unnumbered.
[2]Dion Fortune, *The Machinery of the Mind* (York Beach, ME: Samuel Weiser,
1980), p. 37.

was—something relatively minor. Minor goals are fine.[3] The important thing is that you choose a goal which really matters to you personally. It's important that you choose a goal toward which you do not have ambivalent feelings. If one part of you very much wants to achieve a goal, but another part of you is fearful of achieving it, you're in a no-win situation because emotional conflict produces few, if any, results. When you set a goal, *all* of you must passionately wish to achieve it.

Practical work upon the emotional plane involves the utilization of both form and force. Force is emotion—the desire to achieve a goal. Without this force, there is no magical power. But raw, undifferentiated force does not, by itself, produce successful results. Force must be tamed, as it were. It must be given form. This chapter will illustrate how this can be accomplished.

VISUALIZATION TECHNIQUES

When you feel something strongly, you automatically create in your imagination a picture illustrative of the feeling. You give the feeling a form, in other words—an image. If you are desirous of fame, for instance, you might imagine yourself appearing on a talk show, or publicly receiving an award. If you want greater prosperity, you might visualize yourself living in a lavishly appointed home, or driving an expensive car. And if you are fearful of something, you usually envision the thing you fear in all its gory detail. In short, there is nothing mysterious about giving form to force. It appears to be an instinctive process. Ordinary people do it all the time when they daydream. As Dion Fortune observes:

> The person who habitually indulges in happy daydreams develops a peculiar mental atmosphere which is best described by the word glamorous, and the more

---

[3]Novice magicians are sometimes afraid to tackle major goals at first because they are understandably unsure of their abilities and don't want to risk failure. It might be best in the beginning to set relatively unimportant (but greatly desired) goals. Success with these will create greater self-confidence.

sensitive of the persons with whom he comes in contact
are influenced by it and see him, not as he actually is, but
as he pictures himself in his day-dreams . . . and as the
belief of those about us induces self-confidence as surely
as their distrust chills us, a circuit of action and reaction
is set up which . . . increases in strength as it proceeds.
It is a true saying that nothing succeeds like success.[4]

Ordinary people don't realize, however, that the unconscious mind
is powerfully affected by images, and they tend to daydream care-
lessly. Magicians, on the other hand, closely monitor their day-
dreams, and are quite deliberate in their design of visual images.

Visualization requires no special skills, but there are some important tips you should know about before you begin the design
process:

1. Visualize yourself as already having achieved your goal:
Imagine that you are a woman and that your goal is to attract a
new romance. A good visualization might be:

> *You are reclining lazily on a couch at home, popping bonbons
> into your mouth. You are reading or watching television or lis-
> tening to music, and you are completely happy by yourself. The
> doorbell rings. You open your front door, and outside is a deliv-
> ery person. He has, in his arms, a mammoth bouquet of long-
> stemmed red roses. They are very beautiful, and their scent is
> delightfully fragrant. You cannot resist touching the velvety
> petals. You wonder who has sent these lovely flowers, and look
> for a card. There is none. You have no idea who sent this ro-
> mantic gift, but one thing is clear: someone loves you.*

There are several important points to note about this visualization.
First of all, notice the aura of ease and pleasure which permeates
the imagery: you are lazily reclining on a couch, eating candy, in-
dulging in a favorite pastime, feeling completely happy by your-

---

[4]Dion Fortune, *Practical Occultism in Daily Life* (London: Aquarian Press, 1969),
pp. 17–18.

self. These images are meant to convey to your unconscious that you are not desperate to find a new lover. (Desperation is always counterproductive; see page 97.) Second, even if you do long for a new lover, there is no need to desperately seek one, for someone has already fallen in love with you. In your mind's eye, you have already achieved your goal. Third, the visualization is ethically sound. Your new lover has no face and no name. If you assigned him a name and a face—those belonging perhaps to someone you know and desire—you would be magically manipulating that individual and would later suffer rebound. Fourth, notice all the sensual details included with the imagery: the taste of the bonbons, the ring of the doorbell, the scent of the flowers, the feel of the petals.

2. **Work as many sensual details as possible into your visualization:** The unconscious mind does not distinguish between vivid imagination and material reality. Imagination is made vivid by sensual details. If you can convince your unconscious through their use that a desired event has already occurred, it will work to produce a similar event in reality.

A personal example will illustrate just how literal the unconscious mind can be when it is given sensual detail. A year or so after the experiment described in chapter 4, I decided to specialize in Shakespeare and, intent on sizing up opportunities, attended a performance of *Hamlet* at a local theatre. Everything about this production was exceptional. The acting and direction were superb, the sets and music perfection, the costumes gorgeous—especially Ophelia's, which was a breathtaking drape of yards and yards of heavy white velvet trimmed in gold braid. I remember sitting in the audience and thinking to myself, "I would give anything in the world to be on that stage, in *Hamlet*, with those actors, wearing those costumes." I had a friend in the cast, and after the show was over, I went backstage to see him. He introduced me to various members of the company and showed me around the dressing area. That night at home, I was consumed with the desire to do Shakespeare with the theatre company that had produced *Hamlet*. I had recently read a book on visualization techniques and decided to put them to the test. Here is the visualization I designed for myself:

> *I am seated at a dressing table backstage of the theatre which had put on Hamlet. There are lights around the dressing room mirror, and I can feel their heat radiating toward me. I am putting on greasepaint, can feel its peculiar consistency as I smooth it over my face and neck, and can smell it as well. I can hear about me the chatter of the other actors as they put on makeup and costumes. I want to be sure that my unconscious understands my desire to do Shakespeare, so I see myself wearing Ophelia's white velvet costume. I can feel its weight, and the tightness of the bodice at my waist and against my ribcage.*

Two months after doing this exercise, the theatre held auditions for a non-Shakespearean play. I was hired to play a role, and then a lead in a second play. During the run of the second play, the managing director of the theatre called to say that *Hamlet* was going to be revived. The girl who had played Ophelia was moving away from the area and wouldn't be able to play the role. He said the part was mine if I wanted it, which of course I did. And there I was, wearing the white velvet costume with the gold braid that I had worn in my visualization.

Unfortunately, the girl for whom the costume had been designed was petite and I was not. Since the *Hamlet* costumes had been constructed at great expense, there was no question of a new costume for me. This presented a variety of problems, some of which had startling consequences, not only for me, but occasionally for the audience. Speaking Shakespeare requires that one take great lungfuls of air—enough breath to last through a lengthy speech if need be. The costume's bodice was so tight that I literally could not get enough air into my lungs in one breath, so I had to accomplish this in stages prior to a speech. This process took anywhere from thirty seconds to a minute, depending on how much I had eaten during the day.

The costume's weight also worked against me. In one scene, Laertes was required to show his delight in seeing me by swinging me around in a great circle center-stage. One night he miscalculated distances. Around I went, the heavy velvet skirt swinging wildly outward. All the furniture was wiped off the stage. In another scene, Hamlet was required to toss me violently to the floor, after which I delivered Ophelia's tragic soliloquy. One night, I was well into the speech and, suitably despondent, cast my eyes tragically downward, only to discover the skirt of my costume had fallen to my ankles. The tussle in the previous scene had been too much for the large safety pin I had used to reinforce the other two fasteners. Fortunately, I was wearing petticoats, but getting off the stage gracefully was a bit tricky.

The play had a long run. When we finally closed six months later, the managing director called to say that *Hamlet* was going to be revived yet again, and that I should prepare to do battle with the Great White Velvet. Another long run, and finally it was well and truly over—or so I thought. The next show slated was a Restoration comedy in which I was to play a role. Restoration costumes, like those of Shakespearean productions, feature very full skirts and tight bodices. Without consulting me, the costume department took my Ophelia costume, stripped it of velvet and braid and built the new costume on top of the old frame. So there I was, for a third time, in agony. Never let it be said there is no magic in the number Three.

Be careful what you visualize.

EXERCISE 7: VISUALIZATION

Take some quiet time to design your visualization. Relaxed reverie is best for this. The design needn't be final, but it should be pretty well set in your mind before you begin the actual visualization.

- Take the phone off the hook, seek privacy, and sit or lie down in a comfortable position.

- Invoke your personal and god symbols (see Appendix B).

- Take at least ten minutes to physically relax before you proceed. If you have a relaxation tape which you can play, use it. If you are a practitioner of Hatha Yoga, you might wish to do Savasana, probably the best relaxation exercise ever invented. If you don't have a tape and are not familiar with yoga, soothing music may be helpful. When your body is relaxed, your mind can work miracles, which is, after all, what you are after. Now you may proceed.

- Repeat the following affirmation (or one like it) either in your mind or aloud: "Creating visual images is easy for me. I see clearly." Still relaxed, repeat this affirmation as many times as you like. (If you have developed clairvoyant skills, you can skip this step in the procedure.)

- Do Exercise 1 (page 42) to activate positive energy. (You needn't repeat the affirmation associated with that exercise unless you wish to.) Your purpose here is to elevate your personal vibrational frequences and to energize the area around you. Visualization—or any kind of magical work, for that matter—is more effective after this exercise is performed.

- Perform the visualization in your mind as designed. But don't be surprised if the visualization begins to take on a life of its own—that is, the image may change in a way that you had not originally planned. This is a good sign, as long as the general tenor of the visualization moves in the direction you wish. But if the images begin to move in a manner opposed to your plan, cease visualizing at once. This is a rare occurence, but it does happen. When a visualization stubbornly refuses to cooperate with your conscious intentions, it's usually a sign that your goal is ill-chosen (check with your oracle), or that the visualization design itself is faulty, in which case you must begin the design process again.

- When you have completed visualizing, repeat the following affirmation (or one similar) either in your mind or aloud: "My mental images are easily manifested in material reality." You may repeat this as often as you wish.

- Slowly come back to normal consciousness: wiggle fingers and toes, open your eyes and yawn.

- When you are ready, seal your aura (see page 80).

The second affirmation in this procedure requires a cautionary note. Please be aware that, by repeating this affirmation, you are giving your unconscious mind *carte blanche* to reproduce in material reality *all* your mental images, not just those contained in a formal visualization. Repeated use of this affirmation means that you must avoid unpleasant images engendered by negative emotions. Techniques for removing negative images are discussed on page 103.

MAGICAL FEELING

If you can trick your unconscious into believing that you already have what you desire, it will go to work and produce the good you want. "Them who has, gets," as the adage goes. Visualization is one way to fool your unconscious. The use of magical feeling is another. Sometimes it's easier to use feelings than pictures. Following are two methods for producing emotion on demand for magical purposes: recollection and identification.

Recollection: Think back to an earlier period in your life when you had, or felt you had, the good that you now desire. A personal example will illustrate. Using visualization for prosperity work is difficult for me. Because I'm not very materialistic, I have trouble picturing myself surrounded with luxuries I don't passionately desire. This doesn't mean I don't need money, of course; and when I do, it's necessary to get the message through to my unconscious somehow. To do so I call to mind an early experience. I had a very glamorous grandmother who decided it was time to jazz me up as I approached puberty. On my birthday—I was probably 11 or 12—she gave me a beautiful blue chiffon nightgown, a large bottle of perfume, and a complete set of black lace underwear. Totally inappropriate for my age, but never mind—I was in heaven. I distinctly remember putting on the nightgown, dousing myself with perfume, getting into bed, and thinking to myself, "Ooh, I feel so *rich*." I call up that feeling whenever I'm working magically for greater prosperity.

This technique can be used for any goal. If you are working for better health, call to mind a period in your life when you were perfectly well and full of energy. Remember how you felt. Recapture the feeling. Relive it. Your unconscious will understand and act upon the message.

Many people wish for more love in their lives. Here is a rite utilizing recollection which you can perform when you want a new romance, friendship, or greater love of self (self-esteem).

THE RITE OF APHRODITE'S GIRDLE

Materials needed: One long cord

Optional: Incense of the romantic variety

Love Water

Explanation and preliminaries: Aphrodite is the Greek goddess of love, and she is irresistible. Her beauty and her melodious laugh are usually enough to entice anyone on whom she sets her sights. But occasionally, when there is some resistance to her seductive wiles, she uses a secret weapon: her girdle. This girdle is not one of those rubbery things women wore back in pre-liberation days; it's more like a silken sash or a loose-fitting belt. Her fellow gods and goddesses borrow the girdle whenever they are feeling amorous or want to be alluring. You, too, can borrow it.

An appropriate cord is best bought in the trim department of any fabric store. It should be substantial—not too thick, but not too thin, either. You can use material other than cord if you wish—a leather thong, for example. In a pinch, you can even use thread or yarn, but cord is probably best. Whatever material you use should hold a knot well. Traditionally, its color should be pink, orange, or red (see the color chart on page 123). However, you may use any color which excites your imagination. Length is important. You will be tying many knots in the cord before you use it, so make allowances for this. When the cord is fully knotted—there may be two dozen or more knots in it—it should still be long enough to fit loosely around your waist. The cord should therefore be several yards long when you buy it.

If you choose to use incense for the rite, this can be purchased in any metaphysical store. There are dozens of appropriate varieties available: Aphrodite, Cleopatra, Love Drawing, etc. If you want to use Love Water but can't find it, tell your local metaphysical store to contact me through the publisher of this book.

The Rite:

Gather your materials, take the phone off the hook and seek privacy.

Invoke your personal and god symbols (see Appendix B).

Light your incense, if you are using it. Waft the cord through the incense six times (this being Aphrodite's number).

Seat yourself comfortably, with the cord held loosely in your hands.

Relax and quiet your mind.

Do Exercise 1 (page 42) to activate positive energy.

Think of the qualities you have which make you lovable: a good sense of humor, compassion, warmth, loyalty, wit, a brilliant mind, *joie de vivre*, physical beauty, athletic skills, grace, a lovely voice, artistic talent—any of these, and a thousand others may apply. Don't be modest. No one is eavesdropping.

As you think of each quality, put a knot in your cord. Knot each lovable quality into the cord.

Rest a while.

Call to mind all those who have loved you during the course of your life: parents, guardians, brothers, sisters, relatives, friends, lovers, spouses, children, and beloved pets.

As you think of each person who has loved you, knot that person's love into your cord.

Rest a moment.

Realize that you have been much loved. You are loved now. It is only natural that more love is coming your way.

Feel richly loved.

If you are using Love Water, dab a little on each knot in the cord.

Tie Aphrodite's girdle loosely about your waist.

Come back to normal consciousness.

Seal your aura (see page 80).

Wear Aphrodite's girdle often. Sleep with it under your pillow.

Comments: Loneliness frequently produces desperation, which is dangerous. The more desperate you are to achieve a goal, the less chance you have of achieving it. The unconscious mind recognizes a feeling of desperation, produces more of the same, and thus begins a vicious cycle. A person who desperately seeks romance will never find it. A person who relaxes into pleasurable solitude will find suitors knocking at the door, as in the visualization given earlier in this chapter. This rite instructs your unconscious to produce more of the love you have already so richly known throughout your life. It also builds self-esteem.

No matter what your goal, the trick is to vividly remember a past experience, and then to bask, as it were, in the emotion engendered by the memory. This, in itself, is powerful magic. You can also use the following technique.

Identification: In order to use this method, **identify with a character from fiction or film who has achieved the goal you have in mind.** I stumbled upon this technique quite by accident a number of years ago. I'll tell you the story so you can see how it works.

When my marriage ended, I suffered from the usual emotional devastation and was broke as well. One evening I watched an old and quite dreadful movie on television called *The Egyptian.* The film featured a rather wicked courtesan named Nefer. Nefer gave lavish parties and reclined, always with her gorgeous cat, on a gilt couch to watch the festivities while her personal slave served her rich wine in a beautiful goblet and her personal musician plucked out lovely melodies on a harp. Men fell over their own feet in an effort to give Nefer expensive gifts so that she would favor them.

Ego shattered and poor, I watched Nefer, and thought to myself: This is the way life should be. And when the movie was over, I *was* Nefer. I stayed Nefer for several days. It was quite heavenly. I went out and bought the book upon which the movie had been based, and this extended my "Neferness" for some time. I learned from the book that Nefer was a priestess of the cat-goddess Bast. This was a real bonus because I've always been a cat-person and had a wonderful sleek black cat at home who would happily play companion to my Nefer.

My boss and his wife were in the Orient while all of this was going on. When they arrived back, they gave me a very expensive pearl necklace as a gift. A month later, they gave me a fur coat. My salary was almost doubled in six months. And other people began to give me gifts as well. Not minor gifts; major ones. It was wonderful, but incomprehensible. I hadn't asked for any gifts, and I had done absolutely nothing to deserve them. It took me a while to put two and two together, but when I did, I realized I had stumbled upon an important magical technique.

Patience: there's more to the story. Because Nefer was a priestess of Bast, I began to take an interest in the Egyptian deities. Up until this point, they had left me cold, but now they fascinated me. Browsing through a bookstore one day, I came across Murry Hope's *The Way of Cartouche*. I bought it and devoured it. I was so impressed with her work that I wrote her a fan letter—something I had never done before. Our correspondence soon flourished and I knew that I had found the teacher I had long sought. Murry, being an astute teacher, spotted the weaknesses in my magical education (and character), and made some valuable suggestions. I followed up on these, and thus was able to complete my magical studies. I owe it all to Nefer.[5]

---

[5]This story illustrates the important relationship between the emotional and spiritual planes. Work done upon the emotional plane opens up the portals to the spiritual plane.

Now to practicalities. This technique is not in the least obscure or difficult. It is simply a matter of finding a character in fiction or film who has what you want, and then becoming that character in your imagination. It is, in fact, a role-playing procedure somewhat similar to (but not as formal as) the two techniques discussed in chapter 5.

We all role-play to a degree when we read a wonderful book and identify with a particular character. We close the book, and for a moment we *are* that character. Or we see a film, identify with a particular character, and when it's over, we walk up the aisle and for a few seconds we *are* the character. The trick is to extend the experience so that your unconscious gets the message that you have (your chosen character has) achieved your goal. It will then go to work to produce the good you want.

Look carefully at the "life" of your prospective fictional character before you start to role-play. If you want freedom and a lot of interesting men in your life, you may be attracted to Carmen of book, opera and ballet fame. But while it's true that Carmen had all these qualities in abundance, it's also true that she died young and nastily. If you wish for Scarlett O'Hara's magnetism and business acumen, you had better ruminate on the heavy burdens Scarlett had to carry before you make a decision in her favor. You don't want to give your unconscious an excuse for creating unforeseen problems.

Do *not* choose a living person as role-model. Stepping into the shoes—actually, the psyche—of a living person is seriously invasive, and it will rebound on you.

Stay away from historical personages for the same reason. Those who believe in the existence of parallel universes which contain soul- or essence-fragments will understand why historical role-playing is a psychic mine field. For safety, stick to fictional characters only. There is no shortage of these.

Both of these techniques, recollection and identification, may be combined effectively with visualization. In fact, such a combination is ideal. Using either of the magical feeling techniques, call up the appropriate feeling first and bask in it. Then, feeling that you have achieved your goal, perform your visualization. The emotion behind the mental images and the images themselves cannot fail to impress your unconscious mind with your message.

CLEARING

There is more to magic than creating positive thoughts, feelings, and pictures. It is true that these go a long way toward producing good results, but sometimes they're not enough. It may be necessary to clear out psychological garbage—negative inherited attitudes, irrational thoughts or feelings, etc.—before proceeding with the positive work.

We have touched on the subject of clearing once before, when discussing affirmations (see chapter 4). Affirmations can reverse unwanted attitudes or beliefs which interfere with your desired success. But this takes time. You can speed up the process considerably if you combine affirmations with clearing procedures.

A change of feeling is a change of destiny.[6]

Ideally, psychological clearing should begin at the same time that you create your affirmations—that is, soon after you have set your goal and received the go-ahead from your oracle. I have waited until now to discuss clearing because it's necessary to have a working knowledge of visualization and magical feeling techniques before you can make use of clearing methods.

There are dozens of effective clearing techniques. In fact, emotional clearing could itself be the subject of a lengthy book. In this chapter, we will discuss just four clearing methods, but these should be adequate for most students' needs. However, if you are inspired to create your own procedures, by all means do so. Techniques which you design yourself will always be more effective than those designed by others.

---

[6]Neville, *Feeling Is the Secret* (Los Angeles: G & J Publishing, 1966), unnumbered.

VISUAL CLEARING METHOD

This technique is best used to get rid of verbal expressions which, having wormed their way into your unconscious, negatively affect your behavior or prevent you from achieving the success you desire.[7]

I had a friend who grew up hearing from her mother the rhyme about the little girl with the curl in the middle of her forehead: "When she was good, she was very, very good—but when she was bad, she was horrid." Her mother, best described as a very proper Victorian lady, always emphasized the "horrid" part of the rhyme in an insinuating sort of way, as if she might find a mischievous daughter more appealing than a perfectly behaved one. However, this was in direct contradiction to the beautiful manners she demanded, and got, from her daughter when the girl was young.

My personal opinion is that the mother was torn between her own Victorian upbringing and a natural desire to kick up her heels—to be "horrid"—now and again. But she couldn't allow herself to be horrid, so she projected this desire onto her daughter, who (being "very, very good"—that is, obedient to her mother's wishes) obliged by being as horrid as possible the minute she reached puberty. She carried the trait into adulthood and her romantic life has always suffered as a result. When she realized she had been programmed to "horridness" and wanted to erase the tape, she used this technique. The words she chose to counter the negative programming were, "You are very, very good."

---

[7]This and the following exercise are based upon techniques created by Jonathan Parker of Quantum Quests International for audiotape listening. Readers interested in further work of this nature are advised to write to Quantum Quests, P. O. Box 7000, Ventura, CA 93006–7000 for a catalog.

EXERCISE 8: CLEARING TECHNIQUE

The technique works like this:

- Seek privacy and physically relax for at least ten minutes.

- Invoke your personal and god symbols (see Appendix B).

- Do Exercise 1 (page 42) to activate positive energy.

- Imagine that you are reclining in a very comfortable lounge chair.

- There is a large red button on the arm of the chair. This button is your deprogramming device.

- In front of your lounge chair is a movie screen. The screen represents your unconscious mind.

- Imagine that you see the unwanted verbal expression written in gray letters on the screen in front of you. See the words written as clearly as possible, and think how much you want to remove them from your unconscious.

- When you are ready to remove the words from your unconscious, press the red deprogramming button on the arm of the chair.

- Instantly, a blinding flash of light sweeps across the movie screen. When the light disappears, the screen is wiped clean of words. It is white and shining. The words have been removed from your unconscious.

- Relax a moment.

- See your words of countersuggestion written in gold letters on the screen in front of you. To program the new message into your unconscious, dwell on them long and lovingly.

- When you are ready, return to normal consciousness.

- Seal your aura (see page 80).

Perform this exercise several times—perhaps once a day for several days, or even longer—until you feel that you have effectively removed the negative programming from your unconscious.

CLEARING FEAR

This technique may be used for other purposes as well. To remove irrational fear, for instance, see the words "Fear of _____" written in gray letters across the screen, and fill in the blank with the word, or words, which best describe what frightens you. Deprogram the phrase as outlined. Then see the words "Courage" or "Self-Confidence" (or whatever describes the psychological condition you desire) written in gold letters across the screen in order to reprogram your unconscious.[8] Stress can be removed in a similar manner, as can any other condition which you see as essentially destructive to your purposes.

Upsetting memories, the existence of which no longer serves any purpose, may also be removed with this technique. To remove a memory, see it played out on the screen, just as if you were watching a movie, then destroy it with the deprogramming button. Ideally, the memory should be viewed in black-and-white, but don't worry if you can't manage this. Follow with a visualization—in living color, if possible—showing positive events taking place. Dwell at length on this pleasant scene.

Be absolutely sure you want to remove a given memory before you use this technique. Some upsetting memories serve a purpose and should be retained. A friend of mine owned a metaphysical store located in a rough section of a large city. On occasion, she and the store were subjected to some rather frightening incidents. One involved a knife-wielding psychopath who appeared in the store day after day, terrorizing the owner and her employees. The police eventually took care of the situation and the lunatic never appeared again, but the memory of the incident occasionally flashed across

---

[8]According to Dr. Parker, the color gray is easily removed from the unconscious, while gold is easily retained. Personal experience confirms his opinion.

her mind. Should this memory have been removed? Probably not. Although distressing, it served to remind my friend of the very real dangers which existed on the street outside the shop, causing her to remain security-conscious and constantly vigilant.

EXERCISE 9: ETHERIC CLEARING

There are times when one wants to clear something from consciousness, but the "something" cannot neatly be put into words or pictures, so the previous method can't be used.

The etheric clearing technique can be used to clear out raw abstract emotions such as anger, fear, envy, jealousy, and grief. It may also be used for healing. (If used for healing, however, please remember that the removal of disease may result in the removal of a badly needed psychological benefit; see chapter 4). To use etheric clearing, follow these steps:

- Seek privacy and physically relax for at least ten minutes.

- Invoke your personal and god symbols (see Appendix B).

- Perform the exercise to activate positive energy (see page 42).

- Mentally locate the seat of the emotion or illness, which is causing you distress in your body. If you are angry, for instance, you may feel that the seat of your anger is located in your solar plexus or chest area. Fear may be located in the pit of your stomach, grief in your heart, envy in your eyes, etc.

- Using physical gesture, pull the unwanted emotion or illness out of your body. Place this psychic "matter" in the air above your body. It will remain there until you are ready to destroy it.

- Keep pulling the unwanted matter out of your body until you feel you are free of it. This may take some time.

- Using physical gesture, start to mold the unwanted matter above you into a ball (beach ball size is ideal).

- Take the ball into your hands and, using physical gesture, throw it out about ten feet from you. The ball remains suspended in the air in front of you until you are ready to destroy it.

- You have at your side a ray gun (like those used in *Star Wars*). This ray gun destroys unwanted matter.

- Take up the gun in your dominant hand. Aim it at the ball. Pull the trigger.

- The ball of unwanted matter is destroyed in a blaze of blinding light.

- When the light fades, the ball is gone. Your problem no longer exists.

- Relax for a moment.

- Visualize yourself healthy and happy; or, using magical feeling, invoke happy emotions.

- Come back to normal consciousness.

- Seal your aura (see page 80).

Helpful Tip: Most variety stores carry inexpensive keyring gadgets which produce a variety of sounds, such as death-ray sirens, missile-launcher explosions, or tommy-gun fire, when you press a button. These can be used to add another dimension to the exercise. When you pull your weapon's trigger, press the appropriate button for instant sound effects. This will probably make you laugh at first, but you'll soon discover that the unconscious mind responds well to this trick.

As with the previous clearing technique, be absolutely sure that you wish to be free of the emotion or illness before you perform this exercise. Remember that supposedly negative emotions often serve an important purpose, and so should not be removed. Intense anger, for instance, is a signal that you need to make some changes in your life. Make these, and the anger will disappear by itself. Envy is a strong indication that you are not living up to your potential. Stop being passive and find a way to attain the good that others have. Jealousy indicates that you are insecure and need to bolster your self-esteem. Fear warns you to be cautious. In other words, you should acknowledge your discomfort, pay attention to its message, and take practical action in the appropriate direction. It is only when an emotion gets out of hand—when it seriously, and for no good reason, interferes with your daily life on a continuing basis—that you should clear it out.

LETTER CLEARING

This is a very effective technique recommended by many psychotherapists. In my experience, it's particularly good for getting rid of anger.

The method is simple. Sit down and write a letter to any individual (or organization) who has enraged you. Make the letter as nasty as possible. Be vicious. Rewrite the letter until it says exactly what you want it to say. Polish the grammar and vocabulary. This may take some time—several days, perhaps. Then burn the letter.

This works. When I was in my early teens, two supposed friends did me a serious wrong. I was enraged and hurt, but felt confronting them with my anger was out of the question. They would have found my reaction amusing, and I wasn't about to give them any such satisfaction. So I swallowed the anger and carried on. Time passed. Thirty years later, for no apparent reason, I found myself enraged all over again. I tried to rationalize the anger out of existence, but it wouldn't go away; every time my mind wandered, there it was. Something had to be done. Open confrontation with the two parties (whom I had not seen in the interim) was both ridiculous and impossible, so I settled on writing letters to them.

I wrote and wrote, rewrote and rewrote; the process took several weeks. When the letters were finished, I saved them, then ritually burned them on New Year's Eve so that I could start the New Year fresh. Some time later, I read that one of the parties had died—very prematurely—and was surprised to feel genuine sadness at the news. I took this as proof that my anger had truly been exorcised.

This story may make some readers wonder if one might unintentionally harm the person to whom a letter is directed. The answer is no. In magic, *intention is everything*, and your intention when you write a clearing letter is not to harm the individual in question, but to rid yourself of inappropriate rage. You could conceivably injure the person on the conscious level if you actually mailed the letter. I can't imagine anyone—guilty of wrong-doing or not—enjoying a truly venomous letter. But by burning it, you give your rage back to the appropriate element, fire, and the individual concerned is bypassed entirely. This is a form of recycling on the metaphysical level, and is a safe procedure.

MURRY HOPE'S RITE OF TEARS

This simple and very moving rite was created (or, more accurately, remembered) by Murry Hope, who brought it through from an Atlantean incarnation. It will help magicians to clear themselves of excessive grief or sadness.

Grief caused by the loss of someone or something dear to you is natural, and it should not be suppressed. Psychiatrists say that grief may endure for as long as two years, or for as short a period as six months, depending on the nature of the loss and the griever's degree of sensitivity. They also say it is very important to allow the grieving process to take place naturally, for if this is intentionally (or even unintentionally) blocked, emotional healing will not occur.

There may be times, however, when you are so overwhelmed by sadness, for so lengthy a period, that your health or livelihood—your existence, in other words—is endangered. In this case, grief-counseling is in order. So is this rite.

Materials needed: A chalice or goblet, filled with spring water

Preliminary notes: This is a formal rite created by an experienced magician with a full panoply of magical tools at her disposal, including a properly consecrated chalice. As a beginner you may not have this advantage. If this is the case, you have two options: you can skip ahead to chapter 9, which will instruct you how to consecrate a chalice; or, you can perform the rite as presented using an ordinary cup or wineglass. The latter option is probably best, because if you feel a pressing need to perform this rite, you are probably in no emotional condition to take on any additional burdens. The same applies to the need for spring water. If you must perform the rite and haven't any spring water on hand, use boiled tap water instead. As with all magic, the rite's operative factor is not in the materials used, but in its psychological impact.

Most formal magical rites begin with an invitation to the four elements and end with their dismissal. This one is no exception. Full instructions for these procedures will be given in chapter 9, and you are invited to jump ahead for instruction if you wish. Otherwise, simply skip the steps in question.

The Rite

Invoke your personal and god symbols (see Appendix B).

Perform Exercise 1 (page 42) to activate positive energy.

Invite and welcome the four elements to the rite (see chapter 9).

Invoke your chosen spiritual plane archetype.

Ask your deity to help you understand the reasons for your suffering.

Allow your grief or sadness to well up from within, until your tears begin to flow.

Allow a few tears to fall into your chalice.

Offer your tears as sacrifice.

Plead with your deity to bestow upon you peace of mind and heart.

Drink a little from your chalice.

Plead again with your deity for understanding and peace.

Take your chalice outside and pour its contents into the Earth or a nearby body of water. As you do so, say: "As this water flows away, so also may my tears depart, to be reabsorbed into the great unconscious."[9] (If it is impossible to go outdoors, pour the chalice contents down a bathroom drain.)

When you are ready to end the rite, dismiss the elements (see chapter 9).

Seal your aura (see page 80).

Murry herself has performed this rite, and she assures me it is most effective.

SUMMARY

Upon reviewing the exercises contained in this chapter, the reader will realize that I do not advocate suppression of so-called "negative" emotions. Feelings, particularly of the darker sort, must be acknowledged, and they must be expressed. If they are not, they go underground and secretly create serious havoc in the form of physical disease and other horrors.

But feelings must be *responsibly* expressed. The fact that you feel angry or envious or jealous does not mean that you must automatically act upon that feeling to the detriment of another individual. It's always easy, of course, to blame others for the problems you yourself may have created. And sometimes others really are responsible for your suffering. This is particularly true in childhood, for there is no such thing as a perfect parent or guardian. Practically speaking, however, it doesn't matter who or what has caused your problems. As an adult, you are ultimately responsible for your own safety and happiness, and it is up to you to root out and destroy that within you which prevents you from achieving

---

[9]The water element has a strong affinity with the emotional plane and has always been considered by psychologists to be a symbol of the unconscious, both personal and collective.

the good you desire in life. It's for this reason that emotional clearing is an important part of magical practice.

1. *Clearing* should be performed at the same time that you create your affirmations:

Visual Method: to clear verbal expressions, fear, memory, stress;

Etheric Method: to clear negative emotions;

Letter Method: to clear negative emotions, especially anger;

The Rite of Tears: to clear grief or sadness.

2. Instruct your unconscious mind to reproduce your desires in material reality through the use of:

Visualization (page 88) and/or;

Magical Feeling (page 94) and/or;

Identification with a Fictional Character (page 97).

CHAPTER 7

THE PHYSICAL PLANE

If you work with all four of the elements in your magical operations, you generate six times more power than if you worked with none at all.[1]

The spirits of the elements are a vital key in occult development, not only because it is part and parcel of ritualistic procedure to invoke them, but because to conquer the human traits associated with each element is what initiation is all about.[2]

—Murry Hope

Once you have defined your goal, invoked the assistance of your chosen archetype, created affirmations and incantations, and performed your visualization (or evoked magical feeling), you have generated an enormous amount of energy on the higher planes. This energy must now be brought down to Earth or, to use metaphysical jargon, "earthed" or "grounded." In magic, like attracts like. If you wish to achieve physical results from your magical operations, you must use physical tools.

All physical plane magic involves the four elements: fire, air, water, earth. We shall discuss each element in great detail later on, but first let us take an overall look at the role the elements play in magic.

---

[1]This is a paraphrase of an old metaphysical adage taught me by Murry Hope.
[2]Murry Hope, *Practical Techniques of Psychic Self-Defense* (New York: St. Martin's, 1983), p. 72.

THE FOUR ELEMENTS IN NATURE

The four elements exist in nature on the physical level. We are all familiar with them—everyone knows what fire is, and air. Some of their manifestations, however, are not so obvious.

Take, for example, the plant kingdom. Chili peppers, which are the fruits of the capsicum plant, have a hot, pungent taste, and if classified by element, would undoubtedly be attributed to the fire element. The weeping willow tree, which grows on the banks of streams and rivers, must surely belong to water. The violet, which grows close to the ground beneath the shade of overhanging greenery, seems clearly to belong to earth; wisteria, a climbing vine, must belong to air.

The mineral kingdom may be similarly classifed: red and orange stones look fiery; aqua-blue and green gems seem watery; brown and black stones are earthy; colorless crystals appear airy.

As for the animal kingdom, the lion is associated with fire, the dolphin with water, the eagle with air, and the dog with earth. Some animals are not so easily classified, however, because they belong to more than one element. The duck, for instance, swims (water), walks on land (earth) and flies (air), making it a three-element creature.

Human beings belong to the animal kingdom, and are four-element creatures. We walk and, if given instruction, swim quite well. It's true we can't fly unaided but, thanks to technology, we're well able to get around by air. With protective covering, we can withstand fire for very brief periods. We have learned to adapt ourselves to the elements.

The four elements also exist within the human being. On the physical level, our blood and the heat of our bodies represent the fire element. Our breathing apparatus is airy. Our bodily fluids symbolize water, and earth is represented by our skin and bones. The elements are clearly manifested in human psychology, as well. We shall discuss this a little later.

Everything which exists on this planet may be assigned to at least one element, and this has its use in ritual magic.

THE FOUR ELEMENTS IN RITUAL MAGIC

Before you perform any formal magical ritual, you must make two decisions:

1. You must decide to which element your goal belongs; goals, like natural objects, may be classifed by element.

2. You must decide which natural objects to use in your ritual; these will correspond to your goal and its element.

Having made these decisions, you may proceed with your magical operation. Your use of appropriate physical objects will ground the energies generated by prayer, visualization, and magical feeling. In addition, physical objects will stimulate certain areas of your psyche so that you can, on demand, dredge up enthusiasm, imagination, and emotion for your ritual. Their mechanical use will encourage you to mentally focus on your goal. In short, the ritual use of physical objects will make you more powerful—six times more powerful, according to the adage quoted at the head of this chapter.

Although all four elements (in the form of physical objects) should be used in every magical operation so that you can raise as much power as possible, in actual practice one element is usually emphasized over the others, depending on the goal and the element to which it belongs. This can be illustrated with an example.

Suppose that a female magician is an artist, and that her goal is to sell a painting. She wants to use all four elements in her work and, to this end, she intends to use a candle (fire), an incense (air), a water (water), and a powder (earth). But since creativity and success are ruled by fire, she wants to place particular emphasis on this element. She could use any color candle, but red or orange is more evocative of fire than, say, blue or green. After checking the color chart on page 123, she decides on orange.

Incense, which is compounded from herbs, represents air, so she checks the list of fiery herbs in chapter 7, and settles on cinnamon. She chooses Creativity Water and Prosperity Powder to satisfy the need for the water and earth elements. She decides to incorporate some extra fire symbols into the ritual as well. On her work area (altar), she places a photograph of her painting, and surrounds it with a statue of a cat (animal), a red rose (a flower sacred to Aphrodite, who favors creative projects), and a carnelian gemstone (mineral). Finally, with all this equipment in place, she lights her candle and incense, sprinkles her water and powder about, and proceeds with her incantations, visualization, etc.

Our hypothetical artist has incorporated all four elements into her ritual, but her main emphasis has been on fire. Every symbol, every object which she has gathered relating to this element will make her operation more powerful, for they will stimulate her senses and ignite a fire in her unconscious mind. Her ultimate success depends on inner fire, for it is this which will attract the external fire she desires—creative success—from the environment.

To be successful, you must know how to put the physical elements to work for you. More important, you must know how to identify, activate, and control your inner elements. This involves some knowledge of psychology.

THE FOUR ELEMENTS IN PSYCHOLOGY

The elements exist within the human psyche. The "creative spark" is fiery. Intellectual skills are airy. The emotional nature belongs to water. The practical sense is earthy. The average healthy human being is emotional, creative on some level, materialistically inclined, and able to function intellectually.

Some individuals, of course, are more creative than materialistic (or vice versa), just as some are more emotional than intellectual, or the reverse. Varying degrees of each element in the individual personality account for the different temperament types.

The magical elements correspond to the four psychological functions as defined by the great psychiatrist, C. G. Jung:

Figure 1. The circle of elemental functions.

fire = the intuitive function
air = the thinking function
water = the feeling function
earth = the sensate function.[3]

The Temperament Questionnaire in Appendix A will tell you which function (element) is most strongly represented in your temperament. This function/element is called your primary function. If the test results indicate that you are an intuitive type, then intuition is your primary function, and fire is the element most strongly represented in your temperament. If the four elements (functions) are placed in a circle so that each of them takes up one quadrant, the circle of elemental functions would look like figure 1 (see above).

---

[3]The correlation between the Jungian functions and the four elements is my own, and is based upon years of astrological study and personal observation. Most astrologers and Jungian therapists agree with my attributions. If you'd like to know more about Jungian typology, you might wish to read chapter 8, "Psychological Types," in *The Portable Jung* (New York: Penguin, 1980). For a fascinating look at Jung's theories regarding symbols, see the lavishly illustrated *Man and His Symbols* (New York: Doubleday, 1979).

Notice that fire is placed opposite earth. These two elements represent very different temperaments. The fiery (intuitive) individual is intuitive, idealistic, and spiritual; the earthy (sensate) individual is practical, realistic, and materialistic. It is rare to find a person in whom equal degrees of fire and earth are represented; a strongly idealistic person is usually not very practical, and a materialistic person is not usually highly spiritual.

Notice also that air and water oppose one another in the circle. Again, these two elements represent vastly different temperaments: the airy (thinking) type is very rational; the watery (feeling) type is emotional. Thinking types are usually uncomfortable with their emotions, and find feeling types overly sentimental. Feeling types, on the other hand, are comfortable with their emotions, and find thinking types cold. A very rational human being who is comfortable with emotion is unusual.

Your weakest function is usually (but not always) the one opposed to your primary function. If thinking (air) is your primary function, then feeling (water) is probably your weakest function, and vice versa. Likewise, if intuition (fire) is your primary function, then sensation (earth) is probably your weakest function, and vice versa.

Many years ago, my psychiatrist told me that we are born with one very strong function (the primary), one fairly strong function (the secondary), a third function which is relatively weak, and a fourth which is extremely weak. We develop the primary and secondary functions during the first half of our lives. At midlife, we become bored with functioning the way we always have, and begin to develop the third function. If we live long enough (or consciously work on the project), we may develop the fourth and weakest function. A goal of Jungian psychotherapy is to develop all four of the functions so that one is capable of dealing with life at any level and in any manner chosen.

As a magician, you seek to develop all four of the elements within your temperament for very practical reasons, which will become evident as you progress through this study.

ELEMENTALS

Elementals are the little creatures which animate the four elements. You cannot ordinarily see, hear, feel, taste, or touch them, but this doesn't mean they don't exist; after all, X-rays exist, even though you cannot sense them. You may, however, get to know the elementals through the use of your extraordinary senses, as we shall see later in this chapter.

The four types of elementals are Salamanders (fire), Sylphs (air), Ondines (water), and Gnomes (earth).

Elementals are experts in their own realms. The Salamander knows everything there is to know about the fire element, both physical and psychological; Sylphs are experts on the subject of air; Ondines are experts regarding water; Gnomes specialize in earthy subjects. Elementals are one-element creatures, and as long as they remain imprisoned, so to speak, in their own element they are incapable of learning anything about those elements to which they don't naturally belong.

Elementals aren't entirely happy with this situation. They'd like to progress and evolve, but the only way they can do so is through vicarious association with multi-element creatures, such as human beings. For this reason, elementals seek human companionship. In return for a favored human's "tutelage," they are very willing to give service. The magician who is able to attract a helpful Ondine can look forward to expert assistance in matters relating to love, friendship, healing, and the psychic arts. Gnomes will help with career and financial matters, Sylphs with intellectual pursuits, and Salamanders with creative and spiritual issues.

Elemental assistance is much to be desired because it makes pursuit of a goal easier. Called upon for help, an elemental gladly goes to work on his companion's project. You still need to do affirmations, incantations, visualizations, and all of the other work covered to this point—you can never expect anyone or anything to do all of your work for you—but your path to the goal will be greased, so to speak, and you'll see speedier results than if you had no elemental help at all. Magicians who are able to attract elemental companions have a great advantage over those who are not.

There is, however, a catch. Elementals tend to be selective when it comes to human companionship. The Salamander, for instance, does not care to associate with a human being who is grossly materialistic. Fire is a high-frequency element, and a Salamander prefers to work with someone who is comfortable on the higher planes. Ondines have no interest in helping individuals who are not comfortable with their feelings, because Ondines are entirely at home with watery emotion and have no respect for those who aren't. And so it goes with all the elementals. In short, until and unless you develop all the elements within your character, you haven't a chance of attracting a full panoply of elemental companions. This means you will find the accomplishment of some goals—those which relate to your weakest function or element—very difficult. Furthermore, if you invoke the aid of elementals belonging to your weakest function (element), you are usually inviting trouble. Elementals aren't seriously malicious creatures, but they're not above creating minor problems (examples of which will be given later on) for humans whom they don't respect. You will see that development of the four elements within your temperament is work of a very practical nature.

Some people may have difficulty accepting the traditional concept of elementals as presented here. One or two psychologically-oriented students have asked me if I thought the elementals were nothing more than cordoned-off parts of the individual psyche to which unusual names are assigned, rather than creatures that exist (albeit invisibly) in objective reality. I'm not able to answer this question. I don't know what the true nature of the elemental is. Being psychologically-minded myself, I'm open to the idea that elementals are, if not exactly figments, products of the human imagination. I'm also receptive to the idea that elementals exist in objective reality. If they do, I rather expect they represent something akin to aggregates of sub-atomic particles, and that New Physics scientists will eventually identify and rename them. Physicists today are confirming the existence of a lot of phenomena formerly thought to be superstitious nonsense, so this isn't as far-fetched as it may at first sound. It is quite possible that elementals have both an internal and an external reality.

I met my own elemental companions several years ago, and there came a time when I knew I was going to have to tell my psychiatrist about them. I had been consulting him for many years, and he was somewhat accustomed, I think, to my interior terrain. Nevertheless, confessing to him that I had four invisible elemental companions on board wasn't something I looked forward to. I told my friends to check the local mental wards if they hadn't heard from me in a day or two. I hesitated a bit at the beginning of the appointment, then confessed. When I'd finished, I told my psychiatrist that I felt terribly foolish. "Why?" he asked. "Because" I said, "here I am, describing things which don't exist. I mean, elementals aren't real like this chair or table are real. They're not external realities." There was a brief pause. Then he said, "They are *psychic* realities, Nancy."

DEALING WITH ELEMENTALS

No matter how you regard the nature of elementals, *deal with them as if they are external, material realities.* This serves two purposes: it simplifies communications (talking to something objective is usually easier than talking to something subjective); and it accords them the respect that they deserve, in the event that elementals have some external reality.

Always treat them with courtesy and affection. They detest being bullied. Request their help, don't demand it. Be sure to thank them for their work on your behalf. Elementals appreciate small gifts; appropriate offerings will be discussed later on.

Try to remain conscious of your companions' existence on a daily basis. Elementals wish to share life with their human companions so that they can learn, vicariously, about the elements to which they don't naturally belong. Invite your friendly elementals to participate in your daily activities. They prefer some activities to others; these will be described in later chapters.

If the prospect of working with elementals makes you uneasy, put it off until you feel more comfortable with the project. Be aware, however, that this work cannot be put off forever. All aspiring magicians must sooner or later come to grips with the elements and elementals for, as Murry Hope observes, this is what magical initiation is all about.[4]

---

[4]Murry Hope, *Practical Techniques of Psychic Self-Defense* (New York: St. Martin's, 1983), p. 72.

THE FIRE ELEMENT

Fire flame and Fire burn
Make the Mill of magic turn
Work the will for which we [I] pray
Io Dio, Ha He Yay[1]

—W. G. Gray

FIRE SYMBOLS, TOOLS, AFFINITIES

Affinity: The spiritual plane.

Astrological signs: ♈ (Aries), ♌ (Leo), ♐ (Sagittarius).

Cardinal direction: South.

Elemental: Salamander.

Gender: Masculine.

Magical tools: Candles, oils.

Psychological function: Intuition.

Qualities: Active, hot, dry.

Ritual tool: Wand.

Seasonal affinity: Summer.

Symbol: △ (equilateral triangle, point upward).

---

[1] W. G. Gray, *Magical Ritual Methods* (York Beach, ME: Samuel Weiser, 1980), pp. 215–216. Used by permission.

Table 1. The Attributes of the Fire Element.

| FIERY GOALS | PSYCHOLOGICAL QUALITIES | | FIRE IN NATURE* | | |
	Positive	Negative	Vegetable	Mineral	Animal
Athletics	Courage	Anger	Allspice	All red stones	Badger
Banishing illness	Creativity	Destructive tendencies	Basil	All orange stones	Bear
Competition	Idealism	Hatred	Bay laurel	Agate, red	Cat
Contests	Loyalty	Intemperance	Carnation	Amber	Centaur
Courts, law	Power	Jealousy	Cinnamon	Bloodstone	Coyote
Creativity	Spirituality	Vindictiveness	Clove	Carnelian	Fox
Defense	Strength		Coriander	Diamond	Hawk
Good health			Garlic	Fire opal	Lion
Loyalty			Heliotrope	Garnet	Mouse
Protection			Holly	Hematite	Porcupine
Sex			Hyssop	Iron	Ram
Spiritual issues			Juniper	Jasper, red	Serpent
Strength			Lavender	Lava	Wolf
Success			Marigold	Rhodochrosite	
			Oak	Ruby	
			Pepper	Sulfur	
			Rosemary	Steel	
			Rue	Tiger's Eye	
			Saffron	Tourmaline, pink	
			Thistle	Tourmaline, watermelon	

*Some objects may be classified under two or more elements.

If your goal is of a fiery nature, or if you wish to activate the positive fiery aspect of your temperament, or desire to work with the archetypes of the spiritual plane, you will need to use the fire element in the form of symbols and material objects when you perform your magical operation. Table 1 gives you the information you need to do so.

The fire element may be used for ritual purposes in the form of an outdoor bonfire, a hearthfire, or a candle flame. Since it's not easy to find a place suitable for bonfires, and since many people don't have fireplaces in their homes, candles (which are readily available and usually inexpensive) play an important role in magical practice.

CANDLE MAGIC

Candle magic is quite a complicated procedure, but these steps should lead you successfully through a rite.

1. **Choose an appropriate color:** The color of the candle you purchase is your first concern. You must try to correlate color with the goal you have in mind. The following list will help you decide which color best suits your purpose:

White: cleanses, purifies, raises vibrations to a higher frequency; appeals to spiritual plane archetypes; heals. When in doubt, use white.

Purple: discourages envy and jealousy; generates power for ritual work; energizes the atmosphere.

Blue: soothes anger, gives peace and serenity; good for meditation and relaxation and for issues involving loyalty and dedication.

Green: draws prosperity and abundance; helps to maintain the status quo; heals on the physical level.

Pink: bolsters self-esteem; helps to heal on the emotional level; used by women to attract romance and friendship.

Yellow: dispels grief, sadness, and depression; repels negative energies; attracts platonic relationships; use for intellectual skills and pursuits.

Orange: attracts success; brightens the atmosphere; encourages a light-hearted outlook; assists with creativity on all levels. Women use this color to attract sexual partners, or to overcome sexual difficulties.

Red: gives strength, courage, and energy; use to initiate change. Men use this color to attract sexual partners, and to conquer sexual problems.

Black: absorbs negativity; counteracts spaciness. Use for protection and grounding.

2. **Cleanse the candle:** Having purchased a candle of the appropriate color, your next task is to remove energies infused into the candle during the manufacturing process.

Saturate a tissue with rubbing alcohol and, holding the candle in your hand, cleanse its surface with the alcohol, moving from the candle's base to its top. This expels energy from the candle. (If you are working with a glass-encased candle, clean the exposed wax and the glass with the alcohol.)

It's best to repeat some kind of verbal formula while you are cleansing the candle. This might be something like: "I cleanse this candle of all impurities." Use your own words, and repeat them until you feel the candle has been cleansed to your satisfaction.

3. **Consecrate the candle:** Your next step is to dedicate the candle to your purpose. There are three different methods of consecration, any or all of which may be used:

Carve symbols into the candle. Take a sharp instrument, such as a toothpick or pencil (I use a nut pick) and carve appropriate symbols into the side (top, if glass-encased) of the candle. If you are working for prosperity, for instance, you might wish to use dollar signs, or, if your goal is romantic, hearts. Astrological and element symbols may also be used. Think intensely of your goal while you carve. Better still, repeat a verbal formula, such as an affirmation or incantation, while you do the carving.

Oil the candle. Most metaphysical stores offer a great variety of oils for sale, and you should choose one appropriate to your goal: Money-Drawing, for instance, if you're working to improve finances; Cleopatra (for women) or Satyr (for men) if your goal is romantic or sexual.

Dip your fingers into the oil and anoint the entire surface of the candle with it. If you want to attract good into your life, oil the candle from the top of the candle to its base, thus drawing the good into the candle. If you want to expel something from your life—such as ill health, a bad habit, or an unwanted situation—oil the candle from its base to its top, as you did when you cleansed it.

If you cannot decide which direction to use when oiling the candle, try an alternative technique which belongs to the Africentric traditions. Begin at the middle or center of the candle and apply the oil upward toward the top, then from the center down to the base. Stroke up; stroke down; up, then down; up, then down, until you have oiled the entire surface of the candle. This both draws and expels. If your candle is glass-encased, oil the exposed surface: clockwise (deosil) to draw good; counter-clockwise (widdershins) to expel negativity.

It's important that you use a verbal formula (such as an affirmation or incantation) while you oil the candle, for this focuses your mind on the work at hand.

Spray, sprinkle, or anoint the candle with water. Purchase a water (such as Prosperity, Love, Success, or Healing Water) from a metaphysical store, and pour some into an atomizer or plant mister. Spray the entire surface of the candle as you repeat your affirmation or incantation. If you don't have an atomizer or plant mister, simply sprinkle the candle. Or dip your fingers into the water and anoint the candle as you would with an oil.

Some magicians (myself among them) dislike using oils because they are messy, and because their scent tends to be overpowering. Waters are a good alternative and add a second element to your candle work. However, the water technique is not as psychologically effective as the oil method because oiling a candle is a much more deliberate process than casual spraying. If your goal is very important, I recommend oiling over spraying. (A student once suggested that people working on romantic goals use an oil if they want a long-term relationship, and a water if they want a romantic fling. It's an amusing suggestion—and good psychology.)

A cleansed and consecrated candle should be used for one purpose only. If you prepare a candle for prosperity purposes, don't use it for healing or romance.

You should decide how often, and for how long a time, you are going to burn your candle. You may wish to burn it for ten minutes a day, for instance, or for an hour at a time. Or, you may choose to burn it entirely in one sitting. The time factor depends to some extent on the candle you are using. Large glass-encased candles (the kind available in supermarkets) will burn all day long for several days. On the other hand, small pillar-shaped candles only burn for about an hour. Choose your candle size according to your purpose. If your goal is very important, you may wish to burn your candle every day for several days, which means you must purchase a very large candle. An alternative is to buy several small candles and burn one per day. If you decide on several small ones, remember that you must cleanse and consecrate each of them before use.

Of course you must always extinguish candles before leaving the house or retiring for sleep. Glass-encased candles are the safest to use, but even these are not proof against earthquakes, tornados, hurricanes, or frisky pets. Don't ever forget that fire can be a dangerous element.

When you light your candle, do so consciously. Be aware that fire has an affinity with the spiritual plane. Archetypes are attracted to fire, as religious types have always known. Walk into any Catholic church and you will see great banks of votive candles which people have lit in the hope that their prayers will be heard and acted upon. So, before you do any sort of spiritual plane work—praying or assuming the god-form—light a consecrated candle. You may also wish to make an offering of fire to a beloved archetype.

Be aware also, as you light your candle, that a fire elemental—a Salamander—is present in the flame and that, if you ask politely and are deemed worthy of regard, it will help you to achieve your goal.

SALAMANDERS

Salamanders are the little ethereal creatures who animate the flame of a hearthfire or candle. They will help you achieve your fiery goals, and they will defend you as well. Murry Hope stresses their protective abilities:

> It was taught in olden times, and is still believed by many today, that when the old soul steps on to the path, his first companion is an elemental spirit who will voluntarily guard him and aid him in his studies. I found this to be absolutely true, although I make no claims to being "old" or "wise." My own first companion was a Salamander, who once saved me from what could have been a vicious *physical* attack while travelling.[2]

Murry recently described this incident to me in some detail. She was riding the London underground late one night after having attended a press gathering in the city. She and a male stranger were the only passengers in the car. The man took one look at Murry (who is quite beautiful) and decided she was fair game. When he came toward her in a menacing way, she panicked and mentally screamed to her Salamander friend for help. The man broke out into what actors call "flop sweat"—instantaneous, copious perspiration—and gagged because he couldn't get any air into his lungs. Still struggling to breathe and sweating profusely, he lurched out

---

[2]Murry Hope, *Practical Techniques of Psychic Self-Defense* (New York: St. Martin's, 1983), pp. 72–73.

of the carriage at the next stop and collapsed. Murry was left alone and safe, but she immediately felt remorse and sent the man healing energies. Later, when she described the incident to her teacher, she was told: "It's not necessary to use a sledgehammer to crack a nut."

This story illustrates the positive (protective) qualities of fire as well as its potential for overkill. Fire can be as dangerous on the subtle planes as on the physical, and it's well to keep this in mind. Asked how she would handle the same situation today, Murry said she'd either mentally erect a force-field which would gently (but firmly) push the attacker away, or she'd distract him from his purpose using the energies of the Egyptian archetype Nephthys, who is closely connected to the water element, for water can extinguish fire. Murry theorizes that the ancient Egyptians used Salamanders to guard certain tombs, "which is why so many molesters of sacred Egyptian places met with fiery ends or violent accidents."[3]

Because fire has an affinity with the spiritual plane, Salamanders will help magicians to contact, and work with, their chosen archetypes. This is an important factor in advanced magical work because the gateway to high magic lies upon the spiritual plane. Ambitious magicians should therefore do everything they can to develop the positive fire aspects of their temperaments.

Salamanders gravitate toward human beings whose primary (or secondary) function is intuition, and who embody all the positive characteristics listed under "Fiery Psychological Qualities" in Table 1 (see page 123). They do not care for those who act out the negative qualities listed, because these represent imbalance—fire run amok, so to speak. Nor do they care for those qualities diametrically opposed to the positive fire characteristics. They like courage, for instance, but dislike cowardice. They respect spirituality, but are disdainful of gross materialism. They prefer creators to consumers.

Generally speaking, if your primary function is sensation (earth), you will have difficulty attracting the help of Salamanders.

---

[3] *Practical Techniques of Psychic Self-Defense*, p. 76.

In fact, earthy types may invite trouble if they invoke them too aggressively. It's impossible to predict what form this trouble will take. Murry Hope writes that she knew someone who "couldn't make it with the salamanders and had a series of blown fuses, burned food, and the like."[4] She mentioned to me that the phenomena also included suddenly extinguished candles and blown light bulbs. Dion Fortune wrote that she never had an opportunity to investigate any cases involving disgruntled Salamanders, but theorized that pyromania might be caused by them.[5]

Fortune's view seems a bit drastic. Personal experience with elementals—not just Salamanders—leads me to believe that problems encountered as a result of invoking them are not likely to produce anything so serious as a full-blown psychosis. Sometimes elemental phenomena are more startling than problematic. I once knew a very sane, down-to-earth (sensate) woman who laid a fire in her fireplace, but did not light it. Several weeks later, on a cold rainy day, she wasn't feeling very well and was curled up, reading, on a couch in her living room. Outside, the storm raged. She looked toward her fireplace and thought to herself, "I wish I had enough energy to get up and light a fire." The firewood instantly burst into flames.

This woman was not a magician. She had no interest whatever in metaphysics, nor was she religious. And it's very doubtful that she produced such an extraordinary phenomenon by mind power alone. So what did produce it? It's hard to say. There had been other peculiar incidents in her home prior to this, none of them involving fire, so there were probably several factors at work. My theory, in part, is that the Salamanders were trying to show her—in a rather kindly, albeit startling, way—that there were more things between heaven and Earth than had heretofore been dreamt of in her philosophy. She took a more open view of things esoteric following this experience, and no wonder.

---

[4] *Practical Techniques of Psychic Self-Defense*, p. 80.
[5] Dion Fortune, *Psychic Self-Defense* (York Beach, ME: Samuel Weiser, 1992), p. 87.

If you invoke the Salamanders and encounter problems, you have two options. You can plead with them to desist. If they have any respect for you at all (and they probably don't, or they wouldn't be creating problems in the first place) they'll cease their activities. Or you can appeal to the Ondines (water extinguishes fire) or the Gnomes (earth smothers fire) for help. Although the first is the ideal, beginners will probably end up using the second option. The Ondines are probably your best bet. Do *not* call upon the Sylphs for assistance, because air can whip fire into a raging blaze.

If you're a sensate (earthy) type or anticipate problems with the Salamanders, you may wish to contact them indirectly, and at the same time curry favor with them by presenting them with a thoughtful gift.

GIFTS FOR SALAMANDERS

All elementals appreciate token gifts from time to time. Salamanders, being relatively incorporeal by nature, appreciate psychological, rather than material, gifts. To be specific, they enjoy witnessing an act of courage. So, the next time you must do something brave, be sure to invite the Salamanders along to act as witnesses. If the Salamanders approve of your courageous act, you may find that you have earned their loyalty and assistance.

Since the opportunity to act courageously doesn't come along every day, you may have to try a substitute. Select a fiery herb or a magically prepared powder. Hold the substance in the palm of your dominant hand for a moment and mentally make contact with the Salamanders. Sprinkle the substance into a candle flame or hearthfire as an offering. This is not as effective as performing a courageous act, but the Salamanders will appreciate your generosity, and perhaps will pay attention when you next request their help.

No matter what your temperament type, you should frequently present the Salamanders with a gift, not just to curry favor with them, or to thank them for a job well done. A thoughtful gift lets Salamanders know that you are aware of their existence and that you appreciate them for themselves alone.

THE AIR ELEMENT

Air breathe and Air blow
Make the Mill of magic go
Work the will for which we [I] pray
Io Dio, Ha He Yay[6]
　　　　　　　—W. G. Gray

AIR SYMBOLS, TOOLS, AFFINITIES

Affinity: The mental plane.

Astrological signs: ♊ (Gemini), ♎ (Libra), ♒ (Aquarius).

Cardinal direction: East.

Elemental: Sylph.

Gender: Masculine.

Magical tools: Incense, sound, breath.

Psychological function: Thinking.

Qualities: Active, Cold, Dry.

Ritual tool: Sword or dagger.

Seasonal affinity: Spring.

Symbol: 🜁 (equilateral triangle, point upward, with a horizon-
　　　　tal line drawn through the center of the triangle).

---

[6]W. G. Gray, *Magical Ritual Methods* (York Beach, ME: Samuel Weiser, 1980), pp. 215-216. Used by permission.

Table 2. The Attributes of the Air Element.

| AIRY GOALS | PSYCHOLOGICAL QUALITIES | | AIR IN NATURE* | | |
	Positive	Negative	Vegetable	Mineral	Animal
Addictions (overcoming)	Diligence	Boasting	Acacia	Agate	Cardinal
Communications	Discrimination (intellectual)	Contempt	Benzoin	Amethyst	Crow
Education	Flexibility	Dishonesty	Comfrey	Aventurine	Deer
Group-work	Independence	Frivolity	Elder	Azurite	Dove
Intellectual skills	Joy	Gossip	Eucalyptus	Calcite	Eagle
Organization	Optimism	Paranoia	Gardenia	Cat's eye	Hawk
Speaking	Penetration	Slyness	Honeysuckle	Chrysocolla	Magpie
Tests			Jasmine	Chrysoprase	Owl
Theorizing			Lavender	Citrine	Peacock
Travel			Lemon verbena	Emerald	Raccoon
Writing			Lilac	Flourite	Raven
			Magnolia	Jade	Spider
			Marjoram	Jasper, mottled	Squirrel
			Mints	Lapis lazuli	
			Mistletoe	Malachite	
			Nutmeg	Moonstone	
			Rose	Quartz, clear	
			Sandalwood	Sodalite	
			Sweet pea	Topaz, yellow	
			Vines	Turquoise	
			Wisteria		

*Some objects may be classified under two or more elements.

If your goal is of an airy nature, if you wish to energize the airy aspects of your temperament, or if it's time to do some serious mental plane work, you need to incorporate air symbols and tools into your magical work. These are listed in Table 2 (see page 132).

It was thought in ancient times that prayers attached themselves to particles of incense and were wafted along with them upward to the spiritual plane, where archetypes heard and acted upon the prayers. The modern view is a bit more scientific. According to Dr. Alan R. Hirsch, a psychiatrist and neurologist doing research at the Smell and Taste Treatment and Research Foundation in Chicago, the sense of smell bypasses the thought process and acts directly on the section of the brain that controls emotions.[7] Magicians have always known that scent effects psychological change, and made lavish use of incense.

INCENSE MAGIC

Incense should always be used in conjunction with mental plane work such as setting and writing goals, and creating affirmations and incantations.

Incense is available in all metaphysical stores, and comes in a variety of forms: sticks, cones, and loose powder. There is an incense for every goal: Material Riches or Money-Drawing for financial goals; Aphrodite or Rushing Love for romantic matters. These are herbal or floral blends created by manufacturers who have studied the properties of plants and who (hopefully) have experimented with scent so that they know which materials combine for the greatest psychological effect. Incenses with plainer names (such as Rose or Honeysuckle) are no less effective for magical purposes, provided magicians know their herbs—that is, to which element each herb belongs. Some incense manufacturers are better than others, so you will need to experiment with various brands before you find one which suits you. Personally, I

---

[7] L. Trager, "Business Scents," *San Francisco Examiner*, June 21, 1992.

stay away from the traditional Eastern varieties because I have read that some are compounded with ingredients like cow dung.

If you're distrustful of commercial ingredients, or if you're allergic to some herbal substances, the best thing to do is to make your own incense. This is a very simple matter. First, decide upon the scent you want. This should correlate with your goal. If your goal is spiritual, for instance, you might wish to use fiery heliotrope. If your goal is intellectual, try one of the airy herbs listed in Table 2 (see page 132); if romantic, check the watery herbs listed in Table 3 (see page 146); if career-oriented, decide on something earthy from Table 4 (see page 166). Purchase a roll of self-lighting charcoal tablets from any metaphysical store. Now you're ready. Light your charcoal tablet and immediately place it in a heat-proof container. *Do not hold the tablet in your hand after lighting it*, as it will ignite very quickly and may burn you. Now spoon some of the loose herb onto the charcoal, and enjoy the scent of your fresh herbal incense.

Dried herbs may be purchased in health food stores and in many metaphysical shops. You may also find some sitting in your spice rack; many a magician faced with an emergency has been thankful for his kitchen spices. But the nicest way to obtain herbs for magical work is to gather them yourself from nature, a process known as "wildcrafting."

WILDCRAFTING HERBS FOR INCENSE

Nature is a storehouse well stocked in the materials of magic. And just as an affirmation or an incantation which you compose yourself reinforces your magical work, so gathering and processing your own herbs gives your incense an increased potency. As you seek out and harvest the plants you need, focus on your goals, and remember these simple rules:

1. Look for your herb in an area where there's not much automobile traffic, so that it is free of exhaust fumes.

2. Have a talk with your chosen plant or tree before you do your gathering. Gently tell it that you wish to gather some of its foliage,

and wait a few moments before you do so. This gives the plant time to adjust emotionally to the coming operation.

3. If possible, use your fingers (rather than shears) to gather the greenery or flowers. A gentle human touch is much easier on the plant than a metal instrument.

4. Gather only what you need, and only from foliage that is luxuriant. *Never* denude a plant. Always leave plenty of growth behind.

5. When you have done your gathering, leave behind some token of thanks, such as a coin, unusual stone, or grain of corn. (The jacket I wear for my morning walk has two large pockets which are filled with thanksgiving pennies.) Actually, it's not the gift that counts, but the thought behind it. If you don't have an appropriate gift, mentally thank the plant for its sacrifice.

Wildcrafted herbs may be used immediately for magical purposes, or dried for later use. To dry an herb, lay it flat on paper towels in a dry place, or (preferably) tie its ends onto a string and hang it to dry. The drying process usually takes about two weeks. When dry, strip the herb from its stems and crumble or grind into a powdery consistency.

If making incense appeals to you, and you'd like to emulate the professionals, here is a basic incense formula given me by a manufacturer, who maintains that any good commercial incense should consist of:

> 30 percent resins (such as frankincense, myrrh or kopal);
> 15-20 percent aromatics (such as rosemary, cinnamon or lavender);
> 50 percent (approximately) woodsy materials (such as sandalwood, patchouli, or cedar); and
> Essential oils to enhance the formula.

SUBSTITUTIONS FOR INCENSE

If you don't like incense (you're not alone), or are allergic to its smoke, you may wish to purchase a potpourri pot. This is a small pot which rests on a stand containing a candle. Put water in the pot, float some herbs in the water and light the candle. The heated, herb-infused water will slowly evaporate into the atmosphere and create ideal conditions for mental plane work. Observe that this process makes use of three elements—fire, water, and earth (herbs)—to produce a fourth, air. The key element is fire, for without its heat, the herb-scented water would not evaporate. Fire is always transformative.

Sound created by the human voice or other instruments is another substitute for incense. Words, as we have already seen, are very important in mental plane work. The well-chosen spoken word impresses itself upon the unconscious mind and, like incense, upon the atmosphere as well—hence the importance of speaking affirmations and incantations aloud. Sound without the use of words (called "sonics" by magicians and "toning" by healers) will do the same. Murry Hope, who is a professional singer as well as a magician, and an expert in the use of sonics, writes:

> Every living entity, at every level, possesses a personal keynote or sonic. To know this is to have the power to heal (make whole) or destroy (fragment) the entity in question. In fact, there is also a specific sonic note for every combination of molecules or molecular structure of matter. Familiarity with the sonic keynote of a certain type of stone, for example, plus a knowledge of the *modus operandi* of the sonic system, would enable one to reduce its specific gravity, disassemble its molecular structure and reassemble it in some other location.[8]

If you are able to discover the keynote of any desired objective you could conceivably sound its keynote, infusing the atmosphere with its particular frequency, and thereby manifest that objective. You could also remove (disassemble and reassemble in some other location) undesirable energies. As a magical technique, sonics will probably appeal to musicians and singers, and those

---

[8]Murry Hope, *Ancient Egypt: The Sirius Connection* (Shaftesbury, England: Element, 1990), p. 177. Used by kind permission.

interested are referred to Hope's *Ancient Egypt: The Sirius Connection* for further information.

Sound instruments such as rattles and drums are used by shamans to alter atmospheric frequencies and are all the rage among metaphysicians today. You should take care in your experimentation with these, however, for percussive instruments and the rhythms created through their use can sometimes create disharmonies. As Hope states:

> Some people find certain rhythms or combinations of sounds highly disturbing. I myself cannot cope with the currently favoured "pop" or beat music, for example, or with some modern classical compositions which effect certain dissonants. A high decibel output also disturbs me considerably. This is because both of these things clash with my personal sonic, causing a "juddering" or jarring note which is re-echoed in all the subtle bodies.[9]

The same principle applies to the spoken word. As a magician with years of Shakespearean training behind me, I cannot bear to hear banal or ungrammatical English spoken during ritual, nor can I stand to hear words poorly enunciated; either is enough to make me abruptly quit the premises, ritual be damned. This is one of the reasons I have chosen to remain a solitary magician.

Breath—inner air—may also be substituted for incense. Breathing upon (insufflating) an object can infuse it with desirable energy, or clear it of unwanted influences. There are two methods of accomplishing this. You can draw the desired energy from the universe into your body. Keep drawing it in until you feel full-to-bursting with it. Then release the energy by blowing upon the object to be charged or cleared. Or you can concentrate on your goal so that your mind and body are charged, so to speak,

---

[9]*Ancient Egypt: The Sirius Connection,* p. 178. Used by kind permission.

with it. Then breathe upon the object until you feel it is sufficiently insufflated.

WHEN TO USE INCENSE

A potpourri pot, words, sonics, instrumental sound or insufflation
may be used in lieu of incense in any one of these scenarios, if
desired.

1. **Light incense whenever you are engaged in mental plane
work.** Aside from the activities we have discussed at length in our
discussions of the mental plane, you may also wish to use it for
special projects like writing important letters, school papers, poetry, articles, or books. For inspiration, waft the paper you intend to
use through the incense before you begin the writing process and
keep incense burning as you write. Then pass the written material through the smoke when the project is completed. This insures
that you will write well and clearly, and also that what you have
written will be well received.

2. **Use incense to clear out unwanted energies**, particularly
those which exist upon the mental plane, such as harmful beliefs
or attitudes. Fiery herbs (like rosemary, bay laurel, or pepper)
burned as incense are particularly effective for this purpose.
Smudge sticks, which belong to the Native American tradition
and are composed of bundles of herbs (usually sage and cedar), are
very effective for clearing etheric energies from atmospheres,
objects, and the human aura. Light a stick and carry it about the
area you wish to cleanse. Waft an object through the smoke, or
wave it (at arm's length) through your aura.

Always invoke the good immediately after you have cleared
an atmosphere, object, or aura. Cleansing creates a vacuum
(abhorred by nature) which must immediately be filled with some
desired good, such as love, prosperity, spiritual grace, or healing
energy. You may do this by using another incense representative of
the good you desire, or by using magical tools belonging to the

other elements. You may also invoke the good through prayer, spoken affirmations, incantations, or visualization.

3. **Use incense to consecrate objects,** such as sacred statuary, altar ojects, amulets and talismans, occult jewelry and tools, and important personal objects like wedding or engagement rings. The ancient Romans stuffed hollow images of their gods and goddesses with herbs pleasing to the deities; they believed this imbued the statues with sacred life. The same principle applies to passing objects through the smoke of an appropriate incense. Pass a wedding ring through rose incense, for instance, and the ring will be infused with Aphrodisiac energies. Waft a prosperity talisman through the smoke created by the burning of an earthy herb, and it will take on the power to attract abundance.

Be aware when you light your incense that friendly Sylphs are present who may help you to achieve your goal.

SYLPHS

Sylphs are attracted to magicians who embody all the positive characteristics listed under "Airy Psychological Qualities" in Table 2 (see page 133), and to those whose primary or second function is thinking. Sylphs appreciate individuals who think rationally. They have the greatest respect for those who think for themselves. They detest the herd mentality. They are light, flashing creatures, and they like speed in thought and movement. They dislike plodders and depressives. Intellectuals will find them excellent companions.

Since the water and air elements are diametrically opposed to one another, feeling types usually have problems with the Sylphs. In fact, the human race as a whole probably has more difficulty with air than with any of the other elements. It's said that our bodies are comprised mainly of water, and if one believes (as I do) that physiological conditions are always accompanied by similar psychological conditions, then it follows that humans are very watery (feeling) creatures indeed. And if you're a feeling type, you're probably going to have more than your share of problems with the Sylphs. Relax, you're in good company.

The great Dion Fortune wrote with characteristic humor of her airy tribulations in *Psychic Self-Defence*. She maintained that air is a contentious element and that accidents invariably occur when it is invoked. Her formal initiation into the element (presumably under the aegis of the Golden Dawn), before she knew its reputation, was a disaster. The man and wife team conducting the ceremony had a family fight in the middle of the proceedings, and various pieces of ritual equipment were apparently dropped and broken. Nor did the phenomena end there. For two weeks following the ceremony, Fortune lived in a

> [c]ataclysm of crockery. I smashed my way through two entire tea-sets and all the mantelpiece ornaments . . . [which] just fell off the mantelpiece one by one of their own accord. I actually saw two of them do it.[10]

Fortune was finally "reduced to a tin mug and a tooth-glass." Her teacher, who was amused by the situation, told her that the initiation apparently had not been successful, and advised her to get in touch with the Sylphs, which she did when she took a short holiday in the country. She describes the experience in some detail and mentions that the "air seemed full of rushing golden flames, lying level in the wind. . . . I have never known a more glorious experience. It was indeed the divine inebriation of the Mysteries."[11]

Fortune does not mention having had troubles with any of the other elements, so I assume that air (thinking) represented her weakest element, and that her view of it was therefore negative.[12]

---

[10]Dion Fortune, *Psychic Self-Defense* (York Beach, ME: Samuel Weiser, 1992), p. 85.
[11]*Psychic Self-Defense*, p. 86.
[12]Fortune was born on December 6, 1890 in Laududno, Wales, but her birth time is unknown, so it's impossible to verify my suspicion that she was a feeling type by looking at her natal chart. If my assumption is correct, she probably would have shown one of the water signs on her natal chart ascendant.

But I assume her account to be true, and that she knew what she was talking about when she stated that initiation into the air element tends to scare off magicians.

Her experiences illustrate the sort of difficulties feeling types may face when they involve themselves with air. While these appear to be relatively minor, the quarrelsome aspect she mentions is worth consideration. It's perhaps well to remember that the Christian devil is sometimes referred to as the Prince of the Powers of Air.[13] It's also worth noting that Gypsies hate the wind so much they call it the "Devil's Sneeze." And it's not coincidence that the ritual tool assigned to air is the sword—a symbol more "quarrelsome" than those assigned to the other elements.

Please remember, however, that a force always has two poles, positive and negative. The magician's sword is double-edged, and is used as a surgeon uses a scalpel, to cut out disease so that what is healthy may thrive. Surgery, physical or psychological, is always painful; but ultimately it's a healing force. This lesson was brought home to me when I dreamed, many years ago, of a woman who had (in real life) deliberately attempted to break up several marriages, including mine. In discussing the dream with my psychiatrist, I remember saying, "This woman, as far as I can see, is nothing but a walking force for destruction. I don't understand why such a person exists." He explained to me that such people serve an important purpose: they destroy what is outgrown or unwanted, so that new life may flourish.

The sword penetrates, pierces, cuts out, and cuts through. So does the human mind. Rational thought—the mind's sword—can penetrate to the truth of a matter, pierce through illusion, cut out irrelevancies, and cut through distractions.

If air fosters quarrels, it's because people harbor differences which need to be openly discussed or "aired." Few people like to quarrel; most of us prefer to sweep differences under a rug and hope for the best. Unfortunately, the rug technique doesn't work. Suppressed feelings fester and then explode at inappropriate times

---

[13]The name *Satan* means "adversary."

and in inappropriate places—witness Fortune's initiation ceremony. But an explosion, however inappropriate, is infinitely preferable to suppression, which cuts off communication altogether. If there is no communication concerning differences, there is no way to "clear the air" and there is little hope for peace.

Air is a moveable element. It demands that we move with the times; we must "bend with the wind" or break. The "winds of change" are always accompanied by stress and tension. Left to our own devices, few of us would initiate change, because even if our current situation is painful, it is at least familiar. The unknown is always frightening. Air forces us to confront difficulties, to sever ties, to pierce through illusions, to focus our intentions, to face the unknown—and to change. No wonder it frightens magicians.

But there is still Fortune's "divine inebriation" to consider. If Fortune was, as I suspect, a feeling type, then her experience with air—the most "glorious" she had ever known—serves to emphasize an important principle mentioned earlier. Great rewards await magicians who deliberately work against their natural temperamental grain. Feeling types thus have a lot to look forward to when they conquer the element of air. Indeed, there is nothing like the exhilaration one feels when buoyed up, so to speak, by air. To be released from unhealthy attitudes, addictions, or relationships is to be released from prison. To be released from the fear of change is to be charged with optimism and creative energy. Air gives liberation.

Sylphs will help you with all these tasks. Most important, they will help you to communicate with your unconscious mind. This is what magic is all about. On a more mundane level, Sylphs will assist with difficulties during travel. Recently, Murry Hope's Sylph friend made it possible for her to drive some distance on a badly patched tire; the tire didn't deflate until she reached a mechanic. The same little companion, given plenty of notice, helps Murry find parking spaces.

When out walking on a windy day, I often ask my Sylph friend to blow away any unwanted mental or psychological cobwebs. This is a very refreshing exercise. Diet-conscious magicians should do everything they can to attract air elementals so that they, too, can be slim and "sylphlike."

Sylphs are very beautiful creatures. I, and many other people, have often seen silvery sparkles dancing in the air; I choose to think these are the Sylphs themselves—little darting flashes of light, frolicking about, happy, light, and free.

GIFTS FOR SYLPHS

If you are a feeling type or anticipate problems with the Sylphs, be aware that they enjoy speed and movement. The next time you walk, bike, drive, take the train, or (especially!) fly somewhere, invite the friendly Sylphs along; they will love you for it.

Sylphs also enjoy a gift of flowers. A flower picked from nature (be sure to leave a token of thanks), or purchased will be much appreciated, and may persuade the Sylphs that you are worthy of their regard.

THE WATER ELEMENT

Water boil and Water churn
Make the Mill of magic turn
Work the will for which we [I] pray
Io Dio, Ha He Yay[14]

—W. G. Gray

WATER SYMBOLS, TOOLS, AFFINITIES

Affinity: The emotional plane.

Astrological signs: ♋ (Cancer), ♏ (Scorpio), ♓ (Pisces).

Cardinal direction: West.

Elemental: Ondine.

Gender: Feminine.

Magical tools: Magically prepared waters.

Psychological function: Feeling.

Qualities: Passive, cold, wet.

Ritual tool: Chalice, cup, goblet.

Seasonal affinity: Autumn.

Symbol: ▽ (equilateral triangle, point downward).

---

[14]W. G. Gray, *Magical Ritual Methods* (York Beach, ME: Samuel Weiser, 1980), pp. 215–216. Used by permission.

If the goal you have chosen is of a watery nature, if you wish to activate the water in your temperament, or if you need to do some work upon the emotional plane, you will need to make use of the attributes and qualities outlined in Table 3 (see page 146).

Water's main virtue in magic is that it alters mood. If you've ever had a rotten day at work, arrived home ready to chuck the whole thing, and then gotten into the tub for a long soak, you're already familiar with its marvelous properties. Emotional negativity is washed away by water.

Water also encourages a receptive attitude toward a desired goal. When you generate energy enough to attract what you desire at the material level, you have accomplished only half your task; you must also be emotionally receptive to the incoming good, for if you are not, you sabotage your own efforts.

WATER MAGIC

The water element is undoubtedly the most versatile of all the elements; it can be drunk, bathed in, sprinkled about, used as an anointing agent, and can even serve as a sleep-programming device. Given its great versatility, and its affinity with the all-important emotional plane, one wonders why this element has been so neglected by magicians. I suspect gender is the culprit. Never mind, we shall give the feminine elements the credit they deserve here.

USING WATER TO WASH AWAY EMOTIONAL NEGATIVITY

We've already presented a technique for clearing grief in Murry Hope's Rite of Tears (see page 107). In Murry's Rite, you combine nature's water with your tears and release your grief to the elements. There are several other ways to dissolve negativity as well.

As a magician, your days of unconscious bathing are over. Use your daily shower to get rid of disruptive emotions. Stand under the shower; let the water cascade over you and mentally consign fatigue, depression, pain, confusion, anger, grief, envy, jeal-

Table 3. The Attributes of the Water Element.

| WATER GOALS | PSYCHOLOGICAL QUALITIES | | WATER IN NATURE* | | |
	Positive	Negative	Vegetable	Mineral	Animal
Ancestors	Compassion	Apathy	Apple	Agate, Blue Lace	Crab
Beauty	Comprehension	Depression	Apricot	Amethyst	Dolphin
Cell growth	Conscience	Frigidity	Camphor	Aquamarine	Elk
(restoring)	Devotion	Laziness	Catnip	Azurite	Fish (all)
Centering	Forgiveness	Indifference	Chamomile	Celestite	Heron
Children and	Receptivity	Insolence	Cherry	Chrysocolla	Horse
childbirth	Tranquillity	Instability	Cyclamen	Coral	Jaguar
Family issues			Eucalyptus	Holey stones	Raven
Friendships			Gardenia	Jade	Scorpion
Healing			Hawthorn	Lapis lazuli	Sea birds (all)
Home			Hyacinth	Lepidolite	Shellfish (all)
Hospitals			Ivy	Moonstone	Whale
Love			Lotus	Mother-of-pearl	
Medicine			Melons	Pearl	
Meditation			Mints	Sapphire	
Partnerships			Myrrh	Silver	
Psychism			Narcissus	Sodalite	
Rest and			Orris root	Sugilite	
recreation			Periwinkle	Tourmaline,	
			Rose	green	
			Willow		
			Yarrow		

*Some objects may be classified under two or more elements.

ousy, and fear to the drain. Or get into the tub and allow the water to absorb your negativity. You might even pour a cup of salt into the water; salt absorbs undesirable energies. When you feel the combination of water and salt has done its job, drain the tub. Be sure to immediately invoke the good (love, joy, peace of mind, etc.) after bathing. You may do this with tools belonging to any of the elements, or by the use of prayer, affirmations, incantations, or visualization.

Bathing is an excellent way to prepare for magical ritual. Ritual demands that you put aside your everyday concerns and concentrate on your objectives. Given a difficult day at work, this is sometimes not easy to do. A ritual bath like the water-and-salt one just described will refresh you so that you can focus on your magic. The magic itself will invoke the good you desire.

You may also use water to cleanse an emotionally charged atmosphere. To do this, you must learn how to magnetize water.

EXERCISE 10: HOW TO CHARGE (MAGNETIZE) WATER

- Stand or sit comfortably with a container of the water you wish to magnetize in front of you.

- Invoke your personal and god symbols (see Appendix B).

- Perform Exercise 1 (page 42) to activate positive energy.

- Concentrate for a while on the type of energy you wish to infuse into the water.

- Place the palm of your dominant hand over the water.

- Hold your weaker hand, palm up, at shoulder or waist level, whichever is most comfortable. Your arm may be bent at the elbow; your hand should be relaxed and open.

- Your weaker hand draws the desired energy from the universe. This energy is then channeled to your dominant hand.

- The energy flows out your dominant palm and into the water.

- Continue channeling the energy into the water until you feel it is sufficiently charged.

- (Optional): Before you begin the charging process you may, if you wish, place a crystal or herb into the water. This adds nature's magnetism to your own. (It's best not to drink water charged in this manner unless you are absolutely sure the crystal is clean and the herb nonpoisonous.)

- Seal your aura (see page 42).

Note: Don't be concerned if you can't feel the energy flowing from one hand to the other and into the water. Energy follows thought. If you mentally intend energy to flow in a particular direction, it will do so. Since water doesn't hold a charge for very long, use your magnetized water immediately.[15]

CLEANSING THE ATMOSPHERE

To cleanse the atmosphere with charged water, put the water into a bowl and, with your fingers, sprinkle it about the area you wish to clear. Or, place the water into an atomizer or plant mister and spray the area. It would be wise to repeat an affirmation (such as "I cleanse this place of all impurities") or an incantation while you perform the clearing. Remember to call in the good after you have purified the area.

An alternative to charging your own water is to purchase a prepared water from a metaphysical store. My own Purification Water is specifically formulated to clear out harmful emotional energies. My Peace Water is also helpful, although it wasn't originally created for purifying purposes. A well-known healer in my area moved into a new house, only to discover that some kind of unseen nasty (a ghost?) was in residence. She tried physical clean-

---

[15]To prolong the "life" of your charged water, ask spiritual or elemental energies to add their magnetism to the water.

ing and psychic healing, but nothing worked until she sprayed Peace Water about—which puts an amusing twist on the tombstone expression "rest in peace." Waters may also be used in the bathtub.

You may clear an atmosphere with water through visualization alone. I use the following technique, taught me by Murry Hope, all the time, especially after teaching group ritual work.

EXERCISE 11: MURRY HOPE'S
CLEANSING VISUALIZATION

- Imagine that the area you wish to cleanse is filled up to the ceiling with purifying water.

- You're going to lower the water level in the room through the use of physical gesture and imagination.

- Raise your arms to the ceiling, palms facing the floor.

- Slowly lower your arms. As you do, imagine that the water level is being lowered, and that the water is taking with it all the psychic dirt existing in the atmosphere.

- Imagine that the loaded water is draining into the Earth. You may use physical gesture to press the water into the earth if you wish.

- Pause. Does the atmosphere feel clean? If not, repeat the procedure.

- Seal your aura (see page 80).

Note: You will know the atmosphere is clean if you feel a chill resulting in goose bumps on your arms, or if you feel a cool breeze on your palms as you lower your arms. This technique is so powerful it will cool down a room on a hot summer day.

USING WATER TO CREATE
A POSITIVE EMOTIONAL ATTITUDE

Water not only dissolves emotional blockages, it also creates a receptive attitude toward the good which is coming your way. Use any of the following methods to create a positive emotional outlook.

1. **Soak in water charged with your intention:** Fill your bathtub with water, then charge it using the method described earlier in this chapter. To give the water a further "boost," add crystals or herbs. These should be appropriate to the element governing your goal. For romantic matters, for instance, you could add a chunk of rose quartz or rose petals. For prosperity purposes, bathe with a piece of jade or malachite, and some honeysuckle flowers.

If you intend to add herbs to your bath water, it's probably best to do so in the form of an infusion (strong tea) rather than as a loose powder, as bits and pieces of herbs will stick to your skin and clog the plumbing. (To make an herbal infusion, put a handful or two of the herb into a pot. Cover the herbs with boiling water, cover the pot, and let steep for about twenty minutes. Strain, and pour the liquid into the tub.)

To augment the effects of your bath, burn incense (air) and candles (fire) as you soak in the tub. With herbs or crystals (both of which are earthy) added to the bathwater, you have all four elements working for you. Add prayer or visualization to the mix, and your ritual bath becomes a full-scale magical operation.

2. **Drink charged water:** Magnetize the water with your desire, then drink it knowing that it will circulate through the area of your brain which controls emotions. (Store-bought waters contain ingredients other than water, and should not be drunk.)

You may wish to place the water you intend to charge in the sunlight for a few hours, then charge and drink it. Or place the water under the light of the Full Moon before you magnetize it; the Moon, being the ruler of the tides, governs water and, therefore, the emotions.

3. Sprinkle or spray charged water about your personal space: Magnetize water with your desire, then place it in an atomizer or plant mister and spray it about the atmosphere. Or simply sprinkle it about with your fingers. Even simpler, place the water in a bowl (or ritual chalice) and allow the water to slowly evaporate. Any of these techniques infuses the atmosphere with your intention and the charged atmosphere, in turn, will affect you psychologically so that you become open and receptive to incoming positive energies.

One nice thing about charged water is that (unlike incense) it can be used in public or on the job without anyone being aware of it. Put the water into a paper cup and allow it to evaporate. A paper cup filled with water is not likely to arouse the suspicions of your boss or coworkers.

4. Use charged water as an anointing agent: Dab magnetized water on your body's chakras (energy centers) to make them more receptive to the good that you desire. To open yourself to love, for instance, anoint your Heart and Sex Chakras. To be receptive to prosperity, dab some charged water on your Root (tailbone) Chakra and solar plexus. To be open to spiritual influences, sprinkle a little water on the crown of your head, and anoint your Third Eye (between the eyebrows).[16] You may also use charged water to anoint candles, ritual tools, and important personal objects.

5. Use charged water as a sleep-programming device: Pour some magnetized water into a bowl and place it by your bedside so that, as it evaporates, it will charge the atmosphere in which you sleep. Its physical proximity to you makes this a powerful technique.

---

[16]Joy Gardner's *Colors and Crystals* (Freedom, CA: Crossing Press, 1988) is recommended for readers unfamiliar with chakras and the various energies they govern.

No matter how you decide to use the element of water in your magical work, always be aware that Ondines are present in the water and that, if they regard you well, they will help you to achieve your watery goals.

ONDINES

Ondines have received a lot of attention throughout the ages by artists, who have usually portrayed them as very beautiful creatures, irresistible to men. In fact, their allure has given them a bad reputation. The archetypal mermaid (Ondine) sits in her grotto upon a rock, lazily combing her hair and admiring her image in a mirror.

> [O]nce I sat upon a promontory,
> And heard a mermaid on a dolphin's back
> Uttering such dulcet and harmonious breath
> That the rude sea grew civil at her song,
> And certain stars shot madly from their spheres,
> To hear the sea-maid's music. . .[17]

The passing male who spies this vision is doomed, for she will lure him to her side, capture him, and drag him down into the watery depths where he will perish.

I believe this folktale motif (which exists worldwide) to be a product of masculine psychology. The mermaid represents the water element and the power of emotion. The doomed male, on the other hand, represents either the air element or that of earth; he is usually described as intellectual or very down-to-earth, and not ordinarily given to folly.[18] Like all rational, practical types, he has difficulty acknowledging, accepting, and expressing his feelings. He fears them, in fact, and with good reason, for he is in danger of being swamped by them.

---

[17]William Shakespeare, *A Midsummer Night's Dream*, II, i, 149–154.
[18]Dion Fortune wrote an interesting variation on this folktale in "The Sea Lure," a short story contained in her *Secrets of Dr. Taverner* (St. Paul, MN: Llewellyn, 1978).

It is true that earthy and airy types—women as well as men—fear being overwhelmed by emotion. There is some basis for this fear, as the release of feelings long-denied usually results in an emotional cataclysm far out of proportion to whatever caused it. And there are magical considerations as well. Ondines do not respect individuals who are not comfortable with their emotions, and they will make trouble for those whom they don't admire. I know whereof I speak.

When Murry Hope first came to the United States to conduct a series of seminars, she stayed a couple of days in my home—long enough to observe that I had spent too much time on spiritual plane pursuits. She counseled me to get in touch with the elemental kingdoms and took me literally by the hand to visit a pristine little stream which runs through a glade not far from my home. "Come, dear," she said, marching down to the brook. "I'll show you how to make a gift to the Ondines." Kneeling down on the bank, very close to the water, she took from her purse a small vial of her personal perfume—"They love scent"—and poured a few drops into the stream. "Here, beautiful little Ondines," she said. "This is a gift for you." There was a pause. Then she said, "Look, Nancy! There they are!" I looked down and saw some *things* gobbling up the droplets of perfume. They did not look like mermaids. They looked, in fact, rather like tiny jelly donuts! (Jelly donuts don't have holes like most donuts; they have a depression in the middle where the hole should be.) Not my idea of an Ondine, but never mind. If Murry said these were Ondines, then that's what they were.

A day later, Murry was due to fly home to England, and I took her to the airport. She walked three-quarters of the way down the ramp, turned around and called back to me, "Work with the elementals, dear." Then, as an afterthought, she said, "There'll be some problems, you know," and disappeared from view. I adored Murry (and still do), but I could cheerfully have throttled her at that moment. Problems! What do you mean, problems? What kind of problems, Murry?

The day after she left, I did some serious thinking. I knew I had to work with the elementals and I also knew that if there were going to be "problems," it would be the Ondines who presented them, because I'm a thinking (airy) type. Best, therefore, to tackle them first. I took a small bottle of perfume, and went back to the stream Murry and I had visited, and poured a few drops into it. "Here, little Ondines, here is a gift for you. I'd very much like to be friends with you." No jelly donuts appeared. I could see the perfume drops drifting downstream, but no little jelly donuts gobbling them up. Very puzzling. I went back every day for a week. No jelly donuts. I went back every other week. I must have visited the stream fifteen, twenty times to no avail. Finally, I gave up.

It occurred to me that perhaps I had been able to see the Ondines while in Murry's presence because they loved her enough to appear at her call, and that I just happened to have been there when they did. It also occurred to me that Murry had allowed me to experience something beyond my level of development so that I would persevere in my efforts to get to know the elementals when she had gone. An enlightened teacher who can produce phenomena at will sometimes encourages a student in this manner. To this day, I don't know the truth of the matter. But there was no doubt that the Ondines were snubbing me.

In the meantime, I started to have inundation dreams. Every night for a week, I dreamt that the monsoons had arrived and that my house had a roof like a sieve. The water crashed through the roof, ruining my house and all my furniture. I also developed a sinus condition. I dutifully made notes on all the dreams for my psychiatrist. Then one very rainy day, I was seated in a restaurant, snuffling and snorting and making notes on yet another inundation dream, and the light finally dawned. I had indeed made contact with the Ondines, and they were having their little joke at my expense. I knew that I should ask them to cease and desist. I also knew they were having too much fun to pay any attention to me.

So I decided to have a talk with the fiery Salamanders. Despite the fact that I hadn't attempted to contact them before this, I would plead with them for help. I did this in the restaurant, over lunch. "Dear little Salamanders, I've done a dumb thing, and I need you to get me out of this mess. My unconscious is flooded, and so are my nasal passages. I know I should tell the Ondines to back off, but that's not going to work. Please help!" I realize that what I'm about to say is unbelievable, but it's the absolute truth. My sinuses cleared on the spot. This was encouraging. I went home that night, put on a red flannel nightgown, turned up the heat, and ate chili for dinner—anything to stoke up the fire, so to speak. There were no more inundation dreams and no more sinus problems. But I still hadn't made friends with the Ondines.

Some time later, a friend called for help. Her marriage was rocky and she had intended, on a magically significant day, to perform a small ritual designed to put things right again. But she was sick in bed and wouldn't be able to perform the ritual as planned. I offered to stand in for her. Normally, I don't practice magic by proxy—in fact, I'd never done it before, and haven't since—but I felt inwardly pressured somehow to do the work, so I went ahead. Since the project involved love, which is ruled by water, I went back to the stream with my perfume as an offering, and pleaded with the Ondines to help my friend. And there were the jelly donuts. I realized later that they had finally shown themselves because all of the factors were right. I had acted—out of *compassion*—on behalf of a *female* friend, who was *ill*, in a matter relating to *love*.

I decided to take the initiative and forge ahead. Not long after, I began to make magically prepared waters. I'm often asked what it is about my Waters that makes them so special. I usually don't respond to the question, because most people wouldn't understand the answer—or, if they did, they'd think me certifiable. But the truth is that I'm not responsible for the special quality of my Waters. My Ondine is. She's the one that gives them their lightness and their buoyancy.

I met my Ondine companion along with my other elemental helpers. They all appeared in a clump, as it were, at the same time. The Salamander, Sylph, and Gnome appeared vivid and hearty, but the Ondine barely registered. It was as if she didn't want to meet me, or was extraordinarily shy. This is no doubt due to the fact that water is my weakest element. She is still shy—it's difficult to see her in my mind's eye—but I have no doubt of her presence, or of her loving and faithful service.

Artists' conceptions notwithstanding, there are male as well as female Ondines, though they are in the minority. These male

Ondines are sometimes called mermen. (I once led a group of people in a shamanic journey to the Ondines' grottos so that participants could meet their personal companions. One gentleman met a merman, who rather indignantly insisted that Ondines should not be referred to as mermaids or mermen. The proper name, he stated, is "mermian"—a term which can be applied to either of the Ondine sexes.) All are beautiful (and sometimes vain) creatures who love to splash about in the water and take life at an easy pace. They tend to be playful. Readers with an interest in opera should look closely at the Rhine Maidens in Wagner's *Das Rheingold*. In fact, study of the entire *Ring Cycle* is worthwhile, for Wagner was very knowledgeable about the elemental kingdoms.

GIFTS FOR ONDINES

As you already know, Ondines love a gift of perfume. If you don't wear scent, go to the perfume counter in any large department store and ask for one or two of their sample vials. You may use an essential oil as a substitute, but please remember that oils belong to the fire element, not to water.

Perfume in hand, go to any body of water—a pond, stream, lake, bay, or ocean—and pour out a few drops in offering. If you are lucky, luckier than I first was at any rate, the Ondines will look kindly upon you and shower you with blessings.

MEETING YOUR PERSONAL ONDINE

Ambitious magicians will want to meet their personal elemental companions as soon as they can. The astral (imaginative) journey described here will make it possible for you to meet your personal Ondine helper. The realm of the Ondines has been chosen over that of the Salamanders, Sylphs, or Gnomes because the issues related to the water element—love, friendship, and healing—are of great concern to most people. Moreover, human beings, being very watery folk, are usually able to make contact with this element with ease. If you prefer to meet elementals other than Ondines, you will have no difficulty doing so if you make the adjustments suggested on page 164.

ASTRAL TRAVEL

To use modern scientific terminology, an astral journey requires that you achieve an altered state of consciousness (ASC) so that you can go "out-of-body" to the realm you wish to visit. Saying the same thing in old-fashioned esoteric terms, it requires that you go into trance and use astral projection to reach the desired realm. Stated in plain English, you must first physically relax to the extent that you become unaware of your body, and then imagine yourself in the realm you wish to visit. It's really quite simple.

The technique's simplicity, however, should not lull you into a false sense of security. There are more things between heaven and Earth than are dreamt of in your philosophy, and if you wish to explore the areas which lie between the spiritual and physical planes, you must be prepared to meet these "things." The astral plane is inhabited by a great variety of creatures, some of which—on the lower levels, anyway—aren't particularly pleasant. Some of these are peculiar to the individual, while others are picked up from society at large.

I once knew a woman who, in the course of practicing magic, found herself menaced by a spirit (a demon, she called it) whose only manifestation was the sound of a cellophane cigarette wrapper being crushed. This may not seem very threatening to you, but it was quite terrifying to her. Since she was a smoker and prone to respiratory disease, it's possible that her unconscious was trying to warn her that her smoking habit was dangerous. Whatever the real nature or purpose of the phenomenon, she was badly frightened and gave up magic, at least for a while. I doubt that you will encounter the cellophane demon, because it was probably peculiar to the woman who harbored it. On the other hand, another woman I knew did a magical exercise designed to expose her Shadow—an archetype composed of the darker aspects of the personality which we usually try to ignore or deny—and what appeared was a typical Walt Disney witch, warts, apple, and all. This symbol of evil is recognizable to almost everyone in our society, and is probably encountered by many magicians.

The unconscious mind takes your darker feelings and thoughts and molds them into those forms, personal or collective, which will most frighten you so that you will heed its warnings. Individuals who face their inner demons head-on, usually through the psychotherapeutic process, don't have to fear confronting them while exploring ASCs, because the mere act of acknowledging them effectively exorcises them. But for those who have not squarely faced the ugly or dangerous aspects of their characters, it is quite a different story.

Psychological considerations aside, classical esoteric theory maintains that the universe contains some energies—beings, creatures or whatever one wishes to call them—that are not altogether friendly to humankind which, if suddenly or unexpectedly confronted, could cause a good deal of trauma for any magician operating at levels other than normal consciousness.

My purpose in discussing possible dangers relating to astral travel is not to frighten you to the extent that you don't attempt it, but rather to warn you that safety measures are required for this kind of work—even for those who are experienced and knowledgeable about the Shadow side of their characters. My own psychotherapy has exposed to view most of my inner demons, but even so I would never consider going out-of-body without adequate protective measures.

Never indulge in drugs or alcohol prior to astral travel. To do so is to court disaster. As Dion Fortune said:

> To open the psychic centres and contact other planes does not constitute the whole of psychism. *It is necessary to know how to approach and handle that which is contacted. Drugs do not confer this knowledge, which only comes with experience.* . . . Moreover, a dangerous astral contact may be formed at the very first experiment.[19]

---

[19]Dion Fortune, *Sane Occultism* (London: Aquarian Press, 1967), p. 119. Fortune further states on page 120: "It may be taken as axiomatic that anyone who suggests the use of drugs for raising consciousness is definitely on the Left-Hand Path [i.e., is a black magician] and had best be avoided.

If you don't feel confident enough to attempt astral travel at this point, don't worry. Skip this section and come back to it when you feel prepared.

It is imperative that you perform the personal and god symbols exercises recommended by Murry Hope (see Appendix B) before you attempt this journey, or any other form of astral travel. These symbols will act as your passport and personal security guard while you explore altered states of consciousness.

Shamanic journeys with earthly destinations require that you move downward, at least for a time, before you reach the desired realm. Astral journeys with cosmic destinations—those which require you to leave the planet and move into space—demand that you move upward before reaching your destination. Keeping these principles in mind, you can easily design your own astral travels.

Journeying requires a good deal of physical and mental discipline. When leading groups of people on shamanic journeys, it's been my observation that some individuals have difficulty remaining physically still. This usually reflects a parallel mental unrest. The inability to achieve physical or mental stillness represents a serious obstacle in the path of the aspiring magician. One of the best ways to overcome the problem is through the practice of Hatha and Raja Yoga. Hatha Yoga teaches bodily discipline, and Raja teaches meditation (mental stillness). My own Hatha Yoga teacher included meditation along with physical instruction; it's my understanding that this is normal procedure.

Astral travel plays a large part in the advanced magician's repertoire, and with good reason. It enables them to acquaint themselves with beings who can help them with their projects. There are reasons for journeying beyond the purely practical, however. Knowledge may be gained from beings who belong to other dimensions—and in magic (as in life), knowledge is power.

EXERCISE 12: THE JOURNEY

There are more Ondines eager to meet friendly human beings than there are humans who wish to meet Ondines, so you can fully expect to make the acquaintance of your personal helper on this journey.

If possible, tape the journey instructions before you proceed and keep the tape recorder nearby so that you can move at your own speed, pressing the pause button when you wish.

This journey activates the 2nd Chakra which traditionally relates to the water element; the 4th Chakra, the seat of clairsentience—the ability to feel upon the subtle planes; the 5th Chakra, seat of clairaudience—the ability to hear upon the astral plane; the 6th Chakra, seat of clairvoyance—the ability to see in the subtle dimensions.

Most individuals are naturally endowed with one of the "clair" abilities, some are capable of two, and a few are capable of all three. Energizing the Heart, Throat, and Third-Eye Chakras ensures that at least one of your "clair" abilities will be activated so that you may feel, hear, or see your personal Ondine during the journey itself. If you are an experienced magician and know that you are, say, naturally clairsentient and clairvoyant but hopelessly unclairaudient, you may wish to skip the corresponding steps in the exercise. Beginners should activate all three of the chakras.

The journey itself is expressed in terms of clairvoyance and clairaudience. That is, you are encouraged to see and hear your Ondines during the course of it. If you are clairsentient, you may only sense your Ondine's presence, and you may have difficulty determining the Ondine's name, but you should have no problems otherwise.

- Seek privacy. Lie or sit down, and physically relax for at least ten minutes.

- Invoke your personal and god symbols (see Appendix B).

- You may also, if you wish, invoke the assistance of your chosen archetype or that of your personal guides, helpers, or tutors.

- Do Exercise 1 (page 42) to activate positive energy.

- Focus your consciousness on your 2nd Chakra, in the region of your sexual organs.

- Breathe in and out from your 2nd Chakra. Don't alter your breath; breathe naturally.

- As you inhale through the 2nd Chakra, imagine that the area begins to glow with an orange color. Each time you breathe in, the color becomes more intense, until the area is filled with a vibrant, vivid orange.

- Rest a moment.

- Now turn your attention to your Heart Chakra in the center of your chest.

- Breathe in and out from your Heart Chakra. Keep your breathing natural.

- As you inhale through the Heart Chakra, imagine that it begins to glow green. Each time you breathe in, the color becomes more intense. After inhalation, the area is suffused with a bright, refreshing green.

- Rest a moment.

- Focus your attention on your Throat Chakra.

- Breathe in and out of your Throat Chakra. Let your breathing be natural.

- Imagine as you inhale that your throat area is surrounded by, and infused with, a glorious turquoise color. Each time you inhale, the color becomes brighter and more vivid.

- Rest a moment.

- Focus your attention on your Third-Eye Chakra, between your eyebrows.

- Breathe in and out through your Third Eye. Inhale and exhale naturally.

- Imagine as you breathe in that your Third Eye starts to glow a beautiful violet—the color of light amethyst. With each inhalation, the violet becomes more radiant, more lovely.

- And now, prepare to take your journey.

- Imagine that there is, a short distance from you, a wishing well. In your imagination, walk toward it, and look down into it. It is empty of water.

- You are going to descend into the well. Your journey down will be very comfortable. Descend in any manner which pleases you: float down, fly down, take an elevator down, climb down—whatever seems right.

- Your descent is easy. You feel very relaxed and comfortable as you move downward.

- When you reach the bottom of the well, rest for a while.

If you don't wish to continue the journey, ascend the well now in the same manner you descended. The trip upward will be easy and comfortable. Go to the end of this exercise and thank your guardians.

- The air in the well is cool and refreshing. Breathe deeply of it.

- Opposite you, there is a tunnel. Look down its length. There is daylight at the far end of it. This is your destination.

- Move through the tunnel at a pace and in a manner comfortable to you.

- When you reach the end of the tunnel, emerge from it and study the landscape.

- Before you is a beautiful body of water glistening in the sunlight. There are majestic trees and fragrant flowers nearby.

- Go to the water and sit down comfortably beside it. Dip your hands into it, and feel its cool, refreshing quality.

- Open a small vial of perfume you have brought with you, and pour a few drops into the water, as an offering to the Ondines.

- Tell the Ondines that you have come to meet your personal helper. Politely ask your helper to appear.

- Wait patiently for your Ondine to appear, as it surely will.

- When your Ondine appears, introduce yourself by name.

- Tell your Ondine that you very much wish to form a relationship which will be beneficial to you both.

- Wait for your Ondine's reply, comments, or advice.

- Ask your Ondine's name. Repeat the name aloud several times, so that you will remember it when you return to normal consciousness.

- Talk with your Ondine for as long as it pleases you both to do so. *Do not ask your Ondine for favors.*

- When you are ready to depart, give the vial of perfume to your Ondine as a gift.

- After having assured your Ondine that you will meet again soon, make your departure.

- Return to the tunnel and make your way through it in an easy manner.

- When you have reached the entrance to the tunnel at the bottom of the well, rest for a moment.

- When you are ready, ascend the well easily and comfortably.

- Emerge from the well.

- Thank your guardian symbols, archetype, guides, helpers or tutors for their assistance.

- Wiggle your fingers and toes, stretch, yawn, open your eyes and come back to normal consciousness.

- Seal your aura (see page 80).

If you think you will have trouble remembering your Ondine's name, write it down immediately.

Do not ask your Ondine for favors until you have fully established a relationship with it.

MEETING SALAMANDERS, SYLPHS, AND GNOMES

The foregoing journey can easily be revised so that you may meet any of the other elementals.

To meet Salamanders: Instead of working with the 2nd Chakra (in the 5th, 6th, and 7th step of the exercise), breathe the color yellow into your Solar Plexus Chakra, located between your ribcage and navel. Imagine your destination is the interior of a volcano. Some distance from the volcano is a man-made shaft, containing steps which lead down into the Earth. Move down the shaft and emerge in a chamber close to, but not within, the heart of the volcano. You need not give a present to the Salamanders. The fact that you dared to make the journey is gift enough for them.

To meet Sylphs: Instead of working with the 2nd Chakra (in the 5th, 6th, and 7th steps of this exercise), breathe the color pink through your Heart Chakra. Imagine your destination is the top of a mountain. The mountain is so high and in so remote an area that it is inaccessible to ordinary travelers. At the base of the mountain is an entrance into its heart. The entrance leads you to a long tunnel, sloping downward. At the tunnel's end is a circular shaft leading upward. Ascend the shaft to the mountain's peak. A gift of flowers will be welcomed by the Sylphs you meet.

To meet Gnomes: Instead of working with the 2nd Chakra, breathe the color red into your Root (tailbone) Chakra. Your destination is a secret mine located deep within the Earth. You enter a narrow crevice in a remote valley and find yourself in a large cave. Far across the cave there is a tunnel which leads downward, deep into the Earth. Follow the tunnel until you find the mine. Take a gift of coins, crystals, or jewelry for the Gnomes you meet.

THE EARTH ELEMENT

Earth without and Earth within
Make the Mill of magic spin
Work the will for which we [I] pray
Io Dio, Ha He Yay[20]

　　　　　　　　—W. G. Gray

EARTH SYMBOLS, TOOLS, AFFINITIES

Affinity: The physical plane.

Astrological signs: ♉ (Taurus), ♍ (Virgo), ♑ (Capricorn).

Cardinal direction: North.

Elemental: Gnome.

Gender: Feminine.

Magical tools: Crystals, powders, salts, sands.

Psychological function: Sensation.

Qualities: Passive, warm, dry.

Ritual tool: Pentacle.

Seasonal affinity: Winter.

Symbol: ▽ (Equilateral triangle, point downward, with a horizontal line drawn through the center of the triangle).

---

[20]W. G. Gray, *Magical Ritual Methods* (York Beach, ME: Samuel Weiser, 1980), pp. 215–216. Used by permission.

Table 4. The Attributes of the Earth Element.

EARTHY GOALS	PSYCHOLOGICAL QUALITIES		EARTH IN NATURE*		
	Positive	Negative	Vegetable	Mineral	Animal
Agriculture	Concentration	Dullness	Bayberry	Agate, green	Ass
Antiques	Endurance	Irregularity	Berries	Agate, moss	Buffalo
Buildings	Firmness	Laziness	Cedar	Aventurine	Bull
Business	Industry	Misanthropy	Cypress	Cat's eye	Cow
Construction	Responsibility	Tardiness	Ferns	Chrysoprase	Deer
Fertility	Self-assurance	Unscrupulousness	Gums	Coal	Dog
Investments	Thoroughness		Honeysuckle	Emerald	Dragon
Job and career matters			Horehound	Jasper	Goat
Money			Jasmine	Jet	Jackal
Nutrition			Mosses	Malachite	Mythical satyr
Old age			Musks	Marble	Serpent
Stock market			Myrrh	Obsidian	Stag
			Patchouli	Olivine	Wolf
			Pine	Onyx	
			Sage	Peridot	
			Violet	Quartz, smoky	
			Vetivert	Salt	
				Tourmaline, black	
				Turquoise	

*Some objects may be classified under two or more elements.

When you want to see physical results from your magical operations, or bring out the practical side of your nature, you need to work with the attributes and qualities relating to the earth element (shown in Table 4).

Using the four elements to achieve your goals is rather like using a net to catch fish. When you use the two masculine elements, you make the decision to catch fish, and cast your net out to sea. With the two feminine elements, you haul in your catch. A large catch is worthless if you don't haul it in. On the other hand, hauling in your net does not automatically insure a good catch. The earth element attracts material good (fish). The water element allows you to receive (haul in) the good. Earth and water must work together if you want to enjoy the fruits of your magical labors.

EARTH MAGIC

The earth element has received a lot of attention in recent years, because the use of crystals has become widespread among metaphysicians—so widespread, in fact, that it seems a bit superfluous to include information on crystals here. However, my aim is to give comprehensive coverage of the elements, and since crystals are an important earthy tool, I can't ignore them. I shall give equal space to those lesser known tools: powders, salts, and sands.

Crystals: Crystalline structure traps energy, and therein lies its virtue—and its vice. Crystals, like all objects which undergo processing prior to sale, must be cleansed before they can be used in ritual. When they are clean, they must be consecrated. So, unless you dig your crystal out of the ground yourself, here's the procedure you must follow prior to using it in magical operations:

Cleanse your crystal: There are dozens of ways to clear crystals of undesirable influences. First focus on your intention and then any one of the elements may be used for this purpose.

1. *Fire:* Pass your crystal quickly through the flame of a candle.

2. *Air:* Waft the crystal through the smoke of incense or a smudge stick. Or blow upon it (see page 137).

3. *Water:* Hold the crystal under cold running water for a minute or two.

4. *Earth:* Bury the crystal in salt; submerge it in salted water (water and earth); or, bury it in purifying herbs, such as rosemary, pepper, and bay laurel.

Use whatever cleansing technique appeals to you. I personally prefer the cold running water method, as this is the least invasive way to purify crystals. Gemstones have personalities of their own (which is why we choose one over another) and it's possible to injure them with harsh cleansing methods. Your purpose is not to clear all the life out of a crystal (this would be counterproductive) but to remove any human energies resident in it due to its subjection to cutting and polishing prior to sale. If in doubt as to which method to use, consult your crystal and accept its advice with grace.

Charge your crystal: There are many ways to do this. Work upon any of the four planes can do the job.

1. *Spiritual Plane:* Hold or wear your crystal while you pray to your chosen archetype, or assume the god-form.

2. *Mental Plane:* Hold or wear your stone while you repeat affirmations or incantations aloud. Or, place the crystal on your written goal so that it may absorb your intention.

3. *Emotional Plane:* Hold or wear your crystal while you perform visualization, or do magical feeling or identification with fictional character exercises.

4. *Physical Plane:* Use any of the four elements. Pass the crystal through the flame of a cleansed and consecrated candle of appro-

priate color (fire); waft the crystal through incense smoke, blow your intention into it, or expose it to music or pure sound expressive of your desire (air); soak the crystal in water which has been charged with your intention; or bury the crystal in herbs appropriate to your goal, or in magnetic sand.

Take care of your crystal once it is charged: Carry or wear the stone as often as you can. Gaze at it and handle it often. Sleep with it under your pillow. When it's not in use, keep it wrapped in pure silk or linen. These materials act as insulators and help the crystal retain its charge. Keep your crystal physically clean. It makes no sense to purchase, cleanse, and charge a stone, and then let it gather dust.

Crystals can be overused. I have an amethyst cluster which has faithfully served me for years, and even though I keep it clean it has become dull and dusty looking. It's been overworked, poor thing, and I shall probably have to return it to Mother Earth. To "rev up" a tired crystal, expose it to moonlight (sunlight is too strong for most stones), place it outdoors during a storm, or put it under a pyramid. If these techniques don't work, the stone should be given back to the Earth, with thanks for its hard work on your behalf.

Powders: Powders are comprised mainly of herbs which have been crushed or ground to a powdery consistency. The herbs themselves have power to attract good, but like crystals, they should be charged with your personal energy and desire before they are used in ritual.

To magnetize a powder, hold some of it in the palm of your dominant hand with your fingers folded over it. Use any of the following methods to charge it: think intensely of your desire; pray to your chosen archetype; verbalize affirmations or incantations; or perform visualization or magical feeling. When you feel the powder is sufficiently charged, if you are indoors, open your palm and gently blow the powder to the four cardinal points, so that it will attract the good from all directions. If you are outdoors, scatter the powder in front of your entranceway, back door, and on windowsills. This attracts the good from the environment and brings it home to you. Or you may sprinkle some of the powder into a medicine pouch and wear it to attract good.

Some powders can be used for repelling undesirable influences. If the herbs used for this purpose are powerful (fiery) enough, they need not be given a personal charge, as they'll do the job on their own. Like other powders, they can be blown or scattered about, or sprinkled in pouches. Be sure to dust them into normally overlooked nooks and crannies, where psychic dirt likes to conceal itself. Be sure to immediately call in the good after cleansing the atmosphere.

An alternative to compounding your own powders is to purchase them ready-made from a metaphysical store. My own line includes powders for Blessing, Grounding, Letting Go, New Love, Prosperity, Purification, Relationship Enhancing, and Serenity. I charge them (with the help of my Gnome friend) when I make them, but they should always be magnetized with your personal desire before use.

Sands: Magnetic sand, as the name implies, is actually magnetized. Its properties may be tested with a lodestone or magnet. Its virtue, as you might expect, is that it takes a charge well and is an effective attracting agent. To charge magnetic sand, put some into the palm of your dominant hand, fold your fingers over it and focus on your desire—or use prayer, affirmations, incantations, or visualization to personally energize it. Since the sand is heavy, you won't be able to blow it to the four directions as you can powders, but you can scatter it about indoors and out, put it into a medicine pouch, or spill some into an open bowl where it will attract the good that you desire from the environment. Many magicians mix powders with magnetic sand to give the powder added potency. Magnetic sand (my own included) is available in metaphysical stores.

Take a close look at any product labeled "sand" before you purchase it from a metaphysical store, because some of these are actually salts, and the two products serve radically different purposes.

Regular sand may be charged and used in exactly the same manner as the magnetic variety. If you decide to gather sand from a beach for magical purposes, be sure to leave some token of appreciation behind; or even better, clean up some of the litter left behind by spiritually immature types.

Salts: Salt's main virtue is that it absorbs negativity. Bath salts are a great boon when you want to rid yourself of distressing spiritual, mental, emotional, or physical conditions. All you need do is fill the bathtub with water, pour in the salts, soak for a while and the trouble disappears—or at least fades considerably. Bath salts found in a drugstore will do the job, but those compounded by magicians are even better because they are created with intention. You can easily create your own. All you need is a cup of ordinary, sea, rock, or epsom salt.. But if you'd like to be fancy, add a drop or two of an essential oil (fire) to the salt. Shake the mixture well and pour it into the water. Burn some incense while you soak in the tub, and you will have all four elements working for you: a complete magical operation.

Not all salts sold in metaphysical stores are of the bath variety; some are meant to be sprinkled about. My own Goddess Salts are double-active: they absorb any energies which may prevent you from establishing contact with the desired archetype, and they attract the deity's assistance at the material level. They should be used in conjunction with Goddess Waters, which help you to be receptive to spiritual influences.

Salt may be used as a cleansing agent inside and outside the home. Scatter it on your front porch to capture negative energies before they can enter your house. Indoors, sprinkle it in corners, closets, and out-of-the-way places not regularly cleaned. Place a few grains of salt in your pockets (or a locket) to absorb undesirable energies surrounding you.

It's not strictly necessary to consecrate salt before you use it, but if you're feeling ambitious, you can charge it by the same method described in Exercise 10 (page 147) for magnetising water.

GNOMES

If your goal is earth-related, you will need to invoke the offices of the Gnomes. Gnomes like people who are practical, salt-of-the-earth, industrious types. They appreciate financial acumen. If earth is your strongest element, or if you are a sensate type (which amounts to the same thing), you'll have no trouble attracting their assistance.

If, on the other hand, your strongest element is fire, or you are an intuitive type, be prepared for some problems. It's impossible to predict how these will manifest. The woman whose firewood spontaneously burst into flame (page 129) "lost" several small pieces of jewelry in her home—a typical example of Gnomic mischief. Since she was a very sensible, down-to-earth person, I suspect the cause of the problem had more to do with her environment than with her personality. Her house had previously been owned by a group of people who belonged to a truly bizarre religious cult. When these people moved out, they left some of their possessions behind. It may be that elemental energies were attached, as it were, to some of these objects, forcing the new resident to cope with the attendant problems. In any case, all phenomena ceased when she got rid of everything belonging to the former owners. This is the only incidence of Gnome trouble that has come to my personal attention. Dion Fortune didn't know any Gnome stories either, and what little she had to say on the subject relates more to the psychology of earth than to elemental mischief. Fortune felt that claustrophobia was probably a manifestation of earthy pathology.[21]

Gnomes live deep within the Earth and don't much care for sunlight or exposure. They love the precious metals and gemstones which nestle inside the Earth's core, and their favored profession is mining. Snow White's seven little companions are indisputably Gnomes, Grumpy being the most archetypal.

---

[21]Dion Fortune, *Psychic Self-Defense* (York Beach, ME: Samuel Weiser, 1976), pp. 83–84.

Murry Hope, whose knowledge of the elemental kingdoms is encyclopedic, says that Gnomes are decided grumps and tend to be resentful when asked for assistance. Her own companion ungraciously says, "Do it yourself" when she asks for his help. When she bends to her task, however, she finds him working hard alongside of her. Murry says Gnomides—lady Gnomes—have sweeter temperaments and are rather mother-henish.

Murry's companion is a "stone-Gnome" who loves precious gemstones—a trait he shares with his adopted human—and more than once has encouraged her to buy jewelry she can't afford. In a typical scenario, he will urge her to look in the window of a jewelry shop as she passes. "I don't want to look," Murry says, "because I haven't enough money to buy anything." "Look," he says. She looks, and sees something she admires and would very much like to have. "Get," says her Gnome. "No, I can't afford it." "Get," he says. She goes in, makes the purchase, then wonders how she is going to pay the phone bill. A few days later, an unexpected check arrives which exactly covers the cost of the jewelry.

Lest the reader think that Gnomes maliciously tempt their human companions to frivolous expenditures, I should point out that Gnomes are not frivolous by nature—anything but! Moreover, gemstones and precious metals have been used throughout history as amulets (devices which repel evil) and talismans (objects which attract good luck). So in urging humans to purchase jewelry, Gnomes are in essence attempting to provide protection and good fortune for their companions.

My own companion is a "precious metal-Gnome." I love gold jewelry and have the most extraordinary luck when it comes to finding bargains. Murry maintains there are "healing crystal-Gnomes" and "cash-Gnomes," as well as those already described.

On a very practical level, Gnomes will help you with the forces of gravity—that is, with lifting or moving heavy objects. Ask their advice and they will tell you how to handle something heavy without harming yourself physically. Back sufferers, take note!

GIFTS FOR GNOMES

Astute readers have probably already guessed the gifts Gnomes most appreciate: coins, jewelry, and crystals. Murry Hope taught me her method of making an offering to the Gnomes: Find a private outdoor spot. Look around for a sturdy twig or broken tree branch. Using this, dig a small hole in the ground and place within it a coin, a piece of jewelry (such as an odd earring or cufflink), or a crystal. Say something like, "This is for you, little Gnomes, and may you prosper." Cover the offering with earth and go on your way. If the little Gnomes appreciate your gift, they may return the favor in the form of material success.

OVERVIEW

Before we tackle our next subject—ritual—it's perhaps wise to briefly recap the information we have covered so far, and for me to make a few further comments.

Magic is a four-tiered structure, comprised of the physical, emotional, mental, and spiritual planes.

It is upon the two middle planes—the emotional and the mental—that we work upon ourselves so that we may achieve our goals. We define our goals and then determine, through consultation with an oracle, if it is worthwhile to pursue them. Then, with the help of clearing techniques, we exorcise emotional negativity and ingrained attitudes that are inimical to our success, and replace them with positive psychological attitudes through the use of affirmations, visualization and magical feeling methods.

We appeal for help with our projects from the highest and lowest planes—the spiritual and the physical. If we are courteous and sincere in our approach to spiritual plane archetypes and elementals, and if we are respectful of the objects found in nature (and restrained in our gathering of them), we can expect to receive the loving assistance of non-human energies.

It's neither fair nor realistic to ask deities and elementals to do all our work for us. After all, even though we may love them deeply and gain their confidence, these beings don't exist solely for our benefit. Besides, they couldn't do our work even if they wanted to, for they're not human. Furthermore, no amount of benevolent (albeit invisible) wire-pulling by deities on behalf of a favored human is powerful enough to overwhelm a psyche not emotionally receptive to the benefits bestowed.

On the other hand, there are times when good use of mental and emotional plane techniques alone can't do the job. Sometimes a certain amount of spiritual grace is required for success. But this does not come free; it must be earned.

No matter how one looks at it, magicians must work for their results. Magic is not a lazy person's pursuit. The fact that magic requires a great outlay of time and energy in order to produce results may lead one to ask why its practice is desirable at all. Would it not be simpler and equally effective to forget the whole thing and carry on, just as the average person does? There's no doubt that life would be simpler without magic, but it's also true that magicians get better and speedier results than laymen. The magician who wants to open a store, say, and who has performed a magical operation to ensure its success, will see customers pour into the shop the minute its doors are opened. By contrast, the average person who does not work magically for the shop's success will have to sweat out several days or weeks of minimal sales until word gets round about the establishment's existence and business picks up. The end result may be the same—both stores may prosper—but magicians have the edge. Spiritually, psychologically and physically primed, magicians hit the ground running, as it were—and they can maintain the pace for as long as it suits them to do so.

Knowledge of magical techniques is an enormous advantage in a competitive world.

PART THREE

THE PRACTICE
OF MAGIC

CHAPTER 8

TIMING AND TIDES

It is the interacting set of . . . tides which is all-important to the practical occultist, because so much of his work depends upon them. The charts of these tides have always been kept secret, and some of them are exceedingly complex. As these concern the secret workings, the genuine and legitimate occult secrets, which are only given after initiation . . . students of the occult are probably wasting their time if they try to operate without the necessary charts.[1]

—*Dion Fortune*

Magicians carefully time their magical operations so that they can take advantage of power tides and cycles. Despite Fortune's words, however, there's no great mystery attached to them. Anyone with common sense and a little knowledge of astronomy can work the "charts" out for themselves.

A magical rite performed at an appropriate time is more likely to be successful than one performed at an inappropriate time. The general (but not invariable) rule is to work in harmony with nature.

USING THE SOLAR AND LUNAR CYCLES

To increase the good in your life, perform your rite while the light increases. In the annual (solar) cycle, this means you should work from the Winter Solstice to the Summer Solstice. The Winter Solstice (the first day of Winter, and the shortest day of the year) oc-

---

[1] Dion Fortune, *The Mystical Qabalah* (York Beach, ME: Samuel Weiser, 1984), p. 260.

curs around December 20th. Each day that succeeds it sees more sunlight, until the Summer Solstice occurs, about June 20th.

In the monthly (lunar) cycle, you should perform your operations for increase while the Moon increases in light (waxes)—that is, from New Moon to Full Moon. At New Moon, the Moon is not visible in the sky because it is traveling in conjunction with the sun, and both luminaries move beneath the horizon at dusk. A day or so after New Moon, a slim crescent appears in the sky at twilight and disappears shortly thereafter. The Moon appears to grow in size for the next two weeks, until it reaches its full bright phase. Check the almanac section of your newspaper or any good commercial calendar for New and Full Moon dates.

Ideally, you should perform your magical operations for the increase of good taking both the annual and monthly cycles into consideration. If you are working to increase prosperity, for instance, you should perform your rite sometime between the first day of Winter and the first day of Summer, and while the Moon is waxing. You have about six chances to do this, since each of the six months contains a two-week period when the Moon is increasing in light.

If you want to decrease negativity in your life, you should perform your magical operations as the light decreases. In the annual cycle, this means working from the Summer Solstice to the Winter Solstice. That is, from the first day of Summer to the beginning of Winter. Each day during this six-month period sees less daylight and more darkness.

It's logical to assume that operations for decrease should be performed while the Moon decreases in light (wanes)—that is, from Full Moon to New Moon. However, I do not recommend performing any magical operations during this period. Waning Moon energies are chaotic and can cause unforeseen trouble. Experienced magicians may perform rites during this period if they wish—at their own risk—but beginners should studiously avoid it. It may be justifiably argued that seeking to decrease negativity while the moon increases in light is counterproductive. But, in my opinion, the risks attendant on working with the darkening Moon are much greater than any potential benefits.

I recommend that if you wish to rid yourself of negativity—bad habits, attitudes, addictions, memories, etc.—you perform your rites while the Moon waxes (as close to the Full Moon as possible), during the waning part of the annual cycle, from the Summer Solstice to the Winter Solstice. Magically speaking, the annual cycle carries greater weight than the monthly cycle, and this plan insures that the more important of the two cycles, at least, is utilized.

Astrologically minded magicians may wish to time their operations according to the moon's monthly progress through the zodiac. This is not an astrological textbook, so the zodiacal signs cannot be discussed at length here; suffice it to say that each astrological sign belongs to one of the four elements.[2] If your goal is spiritual and fiery, for instance, it would behoove you to perform your magical operation while the Moon is traveling through one of the fiery signs. Metaphysical bookstores carry a number of good calendars containing all the information needed pertaining to the Moon's monthly movements.[2]

USING POWER DAYS

In addition to working with the solar and lunar cycles, you should attempt to perform your rites on any of the following "quarter" and "cross-quarter" days:

Winter Solstice: Approximately December 20th (check your calendar). The first day of Winter. The shortest (darkest) day of the year. An excellent day for preliminaries. Decide what you want to achieve—what good you wish to increase—over the next six months. Or, if you've already set your goal, perform your rite.

Candlemas: February 2nd (yes, Groundhog Day). The middle of Winter. First signs of Spring are appearing—rejoice! Days are getting longer. Reconsider goals set at the Winter Solstice. Or, perform a rite based upon the goal set at Winter.

---

[2]Classification of each sign by element is given in chapter 7.

Vernal Equinox: Approximately March 21st (check your calendar). The first day of Spring. Day (light) and night (darkness) are of equal length. Planting season. Time to perform magical operations designed to increase good: health, prosperity, love. Work to form beneficial relationships, business and personal; the best time to form ties. Work hard. Go for it.

Beltane: May 1 (May Day). The middle of Spring. The flower month (don't forget to share some blooms with the Sylphs!). Days are of greater length than nights, and the light is still increasing. The brightest and most joyous of the power days. Celebrate nature's beauty. Perform rites for increase. Particularly good for love magic.

Summer Solstice: Approximately June 20th (check your calendar). The first day of Summer. The longest (lightest) day of the year. Nature is in full bloom. Time to plan for the next six months. Decide what you wish to remove from your life. Or, if you have already set this goal, perform a rite to achieve it.

Lammas: August 1st. The middle of Summer. Days are getting shorter; darkness is increasing. First harvest. Give thanks to your archetypes, tutors, guides, and elemental companions for all the blessings they have bestowed on you. Reconsider goals set at the Summer Solstice, or perform a rite based upon those goals.

Autumn Equinox: Approximately September 21st (check your calendar). First day of Autumn. Day (light) and night (darkness) are equal. Leaves are beginning to turn. Harvesting continues. Sever ties that are outworn or unwanted. Perform rites to rid yourself of negativity.

Halloween: October 31st. The middle of Autumn. Darkness is increasing. Final harvest. Leaves are falling. Nature is dying. Time to thank the Earth for all her blessings. Think about and thank ancestors, family members, and friends who are buried within the rich, dark earth. Perform rites to rid yourself of negative attitudes, situations, habits, addictions, and everything you have outlived and outgrown.

USING DAYS OF THE WEEK

There are seven days in the week, and each of these is governed by one of the seven planets known to the Anglo-Saxons who named them.[3] Each day is thought to be suffused with the energy of the planetary deity for which it is named. Magicians attempt to increase the power of their operations by working with the appropriate energies.

Monday: Moon-Day. Since the Moon governs the tides, this is a good day for working on goals which relate to the emotions, and on domestic and purely feminine issues. Excellent for emotional plane work, such as visualization.

Tuesday: Tiu's Day. Tiu is the sword-bearing Norse god of justice; his nature combines qualities of the Greek gods Zeus and Ares. The day of the planet Mars. A good day to work for more energy, greater self-assertion, and on purely masculine goals. As Mars is a fiery planet, it's an excellent day for spiritual cleansing and for getting rid of negativity.

Wednesday: Woden's Day. Woden (Odin, Wotan) is the great Father-God of Norse mythology; his nature is like a combination of the Greek Hermes and Zeus. The day of the planet Mercury. The best day for consulting oracles (especially runes), planning magical operations, writing affirmations and incantations—for work upon the mental plane, in other words. Good for intellectual goals.

Thursday: Thor's Day. Thor, with his thunderbolts, is closely connected to Zeus, the beneficent Greek All-Father. The day of the planet Jupiter, called by astrologers the "Great Benefic." Magicians use this day for working on prosperity issues.

Friday: Freya's Day. Freya is the Norse Aphrodite. The day of the planet Venus. The perfect day for love and friendship operations. Also excellent for artists, their creations, and the selling of same.

---

[3]The planets known to the ancients were the Sun, Moon, Mercury, Venus, Mars, Jupiter, and Saturn. Uranus, Neptune, and Pluto were discovered in relatively recent times.

Saturday: Saturn's Day. The planet Saturn rules over restrictions and boundaries, so operations for setting these are favored. A good day to work for protection, to maintain the status quo, or to freeze the action. Think about what is blocking you from success—and eradicate the obstacles on Tuesday.

Sunday: The Sun's Day. The best possible day to initiate magical activities. Good for all goals, but particularly those which relate to healing and success.

USING PLANETARY HOURS

Just as each day of the week is governed by a planetary archetype, so is each hour of the day. Figuring planetary hours is not an easy matter, especially for those who are not mathematically inclined.

Planetary hours are, in my opinion, the least important of the power tides and they may usually be safely ignored. A cycle's influence is commensurate with its length. The solar cycle (365 days) is the most important tide, followed by the lunar (28 days), followed by the Moon's stay in a zodiacal sign (approximately two and a half days), and the twenty-four hour tide pertaining to each day of the week. By comparison, the influence of a planetary hour is trifling.

There may be times, however, when attention to planetary hours is important. If you are a meticulous type, or if the achievement of a goal is absolutely critical, then you will wish to work with them. Llewellyn publishes an *Annual Planetary Guide* which gives all the instruction you will need for figuring hourly tides.

EXCEPTIONS TO THE RULES

Finding the right date to perform a magical operation, based on the above rules, can be a complicated matter. In fact, it's almost always impossible to do so in actual practice. If you want to work for prosperity, for instance, and are looking for a power day which occurs on a Thursday during the waxing lunar and solar cycles, you probably won't have much luck. Nature does not arrange its tides for the sole benefit of ambitious magicians. And when you factor personal astrological and numerological influences into the equation, the situation becomes even more complex. The trick is to do your best. Is the effort worth it? Yes. When you work in harmony with nature, your chances of success increase immeasurably.

Even if you've managed to find a perfect ritual date, however, it is critical that you be ready on an emotional level to perform the rite when the date you have set rolls around. If too much time has elapsed between the planning stage and the operation itself, this may not happen, and your chances of success decrease accordingly.

Imagine that you have been in the doldrums for several months. You're tired of your normal routine and generally bored with life. You've tried several ways to "rev up" some energy, but nothing has worked and you're stuck. One day, while doing nothing in particular, you have a flash: you need to travel, not just across the bay, but far away—to Europe perhaps. The very thought of it makes your blood race. You haven't felt this excited in a long time. Finances, however, are an obstacle, so you decide to perform a prosperity rite. Alas, it's September and the Moon is just past full—the worst possible time to work for money. Playing by the timing rules, you'll have to wait until late December (the Winter Solstice) to perform your operation. And it'll probably be a while before you see results from the ritual. You realize it'll be a good six months before you see Europe. A long time. Will you be as fired up about the trip in December as you are right now, in September? Perhaps. But will you have the energy and the time to perform the prosperity rite in the middle of the holiday season? Probably not.

In a case like this, jettison the rules and perform the ritual now, while your enthusiasm for the project is at its peak. When you must make a choice between perfect timing and powerful emotion, always go with the emotion. I have many times gone to great lengths to time an operation perfectly, only to find on the appointed day that I have little enthusiasm left for the project. In my early days, I dutifully performed rituals under these conditions. It seemed wasteful to abandon a project after a great outlay of time and energy. But I eventually learned the results weren't worth it. Good timing is no substitute for passion. Occasionally, passion and perfect timing occur together. When this happens, you can expect spectacular results.

WHEN TO EXPECT MAGICAL RESULTS

Walt Disney's fairy godmother waves her magic wand, repeats a special incantation and—*voila!*—instant results. Would it were so in real life. Wands and incantations are effective, but instant results are rare. It usually takes some time for the powers that be (those within and those without) to manifest your desire at the material level or, for that matter, on any other level. In short, you must be patient after you have performed your operation. This isn't easy, especially for beginners; but it is absolutely necessary.

Archetypes, elementals and your unconscious mind need time and privacy in order to work on your behalf. To worry about the outcome of an operation after it has been performed is to seriously interfere with the work-in-progress. Archetypes and elementals do not appreciate a lack of faith in their powers, and they will cease working for you if they think you do not trust them. Furthermore, your unconscious mind will translate your doubts into negative images or feelings which will scotch your efforts to produce positive results. Perform your ritual to the best of your ability—and then forget it. Entirely. Get on with your life.

Actually, if you've done your work properly, you will probably be sick of the whole project. Magic properly planned and performed is an exhausting process. This is just as well, since unused energies are often channeled into fears that an operation will not be successful.

Nature works in seasonal cycles. So does human nature. If your goal is relatively simple and does not require results at the material level, you can expect success in three months or less. A complex or more materialistic goal will take longer to achieve.

A friend of mine, bent upon buying a house in one of the most expensive areas in the country, performed the Prosperity

Ritual contained in chapter 10, and one year—four seasons—later she was successful. I have no idea how much money she started with (she wasn't rich), but she got very speedy results. With her laser-like mental focus, she is a natural magician. Things happen quickly when magical forces are brought to bear upon a situation.

There is also such a thing as beginner's luck in magic; I've often seen it. It's as if the powers-that-be (internal and external) are so deliriously happy when they see you taking charge of your life that they do everything they can to encourage you to make greater efforts.

My own experience leads me to believe that magical results are most often obtained on a power day. If you perform a ritual on, say, Halloween, you will probably see results on the following Candlemas or, if there's a good deal of difficulty inherent in the goal, on the following Spring Equinox or Beltane. Power days are so named with good reason.

WHY SOME MAGIC FAILS

Assuming that you apply yourself to the techniques taught in this book and that you are not neurotic to the point of self-sabotage, your magical operations have an excellent chance of succeeding. But what about the occasional failure?

It's perhaps easiest to illustrate why a magical operation fails with a personal anecdote. In my theatrical days, after I had performed Ophelia in the production of *Hamlet* described in an earlier chapter, the theatre company to which I belonged decided to produce *Othello*. This play contains a role, Desdemona, which every young Shakespearean actress longs to play, and I was no exception. My Ophelia had been a success (despite the catastrophic costuming) and, since I knew the part of Desdemona backward, forward, and sideways, I thought I was pretty much a "shoo-in" for the role. I learned with horror, however, that I had two serious competitors. One was a young, delightfully earthy, and rather worldly woman (an excellent actress) who specialized in character roles rather than ingenues. Aside from her youth, she wasn't right for Desdemona, who is a sweet and very innocent creature. My other competitor was a woman of forty-five years who had thirteen children and very little dramatic (let alone Shakespearean) experience. How anyone could have imagined her as Desdemona was beyond me. Then I learned that she was wealthy, and that she had offered to give the struggling theatre a goodly sum if she were allowed to play Desdemona.

This panicked me, so I went to work magically. It was early days in my esoteric career and the only techniques I knew were goal-writing and visualization. Since these had worked for me before, I put my faith in them and wrote and visualized for all I was worth.

At the audition, the man who was to play Othello told me that my reading had put him to shame—a very generous remark from a seasoned actor. I thought to myself: "Well, if this man thinks I'm that good, the director must surely think so, too." Then the director did something that I had never seen before, and never was to see again, at an audition. He asked the three would-be Desdemonas to remove their shoes and stand in a row. We did so. The wealthy woman was the shortest of the trio; I was in the middle; the other woman was the tallest. The crowd gazed at us for a while. Not a word was said by the director or anyone else. Then we were told to put our shoes back on and sit down. No explanation was ever given, but I presume the director was trying to visually suggest that the wealthy woman, being the shortest, was the best choice for Desdemona. This didn't make much sense, since the leading man was of medium height and certainly taller than any of us, but I guess it gave the director his excuse.

The wealthy woman was given the part and the theatre got its money. The simultaneous loss of the role and of my magical powers (such as they were), not to mention the unfairness of the situation, was quite shattering. But two months later, I understood. My mother died the night *Othello* opened. My father fell apart at the seams and never recovered. I had more important things to do than to play the role of Desdemona.

Some magical operations are doomed from the start. It is not lack of expertise or passion or bad timing that causes the failure. The culprit is life, nature, fate, providence, or whatever one wishes to call it. In Greek and Norse mythology, the Three Fates—known by the Greeks as the Moirae and by the Norse as the Norns—govern the destinies of even the most powerful gods and goddesses. The Fates' decrees are unassailable by magic and are, for the most part, irrevocable. We gods-in-the-making are subject to the same forces.

Consulting an oracle (see chapter 4) is one way to determine if your operation has a chance of success. However, I have known oracles to encourage magicians in pursuit of a goal even in the face of inimical fate. Your unconscious mind (which speaks through the oracle) apparently sees an educational opportunity in the planning and execution of a magical operation and nudges you forward despite the ritual's foreordained failure.

Astrology—which some might justifiably equate with fate—is more reliable. Had my astrological knowledge been more sophisticated when I was pursuing the role of Desdemona, I would have been forewarned. At the time of the audition and for some time afterward, transiting Saturn (hardship, limitation, lessons) was in opposition (an aspect that acts exactly as you'd expect) to my natal Moon (mother) in the sign of Leo (theatrical performance). This pretty well describes what happened. As I have stressed before, astrological knowledge is absolutely indispensable to magicians.

Don't let the possibility of failure discourage you. Remember: if you follow the instructions given in this book, your chances for magical success are overwhelmingly positive.

CHAPTER 9

RITUAL

Ritual is meditation expressed in action.[1]

—Dion Fortune

Ceremonial magic enables man to become an engine capable of harnessing and directing the enormous power that lies within.[2]

—Israel Regardie

The *Encyclopaedia Britannica* defines ritual as "a specific, observable kind of behaviour based upon established or traditional rules," which makes it sound very uninteresting and entirely uncreative.[3] In fact, it is neither. Furthermore, this academic definition doesn't get to the heart of the matter.

As a magician, you use ritual in order to create within yourself a mental state that allows you to give clear and direct instructions to your unconscious mind. Simply put, you perform ritualistic actions which produce a state of light trance, usually at Alpha Level. This subdues the constant clamoring of your conscious mind so that your unconscious mind may easily be reached. Ritual is a means to an end, not an end in itself.

Some individuals are able to successfully practice magic without the use of formal ritual. These people are either natural magicians, born with the ability to penetrate to the deeper levels of the unconscious, or they are very experienced in magic, with minds conditioned by constant practice to reach unconscious depths. For

---

[1]Dion Fortune in her essay, "Guild of the Master Jesus," contained in Charles Field and Carr Collins, *The Story of Dion Fortune* (Dallas, TX: Star & Cross Publications, 1985), p. 283.

[2]Israel Regardie, *The Middle Pillar* (St. Paul, MN: Llewellyn, 1985), p. v.

[3]*Encyclopedia Britannica*, 15th ed., s. v. "ritual."

them, ritual is cumbersome, perhaps even counterproductive. But the majority of people (beginners most of all) need ritual in order to achieve the desired Alpha State.

Ritual is too extensive a subject to cover in any detail here. The *Britannica* lists eighty-seven entries relating to it, and entire books have been written on the topic, usually by scholars who make little or no use of their subject in practice. Murry Hope's *The Psychology of Ritual*, however, was written by a practicing magician, and students interested in a very detailed look at the subject will find Hope's book to be of great value.[4] We shall tackle it in simplified form in this chapter.

THE FOUR PHASES OF RITUAL

All ritual is comprised of four stages:

1. **Preliminaries**: Gather together the materials necessary for your work. These may include candles, oils, incense, waters, powders, crystals, magical implements, writing materials—anything you will need for the practical part of your magical work. Arrange these aesthetically on some convenient flat surface, usually termed for this purpose an "altar." You may also don a robe and various magical accessories, such as jewelry, mask, or headgear. Some magicians take a ritual bath prior to robing; it is debatable, however, whether this practice—an excellent one—belongs to the Preliminaries or to the Opening. In any case, turn your mind away from your everyday concerns during the preliminaries and begin to focus on the work ahead.

2. **The Opening**: This is the phase that produces light trance. It does not matter how you reach Alpha Level. You may create a magic circle, chant, dance, drum, sing, breathe rhythmically, stare into a mirror, or simply meditate. The trick is to lull your conscious mind into a nice doze so that it stops its usual chatter. Men-

---

[4]Murry Hope, *The Psychology of Ritual* (Shaftesbury, England: Element, 1988).

tal chatter is destructive to magic because it acts as a barrier between you and your unconscious mind, and because its content is apt to be critical of your actions. A little voice that says, "You're nuts if you think this mumbo jumbo is going to get you a job" is guaranteed to sabotage an operation.

Your conscious mind should doze during ritual, not sleep. There is work to be done in the next phase, and it's not going to be accomplished if you are "out cold." Deep trance may be good for channeling, but it's not suitable for practical magic. You'll know you're in the right state when you feel relaxed and a little dreamy but, somewhat paradoxically, well able to focus your mind on the work ahead.

3. **The Work Phase**: Having achieved Alpha State, turn to the practical work at hand. Light candles and incense, scatter waters and powders about, call upon your elemental friends, speak to your archetypes, visualize, incant and create symbolic pictures for the edification of your unconscious mind. In short, you practice magic. When you feel your unconscious mind has absorbed your message, close the ritual.

4. **The Closing**: It's important to properly shut down a ritual once the practical work has been accomplished. By invoking your archetype and elementals, and by evoking power from your own mind and heart, you have both generated and attracted tremendous energies. Ideally, the majority of these energies are absorbed or expended during the work phase of the ritual. In actual practice, however, there are usually some energies that are not absorbed by the work and that hang around, so to speak. These must be dispersed. If they aren't, they can cause havoc.

Nonhuman energies having been sent back to their proper realms, you must seal your aura (see page 80). If you don't do this, you will walk away from the ritual with your aura "flapping open like a barn door" (as Murry Hope picturesquely puts it)—easy prey for any good, bad, or indifferent energies that happen to be floating around in your vicinity. Experienced magicians look askance at gurus who do not teach their charges to seal off their auras after meditation or any other form of spiritual work. A wide open aura is dangerously susceptible to foreign influences, not all of which are benign.

CASTING A MAGIC CIRCLE

You may use any method you choose to open and close a ritual; there is no law that says you must do so with the magic circle method. But a properly constructed magic circle undeniably has several advantages over other ritual techniques. Casting a circle creates "sacred space" which encourages you to turn away from everyday concerns and to focus your mind on magical work. The confines of the circle (which is visualized as a sphere of energy) enable you to create in your imagination a protective barrier between yourself and any unwanted influences outside the circle. The circle serves to contain the energies which are "raised" within it, so that they are available to you for your practical work within the circle. No other ritual method, to my knowledge, bestows all three of these benefits.

Some Wiccan groups and other magical societies (such as the offshoots of the Golden Dawn) have, over time, standardized their use of the magic circle to the point where the same formula is used to create the circle at every ritual. Individuals, too, tend to stick with a method which has proven effective for them. Consistent use of a technique that works is good psychology. Solitary magicians need to experiment until they find the right formula.

You have the right to design your own system. In fact, it is best that you do so. Beginners, however, may need some initial guidance, and for their sake, I have designed the following ritual to create and close a "generic" magic circle.

1. **Create the circle using the four elements**: Keeping in mind your need for protection from foreign influences and the desire to contain the energies raised within the circle, face east. (The east is the traditional starting point for circle casting because it represents the place of the rising Sun and Moon—the increase of

light, in other words.) If you don't know where east is, you may designate any direction as "magical east" and begin from there. As you move around the circle (circumambulate), always turn to your right—that is, clockwise. Invoke the elements as follows:

Earth: Use some physical material (such as rocks, crystals, salt, rope or tape) to outline the perimeter of the circle. Or, you may mentally draw the circle with the help of a magical sword or dagger. Use words to focus your mind on the earth element as you create the physical circle. Make up your own, or use William Gray's short incantation on page 165.

Water: Place some spring water in a bowl or chalice and, beginning again at the east, circumambulate to the right while you sprinkle the water about the circle with your fingers. Use words to focus on the water element. Devise your own, or use the short incantation on page 144. Or, you may wish to use this lovely Golden Dawn speech:

> So therefore first the priest[ess] who governeth the works of Fire must sprinkle with the Lustral Water of the loud-resounding Sea.[5]

Air: Starting at the east, circumambulate to the right with incense. Use words—your own, the incantation on page 131, or these belonging to the Golden Dawn:

> And when, after all the Phantoms have vanished, thou shalt see that Holy formless Fire, that Fire which darts and flashes through the hidden depths of the Universe, hear thou the Voice of Fire.[6]

---

[5]Francis King and Stephen Skinner, *Techniques of High Magic*, published by Destiny Books, an imprint of Inner Traditions International, Rochester, VT © 1976, 1991; Saffron Walden, England: C. W. Daniel, © 1976, 1991. Used by permission.
[6]King, *Techniques of High Magic*, p. 74. Used by permission.

Fire: Beginning at the east, move clockwise around the circle with a candle. Create your own words, use the incantation on page 121, or this from the Golden Dawn:

> Holy art Thou, Lord of the Universe.
> Holy art Thou, whom Nature hath not formed.
> Holy art Thou, the Vast and Mighty One,
> Lord of the Light and of the Darkness.[7]

Note: If you decide to use the Golden Dawn verse (which praises the Divine Masculine), for the fire element, you should invoke the Divine Feminine at Step 3 in order to create a balance.

Your circle is now constructed and properly consecrated.

2. Invite the elements (or elementals) into the circle:

Now that you have created a magical "space" in which to work, you must invite into it those powers which can help you to accomplish your goal.

Air: Face east.

Point the fore- and middle fingers of your dominant hand at shoulder height before you, and draw the symbol for the air element (△). The symbol glows yellow.

Using your imagination, expand the symbol until it is quite large.

Verbally invoke the powers of air. Your words may be in prose or verse, elaborate or simple, improvised or formulaic. A simple: "Greetings to the swift air element and to all lovely Sylphs. Please be present for this rite and kindly bestow upon me your assistance" (or words to that effect), is perfectly adequate.

Relax a moment.

Now imagine that you can see a tall mountain inside the symbol before you. It is dawn on a spring day, the air is brisk and you can

---

[7] *Techniques of High Magic,* p. 74. Used by permission.

feel a cold wind blowing in your direction from the triangle. Breathe in the fresh, clean air.

Fire: Move to and face south.

Fingers pointed as before (in "benediction" position), draw before you the symbol representing the fire element (△). The symbol flames bright red.

Expand the symbol in your imagination.

Verbally invoke the fire element.

Relax.

Within the triangle, it is noon on a hot summer day. The sun is shining overhead. You can feel its heat upon your face and on your body. Bask in its warmth.

Water: Move to and face west.

Fingers in benediction position, draw water's symbol (▽) before you. It glitters blue.

Expand the symbol in your imagination.

Verbally invoke the water element.

You see an ocean beach in the triangle before you. It is dusk, a Full Moon shines upon the water, and a few stars glimmer in an autumn sky. The waves crash toward you. Hear their thunder. Feel the moisture in the air. Smell its salty tang.

Earth: Move to and face north.

Fingers in benediction position, draw upon the air before you the symbol for the earth element (▽̶). It glows dark green.

Expand the symbol.

Verbally invoke the earth element.

Within the triangle before you is a forest of evergreens. It is a clear, cool winter night. A slim crescent Moon rides high above the treetops and many stars sparkle overhead. You can hear the soft sounds of wildlife moving through the trees. Feel a cool breeze. Inhale the rich scent of mingled pine and cedar, cypress and fir.

3. **Invoke your chosen spiritual plane archetypes**: Ask the deity (or deities) whom you wish to assist you with your rite to join you in the circle.

Note: If you used the Golden Dawn verse for fire when you constructed the circle (see page 196), you should now invoke the Divine Feminine to create balance.

4. **Do your practical work**: Now is the time to use the magical techniques given in previous chapters.

5. **Close the Circle**: Your practical work done, you must now end the ritual and return to normality. Closing a circle is simpler than opening one. It involves movement to the left ("widdershins") instead of to the right.

Gratefully acknowledge the assistance given you by your chosen archetypes.

Face east. Thank the air element and the Sylphs for their assistance, and politely dismiss them. You might say something like this: "With gratitude and love, I acknowledge the assistance of the air element and all the Sylphs who attended this rite, and now request that they depart this circle in peace and that they return forthwith to their natural realm."

Turn to your left and face north. Acknowledge and dismiss earth and its Gnomes.

Move to your left again and face west. Dismiss water and the Ondines.

Move left once again and face south. Dismiss fire and its Salamanders.

Extinguish all candles and incense.

Seal your aura (see page 80).

If you feel ungrounded, eat or drink something immediately.

Opening and closing a magic circle sounds more complicated than it is in reality. With some practice, the work goes quickly and is very pleasurable.

CONSECRATING MAGICAL TOOLS AND IMPLEMENTS

The following procedure is designed for ambitious magicians who would like to own a full set of properly consecrated magical implements. The instructions given are very simple. Beginners who feel the need for more precise guidance are directed to the blessing rites contained in books written by Wiccans, Norse magicians, Golden Dawn devotees, and others. Consecration rites designed by the leaders of magical groups are usually formalistic and slanted in a particular spiritual direction, and they are effective. No more so, however, than this simple procedure.

1. **Physically clean the magical implement(s)** you intend to consecrate for magical use.

2. **Gather together a lighted candle**, smouldering incense, water, and salt (or earth) to represent the four elements. The colors and scents of the candle, incense and water should correlate with the implement or tool you are blessing. If you are dedicating a wand, for instance, the candle should be red and the incense of fiery scent.

3. **Construct a magic circle**, if you wish, and call upon the various archetypal and elemental energies you want to be present during the rite. It's important to emphasize the element which governs the tool you intend to bless. If you are consecrating a wand, for instance, pay particular attention to the fire element when you invoke the elements. If you're blessing a sword or dagger, concentrate on invoking air. A chalice requires emphasis on water, and a pentacle on the earth element.

4. **Consecrate the object with all four physical elements,** but with special emphasis on the element which governs it. Scatter some salt (or earth) over the implement. Rub some into the tool if this won't harm it (salt corrodes metal). Sprinkle some water upon the tool, then pass it several times through the smouldering incense. Finally, pass it quickly through the candle flame. It's most effective to use some words while you are performing these actions and, as always, it's best if the words are your own.

Here is a variation of a speech contained in an out-of-print historical novel, *The Witches*, which I use when consecrating any new tool. The actions to be performed while repeating the words are indicated in brackets:

> **In the name of my mistress, the fair one, the three-fold one, I bless you with the power and with coming and going; with earth, her body** [scatter salt over tool]; **with water, her womb** [sprinkle water over tool]; **with air, her breath** [pass tool through incense]; **with fire, her spirit** [pass tool quickly through candle flame]; **wherever you be, in heil or ill, each to each everlasting. Without beginning, without end, eternal and illuminated. Be blessed.**[8]

This channels the energy of the goddess in her triple form to you, as you bless the instrument with the four elements. It can easily be altered to call upon the power of the Divine Masculine.

5. **Close the circle.** Your instrument is now dedicated to the magical art, and the circle may be closed.

Note: It's a good idea to sleep with the tool under your pillow for several days following the rite so that the instrument is infused with your personal energy. It is the personal link with the magician, more than anything else, that makes an implement powerful.

---

[8]Jay Williams, *The Witches* (New York: Random House, 1957), p. 131.

For an added boost, tools may be exposed to sun or moonlight on magically significant dates.

USING MAGICAL INSTRUMENTS

As discussed in chapter 5, the use of props and magical instruments can play an important role in the planning and execution of magical operations, especially if you are a "technical" magician. Following is a brief summary of how some of the most commonly used magical implements can be integrated into your rituals.

1. **Place your wand, dagger or sword, chalice and pentacle upon the altar** to represent the presence of the four elements. The wand should be placed in the south, the dagger to the east, the chalice to the west, and the pentacle to the north.

2. **The implements may be used to open the circle.** For instance, magicians may wish to use their wands or daggers to "draw" (with the help of imagination) the perimeter of the circle on the ground, and they may sprinkle the circle with the water contained in the chalice. They may inscribe all the elemental symbols in the air using either wands or daggers. Or, they may draw the fire symbol with the wand, the air symbol with the dagger, the water symbol with the chalice, and the earth symbol with the pentacle.

3. **Magical instruments are often used during the working phase of a ritual as well.** A written goal, for instance, may be placed upon the pentacle, where it will absorb earthy energies, or it may be placed inside the chalice (covered, perhaps, by the pentacle) where it can "incubate" on the emotional level. For healing rites, water within the chalice may be charged and drunk. The wand may be used to direct fiery energy to parts of the body in need of it. The dagger may be used to symbolically sever links with bad habits or attitudes.

Note: Providing only that an instrument is properly matched to its task, there are no rules that govern the use of magical tools. The scope of their use is limited only by your imagination. The more they are used in magical rites, the more effective they become. Love them, use them, and they will serve you well.

CHAPTER 10

A PROSPERITY RITE

The barge she sat in, like a burnish'd throne,
Burnt on the water. The poop was beaten gold,
Purple the sails, and so perfumed that
The winds were love-sick with them; the oars were silver,
Which to the tune of flutes kept stroke, and made
The water which they beat to follow faster,
As amorous of their strokes. For her own person,
It beggar'd all description: she did lie
In her pavilion—cloth of gold, of tissue—
O'er-picturing that Venus where we see
The fancy outwork nature. [1]

—Shakespeare

It's now time to put all the magical and ritual techniques presented in previous chapters to work. I have taught a variation of the following rite for several years to classes comprised of both beginning and advanced students of magic. The ritual is more elaborate in design than the norm (presuming such a thing exists), but the amount of work involved, and the length of time it takes to perform it, will give you an opportunity to put into practice, in a coherent manner, all the techniques discussed heretofore. The experience you will gain is very definitely worth the energy and the time invested. Furthermore, the rite has proven to be very effective.

---

[1]Shakespeare's description of Cleopatra's voyage down the Nile to meet Antony (*Antony and Cleopatra*, II, ii) is surely one of the richest images in English literature.

Preliminary Discussion: You must work with the earth element if you wish to pursue greater prosperity. On a psychological level, this means that you must be down-to-earth, practical, and realistic. Let us, therefore, face some hard facts.

Very few people inherit a fortune; even fewer win the lottery. The majority of people have to earn a living in order to survive and thrive. This ritual isn't going to change these facts. What it can do, however, is give you a financial edge when you need it.

It's recommended that you perform the ritual before you ask for a raise or before you seek a new job. It's probably beneficial to perform the rite once a year in order to ensure a continuing increase in prosperity.

Timing: Ideally, the ritual should be performed during the six-month period between the Winter Solstice and the Summer Solstice (from late December through late June), and while the Moon is waxing. And, it's best if it's begun on the Winter Solstice, Candlemas, the Spring Equinox or May Day—or, failing these, on a Thursday, Sunday, or Friday. Experienced magicians, or those who don't feel a pressing need to work for more money, should stick to this time frame. Novices eager to try out their new skills and those in dire need can scrap the timing rules altogether and carry on.

Materials needed: You will need to assemble the following articles:

1. A candle of any size or shape. It should not be encased in glass. Green, yellow, or gold are traditional to prosperity magic (see page 123), but any color which fires your imagination will do.

2. A prosperity incense. This may be purchased from a metaphysical store, taken from your kitchen spice rack, or wildcrafted. Earthy herbs appropriate to prosperity work are listed in Table 4 (see page 166). If you gather your herbs from nature, be sure to follow the wildcrafting rules contained in chapter 7.

3. A cup of ordinary, sea, or rock salt.

4. A black stone of any size, but the larger the better. Stones appropriate to prosperity work are listed in Table 4 (see page 166). A dark stone found in nature is also fine.

5. A small green or yellow stone. (see Table 4).

6. Two handfuls of prosperity herbs. (see Table 4).

7. A pouch. This may be purchased in a metaphysical store, or you may make one yourself. It may be simple or elaborate, but should not be too large.

8. Five pins. Straight pins are fine, but map pins (found in any stationery store) are better, because they are aesthetically pleasing.

9. Three shiny coins. Any denomination will do.

10. Optional but recommended: A small crystal point to amplify the energies contained in the pouch once the ritual is complete; Prosperity Water to sprinkle about during the ritual; Prosperity Powder and/or Magnetic Sand to scatter about during the ritual, and to go into the pouch when the ritual is complete; personal mementos which symbolize abundance.

Now you're ready to proceed.

DAY ONE: The activities assigned to this day serve to clear out any psychological negativity relating to prosperity issues.

1. Gather all materials needed for the rite.

2. Invoke your personal and god symbols (see Appendix B).

3. Do Exercise 1 (page 42) to activate positive energy.

4. Cast a magic circle or use any other ritual opening which appeals to you.

Note: Henceforth, instructions at the start of each ritual day to "open the ritual" refer to Steps 1 through 4.

5. Consecrate your salt. Follow the procedure described in chapter 7 for charging water, and use some verbal formula during the consecration procedure. Scatter the consecrated salt before your

front door, before your back door, and on windowsills. This will absorb negativity from the atmosphere. Thank the salt-Gnomes for their assistance.

6. Draw water for a ritual purification bath, and place the remaining salt in the tub. Ask the Ondines to help you with the cleansing.

7. Take your black stone into the tub with you and hold it in your dominant hand. Ask the stone-Gnomes for assistance with your work. The salt and the stone will absorb your personal negativity, and the water will wash away prosperity blocks.

8. Perform a meditation while soaking in the tub. What is preventing you from achieving prosperity? What ingrained and counterproductive attitudes toward money did you inherit from your parents? Identify as many bad attitudes as you can.

9. After your purification bath and meditation, light your incense and greet the Sylphs resident therein. (This is the first ritual step toward calling in the good that you desire.)

10. List on a piece of paper all your negative attitudes toward money.

11. Place your black stone on top of the list so that it can symbolically absorb the negativity represented there.

12. Close the ritual and seal your aura.

DAY TWO:

1. Open the ritual (see Day One, Steps 1 through 4).

2. Cleanse your green stone, using any of the methods described in chapter 7. Ask the stone-Gnomes for assistance with your goal.

3. Perform the grounding portion of the aura-sealing exercise on page 80. (Do not perform the second part of the exercise at this point.) Grounding, as you might expect, relates to the earth element. Mother Earth is both creative and rich, and if you wish to

share her bounty, you must first of all share her energy. Grounding makes this possible.

4. Light your incense and greet all Sylphs.

5. Formulate your goal. Be sure to bind the baser aspect, and to use generic safety clauses, both of which are described in chapter 4.

6. Write down your goal on a piece of paper, and place your green stone upon it. This stone will symbolically absorb the positive qualities contained in the goal.

7. Consult an oracle to determine if, at this time, it is appropriate for you to pursue the goal as written. With a positive response from the oracle, proceed to Step 8. With a "qualified go-ahead" from the oracle, go back to Step 5, then proceed. With a negative response from the oracle, do not continue the ritual. Check again with the oracle until you get a positive response, then proceed. If the oracle, over a period of time, indicates that pursuit of your goal is not appropriate, formulate a new goal and start all over again. (For further notes regarding divination, see chapter 4.)

8. Choose or construct affirmations for use during the ritual, and for at least three months following its completion. Write down the affirmations. Tips on creating effective affirmations are contained in chapter 4.

9. Close the ritual and seal your aura (see page 80).

DAY THREE:

1. Do your affirmations in the morning (or whenever convenient) while holding your green stone in your dominant hand.

2. Open the ritual (see Day One, Steps 1 through 4).

3. Do the grounding exercise.

4. Cleanse and consecrate your candle, using any or all of the methods described in chapter 7.

5. Place the five pins at equal distances down the length of the candle.

6. Place your written goal beneath the candle.

7. Place the three coins around the candle.

8. Light the candle and greet the friendly Salamanders. As you proceed with the day's ritual activities, burn the candle down to the first pin.

9. Light your incense from the candle flame, and greet all Sylphs.

10. Pray to your chosen spiritual plane archetype for assistance with your goal (see chapter 5). (Assuming the god-form is not appropriate for this ritual.) Make your plea emotional.

11. Close the ritual and seal your aura (see page 80).

12. Extinguish the candle (even if it has not burned down to the first pin) if you plan to leave the premises or retire for the night.

DAY FOUR:

1. Do your affirmations in the morning (or whenever convenient) while holding your green stone in your dominant hand.

2. Open the ritual (see Day One, Steps 1 through 4).

3. Do the grounding exercise.

4. Light your candle and greet the Salamanders. Burn the candle down to the second pin as you perform the day's ritual activities.

5. Light your incense from the candle flame and greet all Sylphs.

6. Read your goal aloud three times.

7. Pray again to your chosen deity for assistance. Be very emotional.

8. Perform visualization while holding your green stone in your dominant hand. (See chapter 6 for tips on how to create effective visualizations.)

9. Close the ritual and seal your aura (see page 80).

10. Extinguish the candle (even if it hasn't burned down to the second pin) if you plan to leave your home or retire for the night.

DAY FIVE: Perform Steps 1 through 8 as described for Day Four, and then:

9. Bury your black stone. This has been sitting upon the piece of paper containing the list of your negative attitudes toward money, and it has busily absorbed all the bad vibes. It now needs cleansing. Mother Earth will draw out negative energies from the stone and transform them.

10. Close the ritual and seal your aura (see page 80).

11. Extinguish the candle (even if it hasn't burned down to the third pin) if you plan to leave your home or retire for the night.

DAY SIX:

1. Do your affirmations in the morning (or whenever convenient) while holding your green stone.

2. Open the ritual (see Day One, Steps 1 through 4).

3. Do your grounding exercise.

4. Burn your candle (and greet Salamanders) down to the fourth pin during the course of the day's ritual activities.

5. Light your incense (greet Sylphs) from the candle flame.

6. Read your goal aloud three times.

7. Pray to your chosen archetype for help. Be as emotional as possible.

8. Prepare to take a prosperity bath: Brew an herbal tea (as described in chapter 7) from your prosperity herbs and pour the infusion into the tub.

9. Magnetize the water with your intention and desire (see chapter 7).

10. Ask the Ondines to help you achieve your goal.

11. You may, if you wish, burn your candle and incense in the bathroom while you are soaking in the tub. Optional materials (such as Prosperity Water or oils) may also be added to the bathwater.

12. Relax and soak in the scented water for at least ten minutes. Pretend you're a sponge and soak up all the energies contained in the bathwater.

13. Perform a magical feeling or an identification exercise (see chapter 6) while holding your green stone in your dominant hand. *Feel rich.*

14. Perform your visualization, holding your green stone.

15. Close the ritual and seal your aura (see page 80).

16. Extinguish your candle (even if it hasn't burned down to the fourth pin) if you plan to leave your home or retire for the night.

DAY SEVEN:

1. Do your affirmations in the morning (or whenever convenient) while holding your green stone.

2. Open the ritual (see Day One, Steps 1 through 4).

3. Do your grounding.

4. Light your candle—be sure to greet the Salamanders—and allow it to burn down to the fifth and final pin while you perform the day's ritual activities.

5. Light your incense from the candle flame and greet all Sylphs.

6. Burn the list of negative attitudes toward money in a heat-resistant container, then flush the ashes down the toilet. Get rid of them!

7. Read your goal aloud three times.

8. Perform your visualization while holding your green stone.

9. Assemble your prosperity pouch. Put into the pouch your written goal, the five pins from your candle, a little wax from your candle, some incense ash, your green stone, a few leftover prosperity herbs, any optional materials such as Prosperity Powder, Magnetic Sand, or personal mementos.

10. Spit into the pouch. This marks the pouch as yours and yours alone.

11. Dig up your black stone. It has been cleared of negative energies and is ready to absorb more. Place the stone in a spot where it can soak up anti-abundance vibrations from both you and the environment.

12. With gratitude to the Gnomes and to Mother Earth (who has provided you with materials for the rite), bury your three coins in the Earth.

13. Close the ritual, extinguish the candle, and seal your aura (see page 80).

BEYOND THE RITUAL:

1. Wear or carry your pouch with you as often as possible. Sleep with it under your pillow. Place it on your altar when it is not "in use." The pouch's proximity to you will serve to subliminally feed your unconscious mind with the positive energies exuded by the objects within.

2. Perform your affirmations daily for at least three months.

3. Perform your visualization as often as you like.

4. Bury your black stone periodically; best done at New Moon.

5. Recharge your green stone periodically by holding it while you perform affirmations or visualization; best done at Full Moon.

6. Take practical action toward your prosperity goal as soon as possible.

7. Donate some money or time to a favored cause (or needy person). You must give in order to receive.

8. Do *not* plead further with your archetype for help with your goal. Do *not* continue to light candles or incense, or take prosperity baths, after the ritual is completed. Continual badgering of archetypes and elementals will exhaust and disgust them, and they will stop work on your behalf.

9. Forget the ritual. Get on with your life. Results will come when they come.

CHAPTER 11

CONTINUING YOUR STUDIES

[T]he finding of the Teacher is one of the tests of the aspirant.[1]

—*Dion Fortune*

All the gods are one god; and all the goddesses are one goddess, and there is one initiator.[2]

—*Dion Fortune*

The key to advancement in magic is experimentation. No amount of reading or intellectual understanding of the subject can act as a substitute for experience. Experiment with all, not just some, of the techniques presented in this book. Work with methods contained in other books as well. Practice, practice, practice.

You will find that one success leads to another. There will be some failures as well, but you'll find these to be almost as instructive as your successes, for you'll learn which methods do not suit you. Furthermore, a doomed operation will often yield an important bit of knowledge that will act as a key to future successes. Every experiment offers something of value. Experience is everything.

Keep a record of your activities so that when you see results (or don't) from your operations, you can refer back to your notes and determine which techniques produced success and which produced failure. Reward yourself when you succeed. Try another technique when you fail.

---

[1] Dion Fortune, *Sane Occultism* (London: Aquarian Press, 1967), p. 114.
[2] Dion Fortune, *Aspects of Occultism* (London: Aquarian Press, 1962), p. 34.

HIGH MAGIC

Some students wish to move beyond practical magic, and express an interest in high magic, without really knowing what this is. I'm not sure that magicians agree upon a definition, but I think it can be stated safely that it's essentially a spiritual endeavor. As I understand it, high magicians seek to become instruments of the gods, so that they may benefit others by the use of whatever skills they have developed in the course of their magical careers. It is a path that demands an unreserved love of the spiritual plane, a desire to give to others and a great deal of practical experience. Like practical magicians, high magicians may be teachers, healers, inspired intuitives, experts in oracle interpretation, channelers, or just plain magicians (i.e., instruments for change); the difference lies in the fact that high magicians are, above all, mystics. Those active in groups are usually ordained as priests or priestesses.

High magic, in my opinion, cannot be taught. A great love for spiritual plane archetypes and a desire to serve are either present and ingrained in your character or they are not. If you feel drawn to this path, you should learn everything you can about various archetypes and concentrate on the spiritual plane techniques described in this book. Most of all, you should read the works of Dion Fortune, Murry Hope, and Israel Regardie, all of whom qualify as high magicians.[3] Nothing else need be done, at least on the conscious level. The archetypes take care of their own, and will see to your development.

FINDING A TEACHER

It's entirely possible to become quite proficient in magic without studying under a teacher, so the question arises: why seek one at all? There are three good reasons. First, given the benefit of a teacher's knowledge and experience, you'll progress much faster than you would if left to your own devices. Solitary students must

---

[3]There are undoubtedly other authors and teachers who fit the description of high magicians. I am merely recommending those with whom I'm most familiar.

constantly reinvent the wheel, so to speak. This isn't bad; it's just inefficient. The second reason is that a teacher is able to provide a measure of protection while you stumble through unfamiliar territory. The third reason is that the joys and frustrations inherent in the practice of magic cannot be shared with outsiders, for no one but a fellow magician understands them. A teacher can provide you with some companionship.

Assume, for the moment, that you wish to seek out a teacher and want to know how to go about it. On a mundane level, it's really very easy. Almost every metaphysical bookstore offers classes on a variety of subjects, including magic. Visit your local store, put your name on its mailing list and introduce yourself to the owner or the salespeople. Check the place out carefully. If you like the store and the people who run it, the chances are good that you'll like what they offer in the way of events and lectures. Attend the ones that interest you and eventually you'll discover a possible teacher, either in the flesh or through word of mouth. If attending classes isn't possible, you might consider writing to the author of a book which you have admired. Write in care of the publisher; your letter will be forwarded to the author.

Now to the hard part. Good teachers are usually not very accessible (for reasons we'll discuss later), and they're extremely selective when it comes to taking on prospective students. You, as a student, must somehow convince a teacher that you are worthy of tuition.

An old metaphysical adage states that "When the pupil is ready, the teacher appears." Unfortunately for the eager student, "readiness" is not measured solely in terms of enthusiasm. Teachers look for various qualities in students before they will agree to take them on. Different teachers have different requirements, of course, but generally speaking, they look for intelligence, psychological health, dedication, and—believe it or not—a certain degree of skepticism concerning things that go bump in the night. Most of all, teachers want to see evidence that you have studied on your own. Metaphysical stores today are flooded with books on magic, so you have no excuse for saying to a teacher: "Teach me everything that I could learn on my own, if I tried." Make it clear that you have done a lot of reading and experimentation, and the chances are good that the teacher will take an interest in you.

After having read Murry Hope's books and spent some time with her, I timidly asked if she would be willing to take me as a student. "No, dear," she said without hesitation. I managed to roll with this punch, then none too politely demanded: "Why not?" "Because, dear," she said in her usual mild way, "the Path must be trod alone." Since I had spent the previous twenty-six years treading the path alone, and since Murry knew this very well, I was speechless. She left for England a few hours later. But from that day on I referred to her as my teacher, which she indeed became. The moral here is: If, after much consideration, you think you have found the right teacher, don't take no for an answer. It might not work, but it's worth a try. Perseverance is something teachers look for in a student.

Dion Fortune wrote often of mysterious adepts who needed a great deal of solitude to do whatever it is that adepts do. Early on in my career, I was pretty much convinced that these shadowy esotericists were figments, more or less, of Fortune's imagination. I know better now. Esotericists do indeed need a great deal of time to themselves—all the more if they are teachers. Magicians need to experiment, think, meditate, learn, and most of all, to spend time with various helpers such as beloved archetypes, tutors, and elemental companions. Most esotericists are natural introverts who are more at home with their helpers than they are with human beings. Solitary research and experimentation feeds their souls and, incidentally, fuels the charisma which is often their hallmark. So it is not sheer contrariness which makes a teacher say an unhesitating "No" when approached by a hopeful student. It is the teacher's need to insure enough time and solitude for the esoteric pursuits so necessary to his or her continued growth and self-education. The fruits of these solitary activities will eventually be passed on to those students who manage to make it past the barriers.

But consider the other side of the issue. Presuming you have decided that you would like to find a teacher—or that you have one in mind, but are unsure as to whether he or she is a safe choice—what should you look for? I have only my personal experience, some advice given by Dion Fortune in *Sane Occultism*, and a few anecdotes told me by acquaintances to go on, so I'm not an expert on the subject.[4] However, here are some general guidelines which may be helpful.

Look for a strong sense of ethics. An ethical teacher will tell you at the outset that it is not morally permissible to magically manipulate another human being, or to harm any living creature, and that there are serious penalties to be paid for such behavior. Any teacher who says otherwise is unscrupulous and is after your money, your body, your blind obedience, or some combination thereof. Any teacher who neglects to mention his or her ethical principles at the outset is suspect and probably should not be trusted.

Look for sanity. This may be difficult to judge, particularly for beginners and young people, because a magician's view of life differs so radically from that of the layman. Sanity as defined here is more a matter of approach than philosophy held. Dion Fortune recommended that individuals who are under psychic attack go see a Charlie Chaplin movie, because laughter is a bright thing that chases away dark energies. She also recommended that attack victims avoid solitude, eat regularly, and physically avoid the perpetrator of the attack. Eminently sane advice—and effective. Compare this to the approach of a well-known West Coast school of occultism whose teachers see "entities" of malign intent infesting the auras of 99 percent of the population, and who maintain that you cannot advance until you are deloused by a great deal of elaborate (and presumably expensive) ceremony. I have met graduates of this school; they are downright paranoid and in dire need of deprogramming. I'm not denying that malign entities exist or that psychic attack exists, but I do maintain that harping on such things is dangerous because constant negative suggestion of this sort can do a lot of psychological damage.

On the other hand, it's possible to be too positive in one's outlook. One of Murry Hope's teachers once told her that vision

---

[4]*Sane Occultism:* see chapters called "Group Karma in Occult Societies," "Authority and Obedience in Occultism," "The Left-Hand Path," and "Occultism and Immorality."

depends entirely upon perspective: the higher one is able to fly, so to speak, the larger the perspective. Hovering at tree-top level over an idyllic glade, for instance, you see very little but the lovely scene beneath. Fly a little higher, however, and the slums come into view. A teacher who proposes that life, human nature, and magic are all sugar and roses hasn't enough perspective to teach responsibly. Hardship and cruelty exist, and to deny this is dangerous, for we are easily blindsided by what we refuse to acknowledge. Too many metaphysical teachers today are unwilling to look at the darker side of nature, human or otherwise.

I am obviously not suggesting that teachers should spend all their time discussing the uglier aspects of life and magic with you. I'm simply saying that teachers must at least be cognizant of these, and that they should be prepared to issue warnings (and explanations thereof) when they see you courting trouble. One of the primary responsibilities of a teacher is to protect those too new to the game to know how to protect themselves. Simplicity of approach, common sense, and a balanced perspective are the hallmarks of a sane teacher.

The issue of perspective also sheds light on how teachers are able to give guidance. One cannot truly master the physical plane until one has risen above it, metaphorically speaking, and explored the cosmos a little. This is one of the reasons why magicians spend a good deal of time traveling on the astral levels. Exploring other realms gives them a different perspective on earthly life, as do astrological and numerological knowledge. The use of these disciplines gives teachers information on the cosmic and karmic backgrounds and characters of their students so that they may gently guide them onto paths for which they are well suited. Without such guidance, students can waste a lot of time searching for their proper magical niches, so to speak, when they could be honing their magical skills.

Look for evidence of experience. Students naturally expect an author or lecturer to be experienced in magic, but unfortunately not all teachers live up to expectations. I am increasingly convinced that some writers do not practice magic and that they never have. I well remember trying to perform a piece of purely physical magic recommended by a prolific writer on the subject and finding that the operation was physically impossible—not dangerous in any way, just impossible. Had the author known this, he presumably would not have advised his readers to attempt it. Does he perform magic at all? Had he ever? One cannot help but wonder. If you read a book or attend a lecture and like what the teacher has to say, put into practice whatever techniques he or she recommends. If these are workable and lead to eventual success, you're probably on the right track. If, after considerable and successful experimentation, you feel you want to learn more, write the teacher and request personal instruction.

Look for a teacher who stresses safety measures. A teacher who neglects these is either inexperienced, or irresponsible, or both. One of Britain's most experienced Wiccans, Maxine Sanders, recently reviewed a book written by someone who either didn't know anything about magic or didn't care about the reader's welfare. According to Sanders, the author instructed readers how to conjure up a spirit in human form, but offered no advice on preparation for the rite, protection during the ritual, or how to banish the spirit. Sanders rightfully comments that the author is "sadly lacking in a sense of responsibility."[5]

I wish I could say that irresponsibility of this sort is the exception rather than the rule, but I cannot. I have heard a lot of hair-raising stories over the years concerning questionable and dangerous practices indulged in by teachers at the expense of their students. Most recently, I was told a horror story about an internationally respected author who led a group of people in a series of guided meditations. Several people went out of their minds and had to be hospitalized. This is appalling, particularly since the teacher in question had impeccable occult "credentials" and presumably enough experience to prevent such a catastrophe.

What went wrong? The teacher was reportedly working with spiritual energies that had proven troublesome in the past, and clearly should have taken greater-than-usual precautions, but apparently did not. And it would seem that participants were not

---

[5]See *The Occult Observer*, Summer 1992.

screened carefully prior to the experiments. Since not everyone is psychologically equipped to explore ASCs in depth, it is a teacher's responsibility to determine ahead of time whether or not participants are capable of withstanding the rigors of an ambitious program. Those who are not should be eliminated from the group for their own safety. And if unanticipated problems arise during an experiment, as they sometimes do, a teacher should be fully equipped to handle the situation easily and with dispatch. A teacher who is not confident of his or her abilities to handle crises should not attempt this kind of work at all.

In view of the foregoing, you may justifiably ask how you are to know if a teacher of sterling reputation is, in fact, competent to teach. There's no easy answer to this question. My advice, meager though it may be, is to search for evidence of safety measures in an author's works and to query those who have studied with the individual before making a commitment to study with him or her.

Look for a teacher who genuinely loves children and/or animals. Such an individual has a reverence for innocence and non-human life forms, and wouldn't dream of harming a helpless creature. This weeds out the arrogant, sadistic, and antisocial types.

To avoid the paranoiacs, look for a sense of humor. According to the American Psychiatric Association's *Diagnostic and Statistical Manual of Mental Disorders*, those who suffer from paranoid personality disorder are "overrepresented among leaders of cults and other fringe groups" and "have no true sense of humor."[6] There are other signs of paranoia, of course, but usually they aren't immediately obvious, while an utter lack of humor is. Besides, studying under a dour teacher wouldn't be any fun.

Beware of teachers who demand a great deal of money for their services. Those who ask you to give up your life savings and your home should be assiduously avoided. And be wary of teachers who demand too much of your time. It's not necessary to spend long hours each week for several years under a teacher in order to learn magic. You need guidance, then time alone to work

---

[6]American Psychiatric Association, *Diagnostic and Statistical Manual of Mental Disorders* (Washington, DC, 1987), pp. 337–338.

with the information a teacher has provided, then a little more guidance, then more experimentation time. And you need time to read and think. In other words, you need to grow on your own. Besides, most students need to watch their budgets; years of study, even at low rates, can be expensive.

Consider your choice of teacher very carefully before you commit yourself to his or her guidance. A good teacher can bestow many benefits, but a bad one can do irreparable harm. Take your time before settling on a teacher. *Take your time.*

FINDING A GROUP

Some students may wish to supplement their solitary work with group activities, and this can often be quite beneficial. Leaders of magical societies are usually experienced and can give guidance and protection to beginners. Group worship of revered archetypes can satisfy the needs of those who are spiritually inclined. And gregarious types, or those in need of family, will appreciate the camaraderie to be found among like-minded individuals.

Finding the right group to join is as challenging as finding the right teacher. The physical part isn't difficult. Most metaphysical bookstores are aware of groups operating in their localities and some can provide names and addresses of societies interested in attracting new members. The hard part is finding a group with which you resonate and which is safe to join. Since groups are founded by individuals who set the tone, so to speak, for their societies, the criteria used for choosing a good teacher may be applied to groups as well. Don't be afraid to ask questions of anyone—members or store-owners—who might know something about the society before you join it.

Group activities are usually centered more upon spiritual objectives than magical goals. This is one of the reasons why mystical types are drawn to esoteric societies. It is very important, therefore, to look for a group with a spiritual orientation similar to your own. If you are comfortable with the Judeo-Christian tradition and like the Cabala and ritualistic high drama, for instance, you might wish to join one of the offshoots of the Golden Dawn. If you are fond of the pagan deities and like your ritual on the folksy side, one of the Wiccan groups is probably for you. The archetypes honored by Wiccans differ from group to group, however, so you'll need to do some further investigation before making a commitment.

As you continue to develop on your own—that is, apart from your group—be aware that you will probably outgrow whatever society you have joined. Dion Fortune was originally interested in Helena Blavatsky's Theosophical Society, then received tutoring from a Freemason, then joined the Golden Dawn, and finally founded her own Society of the Inner Light, which still exists in England. Freya Aswynn, author of a book on runes titled *Leaves of Yggdrasil*, writes that she was originally a Rosicrucian, then a Wiccan, and is now a Priestess of Odin.[7] Moving from group to group in search of the right niche is not uncommon. Sometimes finding stability within a group—or, more accurately, within a spiritual system—is simply a matter of psychological maturity.

If you are intrigued by the Norse deities, for instance, you might join a group which honors them, only to feel a call later on from the Egyptian archetypes—a change so radical that it necessitates departure from the Norse group. Or if you have a taste for the Cabala, you might join a Golden Dawn society only to discover a distaste for long-winded ritual speeches and a yen for some down-home Wiccan ritual. Some students develop so fast, spiritually speaking, that the sheer pace of their growth prevents them from finding and joining groups. Others are so eclectic in their spiritual tastes that it is impossible for them to find a congenial group. If you are an eclectic type, you are probably better off as a solitary.

If the spiritual limitations inherent in group work are often a problem for serious magicians, so are group politics. Dion Fortune wrote of the "wars" that were taking place among the leaders of the Golden Dawn when she joined it. Murry Hope, who should know, writes:

---

[7]Freya Aswynn, *Leaves of Yggdrasil* (St. Paul, MN: Llewellyn, 1990).

It would appear to require a very stable and well-integrated person to cope with the stresses and personality clashes which inevitably rear their ugly heads at some time or other during group proceedings. These days in particular, psychic groups, lodges and covens appear to mushroom overnight. The initial enthusiasm, however, eventually gives way to dissatisfaction, personal sniping, behind-the-back planning and eventual disintegration—which usually involves a few partnership musical chairs, and one or more of the disenchanted leavers starting up another group on their own.[8]

Spiritual and magical growth appear to take a back seat when power and leadership are up for grabs. No wonder magicians dedicated to self-development tend to quit group work altogether in order to pursue a solitary path or to teach.

The character of a group may change after an important leader leaves, and this may affect individual members. Murry Hope cofounded The Atlanteans in London during the 50's and headed their healing circle for a long time, then left to work as a solitary and to write. Several years after her departure, the group asked her to help them switch from the Atlantean to a Greek orientation, as members could no longer cope with high-frequency Atlantean energies. Dion Fortune wrote of the changes which took place in the Theosophical Society after Blavatsky died, and of the "back-to-Blavatsky" movement which superseded them.[9] Fortune's own group appparently became much enamored of Alice Bailey's work after Fortune's death, then tired of Bailey and returned to Fortune's teachings. *Plus ça change, plus c'est la même chose.*

GROWING INTO MAGIC

Magical and spiritual growth is ultimately up to the individual. A teacher's goal should not be to forcefeed you with intellectual in-

---

[8]Murry Hope, *The Psychology of Ritual* (Shafesbury, England: Element, 1988), p. 53.
[9]Dion Fortune, *Applied Magic* (London: Aquarian Press, 1979), pp. 70–71.

formation, but rather to encourage you to discover the instinctual and intuitive knowledge that exists deep within you, and to develop skills based upon this knowledge. The finest teacher in the world may be able to point the way and to provide some protection during the exploration process, but that is all he or she can do. You must do the rest. There is no other way.

Groups may confer formal degrees of initiation upon members but, contrary to the claims made by some secret societies, these do not automatically bestow magical powers or grant instant access to esoteric knowledge. True initiation occurs as a result of life experience, and it manifests as a deep-level understanding of some issue which has previously proven troublesome or puzzling. Occasionally, it manifests as a startling experience which forces one to alter perspective on some important issue.

An initiatory experience is a signal from your unconscious mind that you have mastered some aspect of existence and that a new challenge lies ahead. It is both an ending and a beginning. Initiation may occur anywhere, at any time. It usually occurs without much fanfare—in a dream, for instance, or after a particularly illuminating therapy session. Most often, it occurs while you are performing some mundane task. It does not occur because you are in the presence of an inspired teacher, or because you have taken part in some dramatic ritual, though either of these may act as catalysts. Initiation occurs only when you are ready, at the deepest level, to move forward.

Magicians dedicated to developing their skills, both practical and otherwise, may study with fine teachers, or join several groups, but ultimately it is the work they do by themselves which makes them powerful. In the end, all serious magicians are solitaries.

APPENDICES

APPENDIX A
TEMPERAMENT QUESTIONNAIRE

The following questionnaire tests readers for the strengths (and weaknesses) of each of the four functions (elements) within their personalities. It is my own invention. My sources include tests devised by psychologists and extensive conversations with a Jungian psychiatrist. Since I am not a psychologist, however, I cannot claim that the questionnaire is in any way scientific. Readers who wish to test themselves using an instrument created by qualified psychologists are advised to take the test offered by David Keirsey and Marilyn Bates in their book, *Please Understand Me.*[1]

INSTRUCTIONS

Answer the questions on pages 227 through 230. An answer sheet is provided on page 231. Decide on answer a, b, c, or d and put a check mark in the proper column of the answer sheet. Scoring is discussed on page 232.

TEMPERAMENT QUESTIONNAIRE

1. **Which type of book or movie appeals to you most?** a. Science fiction and horror b. Humor and satire c. Romantic drama d. Adventures and thrillers 2. **Which are you most proud of, your** b. Mental clarity c. Compassion	3. **Having status is** a. Not important at all d. Very important 4. **Which occupational category would you select?** a. Design and research b. Teaching, journalism, business administration c. Social work, psychology, public relations, practical medicine d. Courtroom law, politics, surgical medicine

---

[1]David Kiersey and Marilyn Bates, *Please Understand Me* (Del Mar, CA: Prometheus Nemesis Book Co., 1984).

TEMPERAMENT QUESTIONNAIRE (CONTINUED)

5. Which would you rather do with a friend?
b. Discuss ideas
c. Share stories of the past

6. Which is worse, to be told that you
a. Are in a rut
d. Have your head in the clouds

7. Which attract you more?
a. People who are imaginative
d. People who are sensible

8. Which do you usually trust more?
a. Your hunches
d. Your experience

9. When under stress, what are you most likely to do?
a. Turn to your imagination
b. Formulate a plan
c. Explore your emotions
d. Take action

10. Which is most distressing to you?
b. To have your plans go awry
c. To misinterpret another person's feelings

11. Do you think genius is more likely to be the result of
a. Inspiration
d. Hard work

12. Which bothers you more?
b. Lack of justice
c. Lack of mercy

13. When making important decisions, do you tend to rely more upon
b. Objective analysis
c. Subjective standards

14. Which quotation are you most likely to agree with?
b. "Justice transcends even friendship."
c. "My friends are my estate."

15. Which do you value the most?
a. Your personal vision
b. The realm of ideas
c. Human relationships
d. The physical world

TEMPERAMENT QUESTIONNAIRE (CONTINUED)

16. **Which statement best expresses your attitude toward time?**
a. The future is the only thing that really matters.
b. History is important because it explains the present and future.
c. Traditions are important and should be maintained.
d. The present is the most important thing.

17. **What distresses you more?**
a. Being pinned down
d. Being fenced in

18. **Are you more likely to be swayed by:**
b. Logic
c. An appeal to your emotions

19. **Is it worse to be**
b. Undiscriminating
c. Too critical

20. **Which would you rather do?**
b. Discuss issues in detail
c. Agree on issues

21. **Which is worse?**
a. To be called a nut
d. To be ignored

22. **Before making an important decision, you**
a. Ignore facts and wait for inspiration
d. Carefully consider all the facts of the situation

23. **Are you more ruled by**
b. Your head
c. Your heart

24. **Which statement usually describes your attitude about the future?**
a. I am extremely optimstic about the future.
b. I think things will get better in time.
c. The future worries me.
d. The future is irrelevant.

25. **What is your natural inclination?**
b. To be fair-minded
c. To be sympathetic

26. **If you had great power, how would you use it?**
a. To change the world entirely
b. To implement important ideas
c. To help those who suffer
d. To control your own actions and, if necessary, those of others

TEMPERAMENT QUESTIONNAIRE (CONTINUED)

27. Which would you prefer to wear?
a. A costume
d. A uniform

28. During leisure time, which would you rather do?
a. Dream about the future
b. Read a book
c. Visit a friend
d. Participate in a sport

29. Which do you consider the greater compliment?
b. To be called cool-headed
c. To be called warm-hearted

30. Which do you trust more?
a. Your imagination
d. The evidence of your senses

31. Is it worse to be
b. Too passionate
c. Too objective

32. Which do you tend to rely upon and trust the most?
a. Inspiration
d. Your skills

33. Which is the more accurate statement?
a. I am more speculative than realistic.
d. I am more realistic than speculative.

34. Which means most to you?
a. To be different
b. To maintain a well-ordered lifestyle
c. To attain emotional unity with others
d. To be self-sufficient

35. Would you rather
a. Be different
d. Fit in with the group

36. Looking back on the past is
a. A waste of time
b. Necessary in order to understand the present and future
c. Very pleasurable
d. Morbid

37. Which is most important to you?
a. Developing a personal vision
b. Adhering to your principles
c. Being loyal to loved ones
d. Being a productive member of a team

TEMPERAMENT SCORES

Number	A	B	C	D	Number	A	B	C	D
1					20				
2					21				
3					22				
4					23				
5					24				
6					25				
7					26				
8					27				
9					28				
10					29				
11					30				
12					31				
13					32				
14					33				
15					34				
16					35				
17					36				
18					37				
19									
Subtotal					Total				

TEMPERAMENT SCORING

Add up the check marks in the a, b, c, and d columns.

Column A represents the intuitive function and the fire element.

Column B represents the thinking function and the air element.

Column C represents the feeling function and the water element.

Column D represents the sensate function and the earth element.

The column which contains the greatest number of check marks indicates your strongest (primary) function/element. This function is natural to you, and is well developed.

The column containing the next–greatest number of check marks indicates your secondary function/element. This function may be nearly as well developed as your primary function. The primary and secondary functions are habitually used and relied upon during the first half of the life span.

The column containing the third–greatest number of check marks indicates a function/element which will require conscious effort to develop. Normally, the urge to develop the third function does not surface until mid-life. Until such development occurs, use of the third function tends to be unreliable.

The column containing the smallest number of check marks indicates your weakest function/element. Its use tends to be unconscious and very unreliable until it is consciously developed. Such development usually occurs late in life and only with great effort.

It is the goal of magicians, and of those who wish to be psychologically well rounded, to consciously develop, as soon as possible, the third and fourth functions/elements within their temperaments.

APPENDIX B
PERSONAL SYMBOL EXERCISES
AND
GOD/GODDESS SYMBOL EXERCISES

The following two exercises are reproduced from Murry Hope's *Ancient Egypt: The Sirius Connection*.[1]

PERSONAL SYMBOL EXERCISE

Lie down or seat yourself comfortably, close your eyes, and take an imaginary journey backwards in linear time to the moment of your birth. Some people I have spoken to tell me that they have visualized this rather like playing a film backwards, so that the end progresses towards the beginning.

Visualise yourself poised to ensoul the embryo that is to become your present self, and enter the womb at the point of your actual conception. Pause for one moment to "feel" the energies surrounding you and become aware of a silver cord which connects the spiritual "you" to its physical counterpart. Then slowly start to move forward in time, passing through your embryonic growth and the drama of your birth. Take hold of the silver cord and pull it along with you as you proceed forward towards the present. As you pass through the experiences of childhood, pause here and there to register a particularly important or traumatic experience or meaningful event, great happiness, pain or new awareness, and *record each incident by making a knot in your silver cord.* Continue your mental travels through your teenage years forward to whichever part of your life you have now reached, *but always imbibing the sensations of each significant episode and knotting your cord accordingly.*

You will finally arrive in the present, trailing your knotted silver cord. Here is what you do next: take the conception end and join it to the point which represents the present, thus creating a

---

[1]The exercises are from Murry Hope, *Ancient Egypt: The Sirius Connection* (Shaftesbury, Dorset, England: Element, 1990), pp. 132–135. Used by permission.

circle after the style of the Ouroborus, the serpent eating its own tail. This circle will represent the sum total of your inner and outer time experiences as related to the "now." Continuing to employ your creative imagination, lay the circle flat and step into the center. You will immediately find yourself gradually sinking fearlessly through a gentle darkness, to eventually touch down in what can only be described as the primordial womb.

This experience will vary with each individual. Keep relaxed, breathe slowly and deeply, and you will find yourself automatically rising, but the way in which you rise will again be unique to you. You may find yourself climbing a flight of steps, flying with new-found wings, ascending the side of a mountain, or being raised in a lift. But ascend you will, and very soon you will arrive at the top of this deep well of your experience. *The first thing you see when you reach the top will be your own personal symbol.*

For example, you may find that after plodding laboriously up a long flight of stairs, upon reaching the top you may notice a window through which you look and perceive a tree in full blossom: that tree will be your personal symbol. Or you may discover a peg upon which hangs a simple hat, in which case that hat will be your symbol. Until you try you will not know, but the important thing is that it must be the first impression that comes to you. No use trying the whole exercise again because you find yourself face to face with a cow, and, not being particularly keen on bovines, you decided to have another go to see if you can find a nice silver cross or an ankh which you would much prefer. After all, the cow was the symbol of Hathor, and to have it as your personal symbol would immediately connect you with the energies of that goddess, as well as indicating that you have possibly served in her temple at Denderah in the linear past!

Having discovered your true personal symbol, always keep it in mind for safety; it will link you with the energies of your group soul, as well as identify you once you are outside the wavelengths of the terrestrial frequencies. Visualise it when going to sleep, when frightened or tired, or when effecting any form of time travel or altered state of consciousness.

GOD/GODDESS SYMBOL EXERCISE

The next symbol you need to know is your god/goddess symbol, which constitutes additional protection since it represents your own personal link with the Infinite—the Center Point of the Universe—call it God, the Goddess, the Ultimate, or whatever.

Having fully familiarised yourself with your personal symbol, relax to a meditative posture and visualise it as strongly as you are able. Then amplify the symbol in your mind's eye until it becomes large enough to create a seat for you to mount or relax into. Should it be a tree, you could recline in its branches; if a swan, you may sit astride its back; a ribbon or piece of cloth can be shaped into a cushion or hammock, and so forth. With abstract or geometrical designs such as a star, a little imagination is needed to make a comfortable seat, but a close look at the headdresses of the ancient Egyptian gods will provide plenty of clues. After all, these were their personal symbols, would you not think?

Once you feel comfortable and absolutely secure in your hold, proceed as follows: start to rotate your symbol clockwise, slowly at first but increasing speed as you spin. Close your psychic eye so that you do not feel dizzy. You may find that you need to give the whole process a little encouraging push to start with, although some people who have tried this have gained momentum with a minimum of mental effort. The time taken is of no consequence, and will again vary with the individual. For a moment or two you will spin and then you will slow down, come to a halt, and land somewhere in outer time. Using your mind's eye, look around: the first thing you see will be an archetype appropriate to you who will greet you or give you some point of reference. You may, for instance, find yourself in a lush meadow where a lady wearing a blue gown and crowned with flowers comes forth to greet you. She may take the wreath of flowers from her head and present it to you—that wreath will be your god/goddess symbol. Note also the nature of the being who greets you. In your terms of reference, it could be a god or a goddess, a maternal or paternal figure, a personality associated with the particular religious faith which has influenced your terrestrial programming, or a cosmic being. But whomever you see will represent the other half of your natural spiritual polarity.

Once established, personal and god/goddess symbols should be used when undertaking any form of psychic or occult work, time travel, or meditation. These are your security codes which will ensure you safe passage through the unfamiliar territories of altered states of consciousness. *Under no condition should* (altered states of consciousness) *be practised when under the infuence of drugs of any kind, medicinal or otherwise, alcohol, or any other stimulant likely to effect a distortion of left-brain logic.* Such chemicals, being unnatural to the human body, create vortices of negative energy which are easily identified by aliens. Therefore, in addition to distorted messages, "bad trips," and the unlikelihood of attracting benign energies, the probability of personal fragmentation resulting in severe mental illness is certainly on the cards. You have been warned!

BIBLIOGRAPHY

Assagioli, Roberto. *The Act of Will*. Baltimore, MD: Penguin Books, 1974.

Aswynn, Freya. *Leaves of Yggdrasil*. St. Paul, MN: Llewellyn, 1990.

Bolen, Jean. *Gods in Everyman*. San Francisco: HarperCollins, 1989.

_____. *Goddesses in Everywoman*. San Francisco, HarperCollins, 1984.

Campbell, Florence. *Your Days are Numbered*. Marina del Rey, CA: DeVorss, 1958.

Campbell, Joseph, ed. *The Portable Jung*. New York, NY: Penguin Books, 1980.

Crossley-Holland, Kevin. *The Norse Myths*. New York: Pantheon Books, 1980.

Cunningham, Donna. *Healing Pluto Problems*. York Beach, ME: Samuel Weiser, 1991.

Diagnostic and Statistical Manual of Mental Disorders. Third Ed., revised. Washington, DC: American Psychiatric Association, 1987.

Fielding, Charles and Carr Collins. *The Story of Dion Fortune*. Dallas: Star & Cross Publication, 1985.

Fortune, Dion (Violet Firth). *Applied Magic*. London: Aquarian Press, 1979.

_____. *Aspects of Occultism*. London: The Aquarian Press, 1962.

_____. *The Machinery of the Mind*. York Beach, ME: Samuel Weiser, 1980.

_____. *Moon Magic*. York Beach, ME: Samuel Weiser, 1978.

_____. *The Mystical Qabalah*. York Beach, ME: Samuel Weiser, 1984.

_____. *Practical Occultism in Daily Life*. London: Aquarian Press, 1969.

_____. *The Problem of Purity*. York Beach, ME: Samuel Weiser, 1980.

_____. *Psychic Self-Defense*. York Beach, ME: Samuel Weiser, 1976.

_____. *Sane Occultism*. London: Aquarian Press, 1967.

_____. *The Sea Priestess*. York Beach, ME: Samuel Weiser, 1978.

_____. *The Secrets of Dr. Taverner*. St. Paul, MN: Llewellyn, 1978.

Gardner, Joy. *Colors and Crystals.* Freedom, CA: Crossing Press, 1988.

Goodrick-Clarke, Nicholas. *The Occult Roots of Nazism.* London: Aquarian Press, 1985.

Goodwin, Matthew Oliver. *Numerology, the Complete Guide.* North Hollywood, CA: Newcastle, 1981.

Graves, Robert. *The Greek Myths.* New York & London: Penguin, 1968.

Gray, W. G. *Magical Ritual Methods.* York Beach, ME: Samuel Weiser, 1980.

Greene, Liz. *Saturn: A New Look at an Old Devil.* York Beach, ME: Samuel Weiser, 1976.

Hall, Calvin S., and Vernon J. Nordby. *A Primer of Jungian Psychology.* New York: New American Library, 1973.

Hay, Louise L. *Heal Your Body.* Carson, CA: Hay House, 1984.

———. *Feeling Fine* (audiotape). Carson, CA: Hay House.

Hope, Murry. *Ancient Egypt: The Sirius Connection.* Shaftesbury, England: Element, 1990.

———. *Essential Woman: Her Mystery, Her Power.* London: Collins/Crucible, 1991.

———. *Olympus, Self-Discovery and the Greek Archetypes.* London: Aquarian Press,1991.

———. *Practical Atlantean Magic.* London: Aquarian Press, 1991.

———. *Practical Celtic Magic.* London: Aquarian Press, 1987.

———. *Practical Egyptian Magic.* New York: St. Martin's Press, 1984.

———. *Practical Greek Magic.* London: Aquarian Press, 1985.

———. *Practical Techniques of Psychic Self-Defense.* New York: St. Martin's Press, 1983.

———. *The Psychology of Healing.* Shaftesbury, England: Element, 1989.

———. *The Psychology of Ritual.* Shaftesbury, England: Element, 1988.

———. *The Way of Cartouche.* New York: St. Martin's Press, 1985.

Jarret, R. H. *It Works.* Marina del Rey, CA: DeVorss, 1976.

Jung, Carl G. *Man and his Symbols.* Garden City, NY: Doubleday, 1964.

Kiersey, David and Marilyn Bates. *Please Understand Me.* Del Mar, CA: Prometheus Nemesis Book Co., 1984.

King, Francis and Stephen Skinner. *Techniques of High Magic.* Rochester, VT: Inner Traditions, 1976.

Larousse Encyclopedia of Mythology. London: Hamlyn, 1968.

Malone, Michael. *Psychetypes.* New York: Pocket Books, 1977.

Neville. *Prayer—The Art of Believing; Feeling is the Secret; Freedom for All; Out of this World; Resurrection* (in one volume). Los Angeles: G. & J. Publishing Co., 1966.

Regardie, Israel. *The Golden Dawn.* St. Paul, MN: Llewellyn, 1984.

_____. *The Middle Pillar.* St. Paul, MN: Llewellyn, 1985.

_____. *My Rosicrucian Adventure.* St. Paul, MN: Llewellyn, 1971.

Shakespeare, William. *The Riverside Shakespeare.* Boston: Houghton Mifflin, 1974.

Waram, Marilyn. *The Book of Neptune.* San Diego, CA: ACS Publications, 1992.

Wing, R. L. *I Ching Workbook,* New York: Doubleday, 1979.

INDEX

A

adept, 73
Adonis, 59
affirmation, 32, 37, 38, 50
  positive energy, 42
  prosperity, 46
  receptivity, 44
  three steps to effective, 39
  tips on using, 45
altered states of consciousness
  (ASC), 157, 158, 220
Amazons, 62
amulets, 139
animal kingdom, 112
angels, 55
anger, 122, 123
ankh, 73
Anubis, 71
Aphrodite, 58, 60, 95, 114, 133,
  183
Apollo, 59, 62, 63
Arachne, 76
archangels, 55
archetypes, 186
  and ego, 76
  Arthurian, 66
  balances character, 62
  Celtic, 65, 78
  choosing, 55, 58
  choosing patron, 59
  contacting, 71

Egyptian, 78
establishing bond, 63
Greek, 78
Norse, 78
Roman, 78
within yourself, 72
Ares, 59, 60, 183
Artemis, 59, 60, 62, 68
Assagioli, Roberto, 23, 26, 81
Astral travel, 157, 159, 160
astrology, 36
Aswynn, Freya, 222
Athena, 59, 60, 62
Atlanteans, 223
atmosphere
  cleansing, 148
aura
  how to seal, 80
Autumn Equinox, 182

B

Bailey, Alice, 233
Bast, 59, 60, 98
Bates, Marilyn, 225
bathing, ritual, 150, 209
Beltane, 182
binding the baser aspect, 29
Blavatsky, H.P., 222
Blessing Powder, 170
Bolen, Jean, 63
breath, use of, 131, 137

C

Cabala, 221, 222
Campbell, Florence, 37
candidates
  for initiation, 7
candles, 121
  cleansing, 124
  color, 123
  to consecrate, 124
  to oil, 125
  to spray, sprinkle, anoint, 125
Candlemas, 181
cards, 33
cellar, 19
Ceres, 59
Chakras, 151, 160, 161, 164
chalice, 144
channelers, 214
circle
  casting the, 194
clearing, 100
  etheric, 104
  fear, 103
  letter, 106
  visual method, 101 (see also
  negativity and *timing*)
colors, 123
conscious mind, 5
consequences
  anticipating, 26
Creativity Water, 113
Crossley-Holland, Kevin, 57
Crowther, Patricia, xvii
crystals, 165, 167, 168
  care, 169
  charging, 168
  cleansing, 167

Cunningham, Donna, 11
cup: see *chalice, goblet*
cycles
  solar and lunar, 179
dagger, 82, 131
days of the week, 183

D

deities
  Celtic, working with, 65; see
  archetypes
Demeter, 59
depression, 124
Devil (Christian), 141
Diana, 59
Dionysus, 62
disease
  positive/negative aspects, 27,
  28
divination, 23, 32

E

Earth Mother, 59
element
  air, 112, 131, 132, 153
  earth, 59, 112, 153, 165
  fire, 70, 112, 121, 122, 133
  functions, 115
  water, 112, 144, 146, 166
elementals, 117, 186
  dealing with, 119
  Kingdoms, 173; see also
  *Gnomes, Ondines,
  Salamanders, Sylphs*
elements (four) 17, 111, 167,
  181, 194, 201
emotion, 18, 153

emotional
  clearing, 38
  negativity, wash away, 145
energy, 124
envy, 123
essence fragments, 99
ethics, 217
Exercises
  One, 42
  Two, 44
  Three, 61
  Four 61
  Five, 80
  Six, 83
  Seven, 92
  Eight, 101
  Nine, 103
  Ten, 147
  Eleven, 149
  Twelve, 159
  God-Goddess Symbol, 54,
    231, 233
  personal symbol, 231

F
Faunus, 59
Fest, Joachim, 77
Fortune, Dion, 3, 4, 7, 9, 10,
    17, 20, 31, 32, 37, 73, 74, 82,
    83, 87, 88, 120, 129, 140,
    152, 158, 172, 179, 191,
    213, 214, 216, 217, 223
Freemasons, 222
Freya, 59, 60, 62, 183
Friday, 183
Frigga, 59
functions

elemental, 115
feeling, 6, 115, 116, 144
intuition, 115, 116
sensation, 115, 116, 165
thinking, 115, 116
weakest, 116

G
Gaia, 59
Gardner, Joy, 151
Gnomes, 117, 130, 164, 165,
    172
  gifts for, 174
  meeting, 164
Gnomides, 173
goal
  achieving, 14, 18
  defining, 24, 111
  expressing it safely, 29
  setting your, 23
  written, 30, 50
goblet, 82, 144
Goddess Salts and Waters, 171
God (Judeo-Christian), 78, 221
god-form, 71
  assuming, 53, 71, 72, 74, 79,
    83
gods/goddesses, see *archetypes*
Golden Dawn, xvii, 74, 194,
    195, 196, 221, 222
Goodrick-Clarke, Nicholas, 77
Goodwin, M.O., 37
Graves, Robert, 57
Gray, William, 20, 48, 121, 131,
    144, 165
Greene, Liz, 11
grief, 107, 124

Groundhog Day, 181
grounding, 80, 124
group
  finding a, 221
  magical
Guinevere, 59

H
hades, 59, 60
Halloween, 182
Hathor, 59, 71
Hay, Louise, 40, 41, 45
healing, 28, 123, 141
Healing Water, 125
health, 27
Hephaestus, 59
Hera, 62
Heracles, 60
herbs, 134, 138, 169
Hermes, 59, 60, 63, 183
High Magic, 214
Hirsch, Dr. Alan R., 133
Hitler, Adolf, 77, 78
Hope, Murry, 3, 20, 53, 54, 55,
  56, 57, 63, 68, 71, 111, 127,
  136, 137, 153, 173, 192,
  214, 216, 217, 222, 223, 231
Horus, 59, 60
hours, planetary, 184
hubris, 76

I
Icarus, 76
I Ching coins, 33
incantation, 32, 47–50
incense, 113, 131, 133, 134
  formula for making, 135

  how to burn, 134
  substitutions, 135
  when to use, 138
initiation,
Isis, 59
Ixion, 76

J
jealousy, 106, 123
Jesus, 10, 55
journey, the, 160
  shamanic
Jung, C.G., 114, 115
Jupiter, the god, 59
  the planet, 183

K
Kiersey, David, 225
King, Francis, 195

L
Lammas, 182
Lancelot, 59
Law of Rebound, 11, 78
Law of Three, 11, 68
Love Water, 95, 96, 125
lunar cycles, see *Moon*

M
magic, 36
  and ethics, 9, 13
  and personal relationships, 12
  and psychology, 4
  candle, 123
  circle, casting, 194
  earth, 167
  ethics, 9, 217

fails, 187
four-tiered structure, 174
growing into, 223
high, 214
how it works, 5
incense, 133
Murry Hope's definition of, 1
water, 145
magical
feeling, 94
incantations, 47, 49, 50
instruments, using, 201
intention, 47, 107
personality
assuming, 83
building, 53, 81
life on, 83
results, 186
structure, 17
studies, 213
tools, 82
tools, consecrating, 199
magnetizing, 70
powders, 165, 169
sand, 167, 170
water, 147, 150
Mars, god, 59
planet, 183
Mary, the Virgin, 55
May Day, see *Beltane*
Mercury, the god, 59
the planet, 183
Merlin, 59
mermaids, see *Ondines*
Mineral Kingdom, 112
Minerva, 59
Monday, 183

Moon, 180, 183, 189
Morrigan, 62, 66
mystics, magicians as, 214
mythology, 89

N
nature
four elements in, 112
Neter, 97, 98
negativity
decrease, 180
removing, see also *clearing*
Neith, 59, 62
Nephthys, 75, 128
Neptune, planet, 11
Neville, 87, 100
numerology, 36

O
Odin, 59, 74, 222
oils, 121
Ondines, 117, 118, 130, 144,
152, 153, 160
gifts for, 156
meeting your personal, 156
oracles, 33

P
Pan, 59, 63
pantheon
Celtic, 65
Parker, Dr. Jonathan, 103
Peace Water, 148, 149
pendulum, 33
seeking advice, 61
using, 61
pentacle, 82, 166

physical illness
  overcoming, 28
plane
  emotional, 18, 87
  mental, 19, 21, 23
  physical, 17, 111
  spiritual, 19, 53, 70, 81, 84
planetary hours, using, 184
Pluto, the god, 9, 59
  the planet, 11
powders, 17, 18, 165, 169
  to magnetize, 169
power days, 181
power
  drive for, 11
  names of, 73
prayer, 53, 113
  effective, 66
  how to, 67
Prince of the Powers of Air, 141
props and costumes, 75
prosperity, 26, 123
Prosperity Powder, 113
Prosperity Water, 125
protecting yourself, 79
psychology, 4, 19, 38, 113, 116, 144, 165
  four elements in, 114
Purification Water, 148

Q
Quantum Quests
  International, 101

R
Rebound, Law of, 11

recollection, 94
Regardie, Israel, 5, 20, 21, 53, 74, 191, 214
religion and magic, 9
repetition, effect on the unconscious, 94
Requests, the Law of Three, 11, 68
Rites
  Aphrodite's girdle, 95
  of tears, 107, 145
  pin and candle, 68
  seven day prosperity, 203
ritual, 191
  four phases of, 192
  magic, four elements in, 113
romance, 26
runes, 33

S
sadness, 124
safety measures, 7, 29, 219
Salamanders, 117, 118, 121, 127
  gifts for, 130
  meeting, 164
salts, 165, 171
  consecrating, 171
Sanders, Maxine, 219
sands, 165, 170
Satan, 141
Saturday, 184
Saturn, the planet, 11, 36, 184, 189
Savasana, 92
sealing, 80
Sekhmet, 73
self-esteem, 72, 95, 123

self
  higher, 56
self-sabotage, 38
Serenity Powder, 26
sexual difficulties, 124
sexual partners, 124
Shadow, 157
Shakespeare, William, 47, 152, 203
shamanic journeys, 159
shamanic traditions, 85
Skinner, Stephen, 195
smudge sticks, 138
solar cycles, 179
sonics, 131, 136
Society of Inner Light, 222
soul fragments, 99
spiritual guide, 56
Spring, see *Vernal Equinox*
Success Water, 125
Summer Solstice, 179, 182
Sun, see *cycles, solar*
Sunday, 184
sword, 82, 131
Sylphs, 117, 130, 131, 139
  gifts for, 143
  meeting, 164

T
talismans, 139
teacher
  finding a, 214
technique, cleaning, 101
temperament, 6
  questionnaire, 6, 57, 115, 225
  scoring, 229, 230
Theosophical Society, 222, 223

Thor, 59, 60, 183
Thoth, 59, 60, 61
Thursday, 183
tides, 179
timing, 179, 204
Tiu, 183
toning, see *sonics*
Trager, L., 133
Tuesday, 183
types
  feeling, 58, 72
  intuitive, 57, 72
  sensate, 58, 72
  thinking, 58, 72

U
unconscious mind, 89, 94, 101, 105, 186
unconscious, collective, 108
Uraeus serpent, 73

V
Valiente, Doreen, xvii, 48
Valkyries, 62
Venus, the goddess, 59
  the planet, 183
Vernal Equinox, 182
visualization, 23, 92, 113
  cleansing, 149
  techniques, 88
visualize yourself, 89
Vulcan, 59

W
wand, 73, 82, 121
Wagner, Richard, 156
Waram, Marilyn, 11

water, 126, 144, 145, 146
  anoiting, 151
  drinking charged water, 107,
   150
  magically prepared, 144
  magnetize, 147
  sleep programming, 151
  spiritual baths, 150
  sprinkles, 151
  using, 150
Wednesday, 183

week
  using days of, 183
Wicca, xvii, 194, 222
Wing, R.L., 33
Winter Solstice, 179, 181
Wodan, Wotan, 183

XYZ
Yahweh, 78
Yoga, 92
Zeus, 59, 60, 183

For over 35 years Nancy B. Watson has practiced magic in the
Western tradition. She has been profoundly influenced by Dion
Fortune and Murry Hope. Since 1981, Watson has studied dream
analysis and, under the guidance of a Jungian psychiatrist, has
worked toward individuation while incorporating her knowledge
of magic into the process. She also practices Hatha and Raja Yoga.
Watson has contributed articles to *American Astrology Magazine*, is a
well-known lecturer on magic and ritual, and is the creator of
Nancy B. Watson's Potions and Tapes, which are sold in metaphysical stores throughout the U.S. and other countries. She currently
lives in northern California.